The Transformation of Rage

Literature and Psychoanalysis
GENERAL EDITOR: JEFFREY BERMAN

1. The Beginning of Terror: A Psychological Study of
Rainer Maria Rilke's Life and Work
DAVID KLEINBARD

2. Loathsome Jews and Engulfing Women: Metaphors
of Projection in the Works of Wyndham Lewis, Charles Williams,
and Graham Greene
ANDREA FREUD LOEWENSTEIN

3. Literature and the Relational Self
BARBARA ANN SCHAPIRO

4. Narcissism and the Literary Libido: Rhetoric, Text,
and Subjectivity
MARSHALL W. ALCORN, JR.

5. Reading Freud's Reading
EDITED BY SANDER L. GILMAN, JUTTA BIRMELE, JAY GELLER,
AND VALERIE D. GREENBERG

6. Self-Analysis in Literary Study
EDITED BY DANIEL RANCOUR-LAFERRIERE

7. The Transformation of Rage: Mourning and Creativity
in George Eliot's Fiction
PEGGY FITZHUGH JOHNSTONE

The Transformation of Rage

Mourning and Creativity
in George Eliot's Fiction

Peggy Fitzhugh Johnstone

New York University Press
NEW YORK & LONDON

NEW YORK UNIVERSITY PRESS
New York and London

© 1994 by New York University
All rights reserved

Library of Congress-in-Publication Data
Johnstone, Peggy Fitzhugh, 1940–
The tranformation of rage : mourning and creativity in George
Eliot's fiction / Peggy Fitzhugh Johnstone.
p.   cm.—(Literature and psychoanalysis ; 7)
Includes bibliographical references and index.
ISBN 0-8147-4194-0
1. Eliot, George, 1819–1880—Knowledge—Psychology.   2. Characters
and characteristics in literture.   3. Psychoanalysis and
literature.   4. Creativity in literature.   5. Emotions in
literature.   6. Grief in literature.   7. Anger in literature.
I. Title.   II. Series.
PR4692.P74J64   1994
821'.8—dc20   94-12908
                       CIP

New York University Press books are printed on acid-free paper,
and their binding materials are chosen for strength and durability.

Manufactured in the United States of America

10   9   8   7   6   5   4   3   2   1

For the Class of 1958
University City High School, St. Louis, Missouri

Contents

Foreword by Jeffrey Berman ix

Acknowledgments xv

Introduction 1

ONE
Self-Disorder and Aggression in *Adam Bede* 24

TWO
Narcissistic Rage in *The Mill on the Floss* 41

THREE
Loss, Anxiety, and Cure: Mourning and Creativity in *Silas Marner* 68

FOUR
Pathological Narcissism in *Romola* 86

FIVE
Fear of the Mob in *Felix Holt* 111

SIX
The Vast Wreck of Ambitious Ideals in *Middlemarch* 132

SEVEN
The Pattern of the Myth of Narcissus in *Daniel Deronda* 159

Conclusion 181

Works Cited 195

Index 203

Foreword

As New York University Press inaugurates a new series of books on literature and psychoanalysis, it seems appropriate to pause and reflect briefly upon the history of psychoanalytic literary criticism. For a century now it has struggled to define its relationship to its two contentious progenitors and come of age. After glancing at its origins, we may be in a better position to speculate on its future.

Psychoanalytic literary criticism was conceived at the precise moment in which Freud, reflecting upon his self-analysis, made a connection to two plays and thus gave us a radically new approach to reading literature. Writing to his friend Wilhelm Fliess in 1897, Freud breathlessly advanced the idea that "love of the mother and jealousy of the father" are universal phenomena of early childhood (*Origins*, 223–24). He referred immediately to the gripping power of *Oedipus Rex* and *Hamlet* for confirmation of, and perhaps inspiration for, his compelling perception of family drama, naming his theory the "Oedipus complex" after Sophocles' legendary fictional hero.

Freud acknowledged repeatedly his indebtedness to literature, mythology, and philosophy. There is no doubt that he was a great humanist, steeped in world literature, able to read several languages and range across disciplinary boundaries. He regarded creative writers as allies, investigating the same psychic terrain and intuiting similar human truths. "[P]sycho-analytic observation must concede priority of imaginative writers," he declared in 1901 in *The Psychopathology of Everyday Life* (*SE* 6213), a concession he was generally happy to make. The only exceptions were writers like Schopenhauer, Nietzsche, and Schnitzler, whom he avoided reading because of the anxiety of influence. He quoted effortlessly from Sophocles, Shakespeare, Goethe, and Dostoevsky, and was himself a master prose stylist, the recipient of the coveted Goethe

Prize in 1930. When he was considered for the Nobel Prize, it was not for medicine but for literature. Upon being greeted as the discoverer of the unconscious, he disclaimed the title and instead paid generous tribute to the poets and philosophers who preceded him.

And yet Freud's forays into literary criticism have not been welcomed uniformly by creative writers, largely because of his allegiance to science rather than art. Despite his admiration for art, he viewed the artist as an introvert, not far removed from neurosis. The artist, he wrote in a well-known passage in the *Introductory Lectures on Psycho-Analysis* (1916–17), "is oppressed by excessively powerful instinctual needs. He desires to win honour, power, wealth, fame and the love of women; but he lacks the means for achieving these satisfactions" (*SE* 16376). Consequently, Freud argued, artists retreat from reality into the world of fantasy, where they attempt to make their dreams come true. While conceding that true artists manage to shape their daydreams in such a way as to find a path back to reality, thus fulfilling their wishes, Freud nevertheless theorized art as a substitute gratification. Little wonder, then, that few artists have been pleased with Freud's pronouncements.

Nor have many artists been sympathetic to Freud's preoccupation with sexuality and aggression; his deterministic vision of human life; his combative, polemical temperament; his self-fulfilling belief that psychoanalysis brings out the worst in people; and his imperialistic claim that psychoanalysis, which he regarded as his personal creation, would explore and conquer vast new territories. He chose as the epigraph for *The Interpretation of Dreams* (1900) a quotation from *The Aeneid* "Flectere si nequeo superos, Acheronta movebo" ("If I cannot bend the Higher Powers, I will move the Infernal Regions"). Although he denied that there was anything Promethean about his work, he regarded himself as one of the disturbers of the world's sleep. The man who asserted that "psycho-analysis is in a position to speak the decisive word in all questions that touch upon the imaginative life of man" (*SE* 19208) could hardly expect to win many converts among creative writers, who were no less familiar with the imaginative life of humankind and who resented his intrusion into their domain.

Freud viewed psychoanalysts as scientists, committed to the reality principle and to heroic self-renunciation. He perceived artists, by contrast—and women—as neurotic and highly narcissistic, devoted to the pleasure principle, intuiting mysterious truths which they could not rationally understand. "Kindly nature has given the artist the ability to express his most secret mental impulses, which are hidden even from himself," he stated in *Leonardo da Vinci and a Memory of His Childhood* in 1910 (*SE* 11107). The artist, in Freud's judgment, creates beauty, but the psychoanalyst analyzes its meaning and "penetrates" it, with all the phallic implications thereof. As much as he admired artists, Freud did not want to give them credit for knowing what they are doing. Moreover, although he always referred to artists as male, he assumed that art itself was essentially female; and he was drawn to the "seductive" nature of art even as he resisted its embrace, lest he lose his masculine analytical power. He wanted to be called a scientist, not an artist.

From the beginning of his career, then, the marriage Freud envisioned between the artist and the analyst was distinctly unequal and patriarchal. For their part, most creative writers have remained wary of psychoanalysis. Franz Kafka, James Joyce, and D. H. Lawrence were fascinated by psychoanalytic theory and appropriated it, in varying degrees, in their stories, but they all remained skeptical of Freud's therapeutic claims and declined to be analyzed.

Most artists do not want to be "cured," fearing that their creativity will be imperiled, and they certainly do not want psychoanalysts to probe their work; they agree with Wordsworth that to dissect is to murder. Vladimir Nabokov's sardonic reference to Freud as the "Viennese witch doctor" and his contemptuous dismissal of psychoanalysis as black magic are extreme examples of creative writers' mistrust of psychoanalytic interpretations of literature. "[A]ll my books should be stamped Freudians Keep Out," Nabokov writes in *Bend Sinister* (xii). Humbert Humbert speaks for his creator when he observes in *Lolita* that the difference between the rapist and therapist is but a matter of spacing (147).

Freud never lost faith that psychoanalysis could cast light upon a wide variety of academic subjects. In the short essay "On the Teaching of Psycho-Analysis in Universities" (1919), he maintained that his new science has a role not only in medical schools but also in the "solutions of problems" in art, philosophy, religion, literature, mythology, and history. "The fertilizing effects of psycho-analytic thought on these other disciplines," Freud wrote enthusiastically, "would certainly contribute greatly towards forging a closer link, in the sense of a *universitas literarum,* between medical science and the branches of learning which lie within the sphere of philosophy and the arts" (*SE* 17:173). Regrettably, he did not envision in the same essay a cross-fertilization, a desire, that is, for other disciplines to pollinate psychoanalysis.

Elsewhere, though, Freud was willing to acknowledge a more reciprocal relationship between the analyst and the creative writer. He opened his first published essay on literary criticism, "Delusions and Dreams in Jensen's *Gradiva*" (1907), with the egalitarian statement that "creative writers are valued allies and their evidence is to be highly prized, for they are apt to know a whole host of things between heaven and earth of which our philosophy has not yet let us dream" (*SE* 9:8), an allusion to his beloved Hamlet's affirmation of the mystery of all things. Conceding that literary artists have been, from time immemorial, precursors to scientists, Freud concluded that the "creative writer cannot evade the psychiatrist nor the psychiatrist the creative writer, and the poetic treatment of a psychiatric theme can turn out to be correct without any sacrifice of its beauty" (*SE* 9:44).

It is in the spirit of this equal partnership between literature and psychoanalysis that New York University Press launches the present series. We intend to publish books that are genuinely interdisciplinary, theoretically sophisticated, and clinically informed. The literary critic's insights into psychoanalysis are no less valuable than the psychoanalyst's insights into literature. Gone are the days when psychoanalytic critics assumed that Freud had a master key to unlock the secrets of literature. Instead of reading literature to confirm psychoanalytic theory, many critics are now reading Freud to discover how his understanding of literature shaped the evolution of his theory. In short, the master-slave relationship traditionally implicit in the marriage between the literary critic and the psychoanalyst has given way to a healthier dialogic relationship, in which each learns from and contributes to the other's discipline.

Indeed, the prevailing ideas of the late twentieth century are strikingly different from those of the late nineteenth century, when literature and psychoanalysis were first allied. In contrast to Freud, who assumed he was discovering absolute truth, we now believe that knowledge, particularly in the humanities and social sciences, is relative and dependent upon cultural contexts. Freud's classical drive theory, with its mechanistic implications of cathectic energy, has given way to newer relational models such as object relations, self psychology, and interpersonal psychoanalysis, affirming the importance of human interaction. Many early psychoanalytic ideas, such as the death instinct and the phylogenetic transmission of memories, have fallen by the wayside, and Freud's theorizing on female psychology has been recognized as a reflection of his cultural bias.

Significant developments have also taken place in psychoanalytic literary theory. An extraordinary variety and synthesis of competing approaches have emerged, including post-Freudian, Jungian, Lacanian, Horneyan, feminist, deconstructive, psycholinguistic, and reader response. Interest in psychoanalytic literary criticism is at an all-time high, not just in the handful of journals devoted to psychological criticism, but in dozens of mainstream journals that have traditionally avoided psychological approaches to literature. Scholars are working on identity theory, narcissism, gender theory, mourning and loss, and creativity. Additionally, they are investigating new areas, such as composition theory and pedagogy, and exploring the roles of resistance, transference, and countertransference in the classroom.

"In the end we depend / On the creatures we made," Freud observed at the close of his life (*Letters*, 425), quoting from Goethe's *Faust;* and in the end psychoanalytic literary criticism depends on the scholars who continue to shape it. All serious scholarship is an act of love and devotion, and for many of the authors in this series, including myself, psychoanalytic literary criticism has become a consuming passion, in some cases a lifelong one. Like other passions, there is an element of idealization here. For despite our criticisms of Freud, we stand in awe of his achievements; and even as we recognize the limitations of any single approach to literature, we find that psychoanalysis has profoundly illuminated the human condition and inspired countless artists. In the words of the fictional "Freud" in D. M. Thomas's extraordinary novel *The White Hotel* (1981), "Long may poetry and psychoanalysis continue to highlight, from their different perspectives, the human face in all its nobility and sorrow" (143n.).

JEFFREY BERMAN
Professor of English
State University of New York at Albany

Acknowledgments

An earlier version of "The Pattern of the Myth of Narcissus in *Daniel Deronda*" appeared in *University of Hartford Studies in Literature* 19 (1987): 45–60.

An earlier version of "Narcissistic Rage in *The Mill on the Floss*" appeared in *Literature and Psychology* 36 (1990): 90–109.

Earlier versions of "Self-Disorder and Aggression in *Adam Bede*" and "Loss, Anxiety, and Cure: Mourning and Creativity in *Silas Marner*" appeared in *Mosaic* 22 (1989): 59–70 and 25 (1992): 35–47 respectively.

I would like to thank the editors, Charles L. Ross, formerly of *Hartford Studies*, Morton Kaplan of *Literature and Psychology*, and Evelyn J. Hinz of *Mosaic*, for their help during the publication process.

I also want to thank Arthur Collins for guiding my independent study of George Eliot and Jeffrey Berman for guiding my independent study of literature and psychoanalysis during my doctoral student days at SUNY at Albany nearly a decade ago.

Finally, I want to thank Douglas Johnstone and Jeffrey Berman for so willingly reading my manuscript prior to publication. I made good use of their suggestions during my final revisions. I am also grateful to the editorial staff at New York University Press for their assistance during the book publication process.

Introduction

George Eliot's fiction synthesizes the intellectual currents of the nineteenth century. As a lifelong zealous reader and self-directed student, Eliot gained not only a rich background in literature and history, religion and philosophy, art, music, and languages (German, French, Italian, Spanish, Greek, and Latin), but throughout her life she kept up with the latest developments in the sciences, including the emerging social sciences of psychology and sociology. Her partner, George Henry Lewes, was also famous in his own right for his substantial writings on a wide variety of subjects, including literature, philosophy, biology, and psychology. Among the eminent names in their shared milieu were Herbert Spencer, the philosopher perhaps best remembered for his "Social Darwinism," Alexander Bain, the British Associationist psychologist, and Charles Darwin, the naturalist whose theories Lewes studied closely and with whom he corresponded on occasion. Much of the literary criticism on George Eliot has illuminated the influences of such contemporaries on her art. Her fiction writing, however, is far more than a synthesis of the thinking of other intellectuals. Her approach to fiction and her insights were her own, and although she "epitomizes" her century, as Basil Willey expresses it (*Century* 260), her fiction was also unique in its time.

Literary criticism in the twentieth century initially established George Eliot's position as a great writer by virtue of the "universality" and "profoundly moral character" of her themes, as Alan D. Perlis explains it (xv). Critics have long noted Eliot's concern with the theme of growth in her central characters from egoism and/or self-delusion to self-knowledge and a capacity for empathy. Critics of the fifties and sixties, influenced by the New Critical emphasis on textual analysis, helped readers appreciate the formal qualities of Eliot's art: the complex designs of her novels, the unifying imagery and symbolism, the rich sense of time and place that her writing evokes, and the psychological insight that distinguishes her characterizations from the novelists that preceded her. In the seventies and eighties, an explosion of interest in Eliot is reflected in the quantity, excellence, and variety of the criticism, which has added deconstructionist, feminist, and psychoanalytic dimensions to readers' understanding of her work. In addition, as Perlis notes, criticism in those decades has demonstrated that "the social context of Eliot's work is so rich and complicated that historical, sociological, philosophical, and, perhaps most important, scientific events and discoveries, are intricately bound in the lives of Eliot's characters" (xiv). Despite the general acceptance of Eliot's position as one of the great English novelists, however, many critics have also seen flaws in her work which they often express in terms of her self-involvement with her idealized characters and/or the closely related problem of the forced endings of many of her novels. It was through my study of psychoanalysis, in conjunction with my work on George Eliot, that I began to see the connection between the artistic flaws in the novels and the author's personal conflicts.

I also began to see the connection between the author's personal conflicts and her denial of aggression in her idealized characters—a subject that has increasingly attracted the attention of critics. U. C. Knoepflmacher suggests in his bibliographic essay that the subject of aggression in Eliot's fiction is one "worth considering more fully" by "practitioners of the psychoanalytical approach" (*Victorian* 257). In recent years, literary critics such as Carol Christ, Sandra M. Gilbert and Susan Gubar, William Myers, and Dorothea Barrett have noted Eliot's apparent concern over the murderous potential of anger, a concern reflected, as Gilbert and Gubar observe, in her tendency to create idealized heroines who "repress anger" and "submit to renunciation" (490). My study, the first book-length psychoanalytic treatment of the subject of aggression in George Eliot's novels, thus constitutes an attempt to respond to the need articulated by Knoepflmacher and other modern critics.

During the course of my psychoanalytic study of George Eliot's fiction, I moved from my initial interest in the subject of narcissism, as reflected in my first published essay on *Daniel Deronda* (1987), to a more particular focus on aggression: the ways in which it is portrayed in the characters, the ways in which it is denied by the author, and the ways in which it affects the author's creative process. While I began by applying the theories of two contemporary psychoanalysts, Otto F. Kernberg and Heinz Kohut, to my study of the novels, I discovered after the publication of my essays on *Adam Bede* (1989) and *The Mill on the Floss* (1990), that I needed to return to the writings of Sigmund Freud in my attempt to understand the character Silas Marner's obsessive-compulsive behavior and its relationship to rage. At the same time, I also read the works of contemporary psychologists—behaviorists, cognitive psychologists, and psycho-pharmacologists—who offer differing perspectives on the obsessive-compulsive disorder. It was this year-long attempt to understand obsessions and compulsions (at the same time as I was writing my essay on *Silas Marner*) that resulted in a breakthrough in my thinking about George Eliot, for in the process I had uncovered the connection between rage and loss, and formulated my thesis that George Eliot's fiction writing was her constructive response to unconscious mourning over the loss of her parents—a thesis that was bolstered by my study of Margaret S. Mahler's work on the process of separation-individuation, and John Bowlby's work on attachment, separation, and loss.

While I was writing the *Silas Marner* essay, I also began to perceive what turned out to be a pattern, reflected in the timing and content of the published writings, of Eliot's responses to the anniversaries of deaths in her family. My discovery of George H. Pollock's *The Mourning-Liberation Process*, which includes a review of the psychoanalytic literature on anniversary reactions, provided theoretical support for my observations. The anniversary reaction, as I. L. Mintz explains it, is a response to the unconscious sense of time. It is a "time-specific variant of the repetition-compulsion"—a psychological response "arising on an anniversary of a psychologically significant experience which the individual attempts to master through reliving rather than through remembering" (720). The anniversary reaction is characterized by some form of reenactment of events at a time when the mind associates present circumstances with one or more traumatic events of the past. Such reactions can occur at yearly, decade-long or other intervals, or at a particular time of day, month, or year; they can also occur in relation to the ages in a person's life (or in the life of a loved one) with which traumatic events are associated. Such reactions may also be a sign that the necessary process of mourning for a lost loved one is not yet complete. Pollock's assertion that the repeating patterns in an artist's creative work are manifestations of the mourning process (1:127), taken together with the psychoanalytic literature on the variety of forms of anniversary reactions, supports my view of Eliot's fiction writing as her constructive response to her sense of loss.

It will no doubt help my readers if I place my psychoanalytic sources in the context of the history of the psychoanalytic movement. Sigmund Freud's daughter Anna (1895–1982), whose work is described in detail in Elizabeth Young-Bruehl's biography, carried on and expanded the work of classical psychoanalysis, with its emphasis on the resolution of the Oedipus complex in the treatment of adult neurosis, into her observations and treatment of young children who had been separated from their parents during World War II. Although she continued to focus her theoretical attention on the oedipal period (187), her insights into the needs of pre-oedipal children laid the groundwork for further research in early child development, including that of John Bowlby, who sees his own work as building on such early studies (1:24). In her Hampstead War Nursery in England, Anna Freud observed the importance for language development and toilet training of an ongoing emotional bond with a mother figure, and consequently decided to organize the children in small groups with a "mother" responsible for each one (Young-Bruehl 252). She had found that when children are separated from their mothers, developmental inhibitions set in and regressions occur, but that "once a stable relationship with a surrogate mother had been established by one of the women at the clinic, the superficial signs of symptomatology disappeared and 'the children began to develop in leaps and bounds'" (Roazen 457). She also found that when the deprived and/or separated children are provided a substitute mother, good object relationships result, aggression becomes bound and its manifestations reduced to normal quantities (Young-Bruehl 322). Anna Freud's insistence on working with children in the context of their families and her belief in helping the child by encouraging changes in maternal behavior amount to an acknowledgment of the importance of environmental factors in human development.

Although Melanie Klein, the British analyst (1881–1960), differed in many ways from Anna Freud in both the theory and technique of child analysis (Young-Bruehl 160–86), she shared with her rival the emphasis on the importance for development of the child's interactions with the mother. However, in contrast to Anna Freud, who emphasized the relationship between the child's inner and outer worlds, Klein, drawing her inferences from her analytic work, focused on the internal world of the small child, which she saw, as Peter Gay expresses it, as "a mass of destructive and anxious fantasies" (468). Klein's work marks the beginning of the development of object relations theory, an approach to psychoanalysis that focuses on the internalized objects, or images, that are created from the child's introjection of parental figures. As defined by Jay R. Greenberg and Stephen A. Mitchell in their review of the history of the concept in psychoanalytic theory, the term "object relations" refers to "individuals' interactions with external and internal (real and imagined) other people, and to the relationship between their internal and external object worlds" (13-14).

Klein's ideas are perhaps most clearly summarized by Hanna Segal, in a collection of lectures that comprise her *Introduction to the Work of Melanie Klein*. Although most psychoanalysts now question much of Klein's theory, many have also found that her notion of the "depressive position," which she believed occurred during the second half of the first year of life, illuminates the difficulty of the young child's acceptance of the fact that the mother is a person apart from itself. In Klein's view, the beginning of the depressive position is marked by the recognition of the mother as a whole person (viii-ix). At that time, the infant experiences feelings of "mourning and pining for the good object felt as lost and destroyed, and guilt . . . which arises from the sense that he has lost the good object through his own destructiveness" (70). Klein believed that this experience of depression "mobilizes in the infant the wish to repair his destroyed object or objects" (72), and that "its working through is accompanied by a radical alteration in his view of reality. . . . The infant becomes aware of himself and of his objects as separate from himself" (73). Klein's theory thus establishes the connection between mourning and development—a connection currently under more thorough investigation by such contemporaries as the American psychiatrist George H. Pollock, who recently published his two-volume work on what he calls *The Mourning-Liberation Process*.

Unlike Anna Freud and Melanie Klein, who began their careers as teachers, Margaret S. Mahler (1897-1985) began hers as a pediatrician, although she knew from the outset that she also wanted to pursue her interest in psychoanalysis. Following her emigration from Vienna to the

United States (via London) in 1938, her professional interest gradually shifted from her research and therapeutic work in childhood psychosis to her research in what she called the "separation-individuation process" in normal children. As she expresses it in her *Memoirs*, "For me, the general problem of identity, and especially the way in which one arrives at a sense of self, has always been primary," because of her belief that "it is only out of such knowledge [of the processes of normal development] that we can formulate those strategies of primary prevention and early intervention that hold out the greatest hope for humankind" (136–37). As Paul Stepansky observes in his "Introduction" to her memoirs, Mahler is now "widely regarded as one of the outstanding students of early childhood development of our century" (xiii). Stepansky goes on to define the separation-individuation process as "the series of stages marking the infant's gradual intrapsychic 'separation' from the mother and correlative understanding of himself as a distinct individual in a world composed of other equally distinct individuals—as an individual, that is, with a subjectively felt sense of identity" (xvii). Mahler explains in her best known work, *The Psychological Birth of the Human Infant*, that whereas separation-individuation is an intrapsychic process, her research, which was based on observations of the behavior of mothers with their young children, was guided by the conviction that "this process could be inferred from behaviors that were indeed observable" (23).

Mahler emphasizes that she uses the term "separation" to refer to "the sense of being a separate individual, and not the fact of being physically separated [or emotionally isolated] from someone" (*Birth* 9). Yet much confusion has resulted from others' misunderstanding of her use of the word. To put it in terms of object relations theory, Mahler's "separation" refers to the essential (for the development of a sense of identity) human intrapsychic process of separation of self-image from parent images. To present human development in such terms is not to deny the need for human attachment throughout life—a need justifiably stressed by the "attachment theorists." On the contrary, Mahler herself stresses that separation-individuation is a precondition for what she calls "true object relationship" (6). The view that attachment theory and the theory of separation-individuation are antithetical, as articulated for example by Daniel Stern in *The Interpersonal World of the Infant* (240–42), is, I believe, based on a misunderstanding of Mahler's intent. Indeed, what Mahler and the attachment theorists have in common is their understanding of the young child's development as necessarily occurring *in relation* to the people in his/her environment.

In contrast to Anna Freud, Melanie Klein, and Margaret S. Mahler, whose work was focused on child development, Otto F. Kernberg, an American professor of psychiatry and training analyst, bases his theoretical formulations on his extensive experience with severely disturbed adult patients. He is probably best known for his classic work, *Borderline Conditions and Pathological Narcissism*, which, as he explains in his preface to the book, is the result of "thirteen years' effort to develop a concept of [the psychopathology, diagnosis, prognosis, and treatment of borderline conditions] in the light of contemporary ego psychology and psychoanalytic object relations theory." As Greenberg and Mitchell explain, Kernberg "derives most of his inferences from the transference reactions characteristically manifested [by such severely disturbed patients]" (328).

Like Mahler, Kernberg sees individual development as necessarily occurring in relation to others in the environment. Emphasizing the importance for the formation of identity of separating self and object images and "integrating libidinally determined and aggressively determined self- and object-images" in the early stages of life (162), Kernberg defines the self as "an intrapsychic structure consisting of multiple self representations and their related affect dispositions." He explains that "the normal self is integrated, in that its component self representations are dynamically organized into a comprehensive whole." This normal integrated self relates to "integrated object representations, that is, to object representations which have incorporated the 'good' and 'bad' primitive object representations into integrative images of others in depth" (315–16).

When early self and object configurations are not successfully differentiated and integrated, severe disturbances result and persist into adulthood. Kernberg believes that what he calls the "narcissistic personality," for example, has a pathological self-structure, originating in the second half of the oral stage, in which "there is a fusion of ideal self, ideal object, and actual self images as a defense against an intolerable reality in the interpersonal realm"; at the same time, "unacceptable self images are repressed and projected onto external objects, which are devaluated" (231–32). The narcissistic personality's inflated self-concept thus consists of a confusion and distortion of self and parent images. Kernberg is not certain of the cause of this pathological fusion of early self and object images, although his clinical experience suggests that the background of his narcissistic patients often includes "chronically cold parent figures with covert but intense aggression," with the result that these patients have sought refuge in their own physical attractiveness or special talents "against the basic feelings of being unloved and of being the objects of revengeful hatred." Moreover, Kernberg believes that it is hard to tell to what extent the development of the "pathologically augmented development of oral aggression" in such patients "represents a constitutionally determined strong aggressive drive, a constitutionally determined lack of anxiety tolerance in regard to aggressive impulses, or severe frustration in [the] first years of life" (234–35). Thus he points to the aggressive drive that he believes is innate in the individual, at the same time that he stresses the child's interaction with others in the environment. In his treatment of narcissistic personalities, who, he emphasizes, tend to project their aggression onto others, Kernberg attempts to get the patient to recognize the aggression that is actually coming from within.

Like Kernberg, Heinz Kohut (d. 1981) was widely regarded as a leading professor of psychiatry and training analyst. Also like Kernberg, Kohut became best known for his work on psychological problems that persist into adulthood when individuals have not completed the intrapsychic process of differentiating and integrating infantile self and object images. In contrast to Kernberg, however, Kohut includes in his definition of "narcissistic personality disorders," as described in his first book, *The Analysis of the Self,* a broader range of personality and behavior problems. He sees such narcissistic disturbances in the context of what he calls "self-psychology," the term he applies to his well-known and much-debated theoretical system. Although many writers see Kohut's system as antithetical to the mainstream of psychoanalytic theory, Kohut himself asserts, even in his last theoretical work, *How Does Analysis Cure?* (1984), that although self-psychology is "still unassimilated by the majority of analysts, . . . it is in the mainstream of the development of psychoanalytic thought" (95). Rather than a "deviation from traditional theory," Kohut considers it "an expansion of analytic understanding" (208). In an earlier work, *The Restoration of the Self* (1977), Kohut explains his (now) widely misunderstood "principle of complementarity" (279): his notion of retaining the concepts of traditional psychoanalysis, while adding to them what he sees as a new dimension of self-psychology. To cite an example: Kohut views the Oedipus complex *in the context of* the child's developing self-structure; he writes that "the presence of a firm self is a precondition for the experience of the Oedipus complex. Unless the child sees himself as a delimited, abiding, independent center of initiative, he is unable to experience the object-instinctual desires that lead to the conflicts and secondary adaptations of the oedipal period" (227). By adding the dimension of self-psychology to such classical concepts, Kohut hopes that therapists can "perceive configurations that would otherwise have escaped [their] notice" (*Cure* 84).

Kohut defines psychoanalytic cure in terms of structural completeness: that is, "when an energic continuum in the center of the personality has been established and the unfolding of a productive life has thus become a realizable possibility" (*Cure* 7). Kohut explains in *The Analysis of the Self* that under optimal circumstances the young child experiences gradual disillusionment with his parent figures—a process that results in "gradual . . . internalization" or the gradual "acquisition of permanent psychological structures which continue, endopsychically, the functions which the idealized self-object had previously fulfilled." If a child suffers a traumatic loss or disappointment in the parent figure(s), however, "the child does not acquire the needed internal structure, his psyche remains fixated on an archaic self-object, and the personality will throughout life be dependent on certain objects in what seems to be an intense form of object hunger. The intensity of the search for and of the dependency on these objects is due to the fact that they are striven for as a substitute for the missing segments of the psychic structure" (45). Therapy involves a process of "transmuting internalization," achieved through a "narcissistic transference" with an empathic therapist who attempts to provide the supportive milieu that is necessary for the patient to rework the past and begin to grow again (*Cure* 4).

Perhaps Kohut's greatest difference from Kernberg is his belief that aggression is not a "manifestation of a primary drive that is gradually unveiled by the analytic process, but . . . a disintegration product which, while it is primitive, is not psychologically primal" (*Restoration* 114). He sees aggression in the transferences of his adult patients as reactions to empathic failures on the part of parent figures. He explains that through the therapeutic process, the patients can reconstruct and work through "the traumatic states of early life" that resulted from the "noxious childhood environment." At the same time, through the process of transmuted internalization that occurs in therapy, the patient will attain new psychological structures, with the result that the propensity for rage will be reduced (261).

John Bowlby, the eminent English psychiatrist, researcher, and teacher in the field of personality development, is best known for his pioneering three-volume work on *Attachment and Loss*, a work which explores the child's need for the ongoing, reliable presence of attachment figures. In his volume on *Attachment*, Bowlby explains his belief that it is instinctive (for survival) in children under age three to maintain proximity to the mother, or attachment figure (1:134). Moreover, observing that social interaction with the child is the most important factor in the formation of such necessary attachment, he asserts that the child's need for the mother exists apart from the gratification of physiological needs (1:361ff). Following Sigmund Freud's idea that childhood trauma causes disturbances in later life, Bowlby regards the young child's separation from the mother as traumatic within the definition proposed by Freud (1:10, 11).

In his volume on *Separation*, Bowlby is careful to distinguish his own use of the term "separation," as referring to a physical separation between child and parent, from Mahler's use of it as "an intrapsychic process which results in 'differentiation of the self from the symbiotic object'" (2:23). Thus, by implication, his work is not to be seen as contradictory to Mahler's, but as concerning separate, although closely related and sometimes overlapping, issues. Bowlby does not concern himself with the child's inner life, including early childhood fantasies of union with parent figures; he restricts himself to descriptions of the child's behavior in relation to others in his environment. Throughout his writings, Bowlby explains in detail the ways in which he increasingly departs from the terminology of Freudian and object relations theory, as he extends his own use of terminology from the fields of ethology and cognitive psychology in his attempts to account for human attachment behavior.

Building on Freud's insight that "missing someone who is loved and longed for is the key to an understanding of anxiety," Bowlby stresses that it was not until late in his career that Freud accorded separation anxiety "the central place in what was to be his final theory of anxiety," which was articulated in the 1926 work, *Inhibitions, Symptoms, and Anxiety* (2:27). The child's reaction to separation, Bowlby observes, also includes anger. Like Kohut, Bowlby has moved away from the traditional psychoanalytic drive theory of aggression, as his observations have led him to see aggression as reactive, rather than primary. Placing his theory close to W. R. D. Fairbairn's frustration-aggression hypothesis, he then points to the paradox that "following experiences of repeated separation or threats of separation, it is common for a person to develop intensely anxious and possessive attachment behavior simultaneously with bitter anger directed against the attachment figure, and often to combine both with much anxious concern about the safety of that figure" (256).

In his volume on *Loss*, Bowlby describes the effects on children of the loss of parents to death. He concludes that "clinical experience and a reading of the evidence leaves little doubt . . . that much psychiatric illness [in adults] [including many cases of anxiety state, depressive illness, and hysteria] is an expression of pathological mourning" (3:23). Arguing that psychoanalysis generally has given scant weight to environmental factors in its assessment of such illnesses as depression, Bowlby believes that depressions in adults that have typically been characterized as endogenous, are (often delayed) reactions to loss (3:253). His account of studies of the consequences for adults of the loss of parents in childhood and adolescence lends support to my view that George Eliot, whose mother died at what I believe to be a critical time in her adolescence, suffered from unconscious mourning for most, if not all, of her life.

As I look back on my study of George Eliot, I am impressed by her remarkable capacity for growth. Each shift in her circumstances, no matter how painful, eventually resulted in a new level of accomplishment. Moreover, the pattern of ongoing intellectual, creative, and emotional growth that began early in Eliot's life continued throughout her fiction-writing career. I will argue that it was through her intellectually demanding work that she was initially able to defend herself against the inner rage that followed from her sense of loss, and through her fiction writing that she was ultimately able to achieve her sense of identity. To put it in Kohut's terms, her intellectual and creative work served to provide her with the necessary process of self-strengthening that would finally ease the depressive symptoms of her rage.

Born Mary Anne Evans into a conventional Warwickshire (Midlands) household in 1819, her first major early childhood loss, as I will argue in my chapter on *Silas Marner*, seems to have been her sense of disconnection from her mother following the deaths of newborn twins when Mary Anne was a toddler; her mother, who suffered from ill health afterward, appears to have been virtually missing from Mary Anne's life after that time. The Evans household at Griff provided her with other attachments, however, and she became very close to her older brother Isaac, her chief playmate before their school days, and to her father, who apparently treated her as his favorite of the three children of his second wife. When Isaac was eight years old, he was sent to a boarding school near Coventry, at the same time that Mary Anne, age five, was sent with her older sister Chrissey to a boarding school three miles from home. The two girls came home only occasionally, on Saturdays and holidays. The young Mary Anne's reaction to the separation from loved ones at home is evident in the middle-aged Eliot's lingering memory, as John Cross, her husband during the last six months of her life, records, of "the difficulty of getting near enough the fire in winter, to become thoroughly warmed, owing to the circle of girls forming round too narrow a fireplace. This suffering from cold was the beginning of a low general state of health: also at this time she began to be subject to fears at night. . . . she told me that this liability to have 'all her soul become a quivering fear,' which remained with her afterwards, had been one of the supremely important influences dominating at times her future life" (8–9). Mary Anne's early childhood closeness to her brother was never restored. According to Eliot's biographer, Gordon Haight, Isaac, whom she now saw only on holidays, began to grow away from her, and Mary Anne turned to books for consolation (*Biography* 7). Thus began what I see as a lifelong pattern of response to loss.

In 1828, Mary Anne was sent to Mrs. Wallington's Boarding School in Nuneaton, where she studied English, drawing, French, and piano, and where she came under the influence of the principal governess, Maria Lewis, a devoted Church of England Evangelical who was to remain a close friend for many years, even after Mary Anne left the school. During her four years at Mrs. Wallington's, following Lewis's example, Mary Anne read repeatedly the whole King James version of the Bible, at the same time that she developed the habit of introspection. In Haight's view, these early practices contributed both to the later development of her "vigorous prose," and to her extraordinary capacity for psychological analysis (9). When she had mastered the offerings at Mrs.

Wallington's school, her parents were advised to send her to the Misses Franklins' school in Coventry, which she entered in 1832. There she studied English, French, history, arithmetic, drawing, and music. She seems to have excelled in every subject; she was remembered by a fellow student as "immeasurably superior" to the others (Laski 16–17). At the Franklins' school she also dropped her Midland dialect as she learned a more "cultivated" version of English pronunciation (Haight, *Biography* 11), and she was exposed to the writings of many English authors, including Shakespeare, Milton, Isaac Watts, Pope, Young, Cowper, Southey, Moore, and Byron. She also read historical novels by Bulwer Lytton, Scott (her lifelong favorite), and G. P. R. James, and wrote her own first piece of fiction, "Edward Neville," a romance that reflects the influence of her current reading; it begins "on a bright and sunny morning toward the end of the Autumn of the year 1650" when "a stranger mounted on a fine black horse descended the hill which leads into the small but picturesque town of Chepstow" (Haight, *Biography* 10–15; text 554–60). Mary Anne participated in the serious religious life of the school, where conversion was taught to be the beginning of the religious life. In Haight's view, her increasing interest in the "gloomy Calvinism" that had resulted in new practices of self-denial only served to increase the distance from her brother, who had "imbibed High Church views" at his own school (19).

Because of her mother's worsening health, the term ending Christmas 1835 was the last spent at the Franklins' school. Mrs. Evans died on February 3, 1836. According to Cross's account of Mary Anne's reaction, "the mother died, after a long and painful illness, in which she was nursed with great devotion by her daughters. . . . to a highly wrought, sensitive girl of sixteen, such a loss seems an unendurable calamity" (15). Ina Taylor's biography also stresses the severity of Mary Anne's reaction to her mother's death, which besides involving so much torture for her mother, had "symbolized [for herself] the end of childhood and the orderly world of school" (23). Haight suggests that her mother's illness and death were the source of a marked increase in Mary Anne's "religious zeal" (*Biography* 22). Certainly her life changed drastically and permanently. For a little over a year afterward, she and Chrissey kept house for their father, until Chrissey's marriage on May 30, 1837. On that day, Haight notes, Mary Ann, as bridesmaid, signed her name in the register for the first time without the final e (22). Cross writes of the wedding day that "one of Mr. Isaac Evans's most vivid recollections is that on the day of the marriage, after the bride's departure, he and his younger sister had 'a good cry' together over the break up of the old home-life, which of course could never be the same with the mother and the elder sister wanting" (15).

From 1837 until her brother Isaac's marriage in 1841, Mary Ann took on the role of housekeeper at Griff. Besides her domestic responsibilities there, she also spent time in the community doing charitable works, such as "visiting the poor and organising clothing clubs." "Over and above this," as Cross reports, "she was always prosecuting an active intellectual life of her own" (17). Besides taking private lessons in German, French, Italian, Greek, and Latin, she continued her music lessons and pursued her own reading, especially in works related to theology. Except for one letter dated a few months before her mother's death, the surviving letters of this period, many of them written to her friend Maria Lewis, begin in May 1838. The language of the letters is stilted, at the same time the tone is ardent; they reflect Mary Ann's struggles to live up to the ideals of nineteenth-century evangelical Christianity, with its demands for daily Bible study, self-examination, and self-denial. One aspect of her strained religious practice is her dutiful attitude toward reading. Questioning the value of most fiction, she writes Lewis in a long letter on the subject, that "as to the discipline our minds receive from the perusal of fictions I can conceive none that is beneficial but may be attained by that of history" (Eliot, *Letters* 1:23). Her close involvement with her family is also reflected in her frequent expressions of interest in Chrissey's rapidly growing family, and in her anxiety over how her brother's impending marriage might affect her own position at Griff (1:50, 59). At this stage she had also begun to think of publishing her own writing. She spent six months beginning in 1839 working on a Chart of Ecclesiastical History before a similar work was published first by someone else. Her own first publication, a poem in the *Christian Observer*, appeared in January 1840. Cross observes of this period in her life that although Mary Ann was free to pursue her own interests, her life was "very monotonous, very difficult, very discouraging." At the same time, he feels, she also experienced "the soothing, strengthening, sacred influences of the home life, the home loves, the home duties" (17). He concludes by remarking that "the very monotony of her life at Griff, and the narrow field it presented for observation of society, added immeasurably to the intensity of a naturally keen mental vision, concentrating into a focus what might perhaps have become dissipated in more liberal surroundings" (18).

With Isaac's marriage coming up, Mr. Evans solved the problem of his and Mary Ann's living situation with the decision to move with Mary Ann to Foleshill, near Coventry, and leave the house at Griff to Isaac and his wife, who married on June 8, 1841. After only a short time in the larger community of Coventry, Mary Ann began to benefit from the fresh opportunities offered by her new surroundings. With more time for her own studies, she attended lectures on chemistry, continued her language lessons, and read more widely. She also met new people, including Charles and Cara Bray, who became lifelong friends. As Charles was notorious for his progressive views, Mary Ann's friendship with him contributed to her growing sense of conflict with her family. The well-known "Holy War" with her father, beginning in January 1842 with her refusal to go to church, marks her open rejection of Christianity as she knew it—a shift in point of view which Haight believes would have happened with or without the influence of the Brays (*Biography* 39). Mr. Evans was so upset that he very nearly insisted that Mary Ann leave the household, and indeed, she did visit Isaac at Griff for a few weeks. With the help of other relatives, however, she and her father finally reached a compromise whereby "Mary Ann agreed to attend church with him as usual, and he tacitly conceded her the right to think what she liked during service" (Haight 44). The shift in her attitude is reflected in her letters. Her correspondence with Maria Lewis is replaced by letters to her new friends, and her style and tone seem more natural, as she emerges from the hold of evangelicalism on her mind (*Letters* 1:117 ff.). At this stage, she was also becoming known in the community for her intellectual capacities. By 1844 she had been invited to do a translation of Friedrich Strauss's *Das Leben Jesu,* a fifteen-hundred page project which took her two years to complete. When the book, *The Life of Jesus,* was published in June 1846, she was not credited for the translation, and she was paid only twenty pounds for the work (Haight, *Biography* 53–59).

During the three years following, until her father's death on May 31, 1849, Mary Ann's time was increasingly taken up with his care, although at this stage she also began to publish reviews and essays in the Coventry *Herald.* Toward the end of her father's life, she found solace in work on a translation of Spinoza's *Tractatus Theologico-Politicus*. She suffered a severe reaction to Mr. Evans's death, which, besides leaving her without a parent, also left her without a home. After the funeral, she took a recuperative trip to the Continent. Upon her return to England, after a series of family visits, she made a decision to live temporarily with her friends the Brays. It was during her stay at their home that John Chapman, a publisher who knew of her as the translator of Strauss, offered her the opportunity to write the notice of Robert William Mackay's *Progress of the Intellect* for the *Westminster Review,* a quarterly journal established in 1824, which had become, as Rosemary Ashton describes it, "the chief organ [in Britain] of political, philosophical, and religious radicalism" (*GHL* 29). When Mary Ann delivered the completed article to Chapman's place of business and boardinghouse in London in November 1850, she also began a trial visit of two weeks, during which she made the decision to move to London to work for him, beginning in January 1851.

Mary Ann's initial stay in London in early 1851 was marred by her much-discussed flirtation with Chapman, a notorious womanizer whose jealous wife and mistress teamed up to drive her out of the household by the end of March. Soon afterward, however, Chapman had the opportunity to purchase the *Westminster Review,* and although he was to be the nominal editor, he desperately needed Marian (as she had begun to spell her name in the spring of 1851) to do the work. She agreed to write the "Introductory Prospectus," and eventually the two women in Chapman's household agreed to her return to do editorial work there, beginning in September 1851. Despite the difficult personal adjustment to her new literary life in London, "The work she had been brought there to do was superbly done," as Marghanita Laski expresses it in her biography (38). Although as her letters at the time reveal, her two years at the Chapman establishment were marked by ill health, depressions, and shifting loyalties to men, they are also distinguished by the quality of her editorial work, and by her "grasp of the needs and problems of the paper" (Laski 38). By all reports, however, she was paid little or nothing for the work, although she probably received free room and board (Laski 38–39; Haight, *Biography* 91).

During her years at the Chapmans' household, Marian also formed her lifelong friendships with Herbert Spencer and George Henry Lewes.

The friendship with Lewes became a love affair, probably by the fall of 1853, when Marian moved into her own lodgings, although she continued to do editorial work for Chapman. She had also begun working on a translation of Ludwig Feuerbach's *Das Wesen des Christenthums*, a substantial work for which Chapman had agreed to pay her two shillings a page, or thirty pounds. When the book, *The Essence of Christianity*, was finally published in July 1854, as "Number VI of Chapman's Quarterly Series," the translator's name, Marian Evans, appeared on the title page. That same month, she left England for a trip to the Continent with Lewes.

Marian's decision to elope with Lewes, a married man, naturally created a scandal. Although Marian was not the cause of Lewes's permanent estrangement and attempted divorce from his wife Agnes, such a liaison could not be condoned in Victorian England, and Marian was socially ostracized. It was not until late in her career that she finally experienced a degree of social acceptance. Lewes's marriage had begun to deteriorate, as Marian's friend Charles Bray explained it to a mutual friend, "when Mrs. Lewes after the birth of her 3rd child took one of those strong and unaccountable dislikes to her husband that sometimes does occur under similar circumstances amounting to monomania and [I have also heard] that Lewes was most sincerely attached to his wife and greatly distressed by it" (qtd. in Ashton, *GHL* 156). No doubt the couple's belief in free love also contributed to the deterioration of the marriage. After bearing Lewes's fourth son, Agnes had born his friend Thornton Hunt's child and become pregnant with a second; at that point Lewes seems to have given up on his relationship with Agnes. Whatever the complex causes of the failed marriage, Lewes and Marian soon became "most sincerely attached" to each other. As they established on their trip to the Continent what became their lifelong pattern of helping each other with their work, they also found strength in each other's company. They managed to support themselves on the income they received from their writing. At the time, Lewes was working on a biography of Goethe, along with some columns for the *Leader*. During the eight months in Germany, Marian wrote articles for the *Westminster Review* and the *Leader*, translated a German article on "The Romantic School of Music," worked on her translation of Spinoza's *Ethics*, translated passages of Goethe for Lewes's biography, and when Lewes was ill, wrote down articles that he dictated. She also read intensively, especially in German literature (Haight, *Biography* 173–74).

When they returned to England, Marian spent five weeks writing and reading alone in Dover while Lewes worked out the details of his permanent separation from Agnes. During that time Chapman invited her to take on the "Belles Lettres" section of the "Contemporary Literature" reviews in the *Westminster Review*. Haight records that during the seven quarters that she covered the section, "The 'Belles Lettres' . . . noticed 166 different books, and Marian doubtless looked at many more that were not worth mention." As he observes, "The work gave her a close practical acquaintance with the literary market-place." During this period she also wrote thirty-one articles for the *Leader*, one two-part article for *Fraser's*, four articles for the *Saturday Review*, and five long articles commissioned by Chapman for the *Westminster* (186).

Lewes's biography of Goethe, published in November 1855, received excellent reviews. Marian continued to write articles for the *Westminster* and the *Leader*, although her translation of Spinoza was her main task for the early months of 1856. She finished it in February, but it was never published; the manuscript remains at the Beinecke Library at Yale University (200). In May, Lewes's interest in marine life took them to Ilfracombe, where he did research for his *Sea-side Studies*. During their stay there, Marian wrote what Haight calls "one of her finest articles for the *Westminster*," "The Natural History of German Life" (201). From Ilfracombe they went on to Tenby for a five-week stay at the coast, again for Lewes's zoological research. There Marian experienced a fresh sense of well-being. On July 20 she wrote in her journal, "I do not remember feeling so strong in mind and body as I feel at this moment" (qtd. in Haight, *Biography* 206). By September, she had begun to write fiction.

Eliot explains in her journal, in "How I Came to Write Fiction," that September of 1856 had marked the beginning of a new era in her life (*Letters* 2:406). Her sense that the date marked the beginning of a new stage lends support to my view that the timing of her decision to write fiction, which occurred twenty years after her mother's death in 1836, constituted a positive anniversary reaction that signified the beginning of her release from mourning. I also believe that the publication of her last novel, *Daniel Deronda*, twenty years later, in 1876, signified a (perhaps partial) resolution of her sense of loss, as well as the fulfillment of her hard-won sense of identity as an artist. I will therefore argue in this book that Eliot's fiction is an example of Pollock's idea that an artist's creative products may represent "aspects of the mourning process itself" (1:127). Eliot's expressed sense of renewal in the summer of 1856 suggests that she began her fiction writing from a position of strength. Both her rich background of accomplishments and her stable relationship with Lewes had contributed to her readiness for new growth.

Eliot explains in her journal entry that although she had always had a "vague dream" of writing a novel, it was not until after her return from the Continent with Lewes that her "greater [than expected] success . . . in other kinds of writing" convinced them both that it would be worthwhile for her to try fiction. At Tenby, Lewes began to urge her to start immediately, but she deferred because of more pressing projects, until "one morning as I was lying in bed, thinking what should be the subject of my first story, my thoughts merged themselves into a dreamy doze, and I imagined myself writing a story of which the title was 'The Sad Fortunes of the Reverend Amos Barton.'" Deciding to make her dream a reality, she came up with the plan to write "a series of stories containing sketches drawn from my own observations of the Clergy, and calling them 'Scenes of Clerical Life' opening with 'Amos Barton.'" When "Amos Barton" was completed, Lewes helped her by proposing to John Blackwood, the publisher of his series of "Sea-Side Studies," a series of "tales and sketches illustrative of the actual life of our country clergy about a quarter of a century ago; but solely in its *human* and *not at all* in its *theological* aspect; the object being to do what has never yet been done in our Literature, for we have had abundant religious stories polemical and doctrinal, but since the 'Vicar' and Miss Austen, no stories representing the clergy like any other class with the humours, sorrows, and troubles of other men" (2:269). Lewes did not, however, reveal the identity of the author.

Eliot's first fictional characters were thus based on real-life figures from her childhood. The character Amos Barton was based on the Reverend John Gwyther, the curate who had officiated at Mrs. Evans's funeral and Chrissey's wedding (Haight, *Biography* 211). The title character in the second story, "Mr. Gilfil's Love Story," was drawn from memories of the Reverend Bernard Gilpin Ebdell, the vicar who had christened Mary Anne; as Haight stresses, however, "the plot is entirely imaginary" (221). In the third and last of the stories, "Janet's Repentance," Mr. Tryan is an "idealized portrait of Mr. Jones, the Evangelical curate at Nuneaton" during Mary Anne's schooldays at Mrs. Wallington's (227). The fact that the characters were drawn from the author's memories of real-life figures did not go unnoticed. In Warwickshire in particular, much curiosity was aroused as to the identity of the author, who had assumed the pen name of George Eliot. Most people thought the writer must be a clergyman; Charles Dickens was the only person to guess (from the domestic details) that the author was a woman (Laski 55). It was not until she had begun to write *Adam Bede* that Eliot revealed her identity to her editor, John Blackwood. After the novel's publication, as Haight records, the truth of its authorship "was spreading generally in literary circles" (*Biography* 287). The attempts by an imposter, a clergyman named Joseph Liggins, to claim credit for George Eliot's work contributed to her gradual (although reluctant) willingness to let her identity be known to the public, although more than anything else, it was the "extraordinary success of *Adam Bede*" that finally "lifted the veil of anonymity" (297).

Throughout the process of publishing *Scenes of Clerical Life* (1857), Blackwood responded favorably, although with honest criticism, to the manuscripts he received from the unknown author (Eliot, *Letters* 2:272, 275, 297). Judging from their correspondence, however, neither Eliot nor Lewes could accept the constructive criticism that might have helped the new fiction writer avoid mistakes later in her career (274, 299). Blackwood's expressed "fear [in regard to "Gilfil"] that [Eliot] huddles up the conclusion of his stories too much" (323) was a criticism that turned out to be prophetic. Although his comment was noted by the author, she seemed not to understand how to work on the problem; she answered that "conclusions are the weak point of most authors, but some of the fault lies in the very nature of a conclusion, which is at best a negation" (324). Blackwood's response to the first part of "Janet's Repentance" also anticipates later comments about Eliot's bleak presentation of provincial life. He wrote, "I should have liked a pleasanter picture. Surely the colors are rather harsh for a sketch of English County Town life only 25 years ago" (344). Arguing that the reality had already been softened enough, Eliot responded, "The real town was more vicious than my Milby; the real Dempster more disgusting than mine; the real Janet alas! had a far sadder end than mine" (347). At this point, Lewes added (in a separate letter) his opinion that "I was in raptures with 'Janet's Repentance' when Eliot first read it to me and declared it to be the finest thing he had written" (351). Blackwood responded, characteristically, with reassurance (352). Yet when he ventured still another criticism of a scene in "Janet's Repentance," Lewes, revealing what turned out to be a lifelong tendency to protect Eliot from criticism, finally wrote, "Entre nous let me hint that unless you have any *serious* objection to make to Eliot's stories, *don't* make any. He is so easily discouraged, so diffident of himself, that not being prompted by necessity to write, he will close the series in the belief that his writing is not relished. . . . *Don't allude to this hint of mine.* He wouldn't like my interfering" (363–64). Although the next letter from Blackwood expresses admiration for the ending of "Janet's Repentance" (371), Eliot apparently still rankled from his earlier criticism. As she recorded in her journal, "I had meant to carry on the series beyond 'Janet's Repentance,' . . . but my annoyance at Blackwood's want of sympathy in the first two parts of 'Janet,' . . . determined me to close the series and republish them in two volumes" (410).

Despite their tentative beginnings, Eliot, Blackwood, and Lewes nonetheless developed a good working relationship over the years that followed. Blackwood was still Eliot's editor, except for a short rift over the publication of *Romola*, when she wrote her last novel, *Daniel Deronda*.

George Eliot was paid generously for her fiction. After 1857, she and Lewes, who was also doing well with his publications, no longer had to worry about money, and Eliot was able to give up her article writing. *Scenes of Clerical Life* was well received in literary circles, and although there were only three reviews, they were encouraging (Laski 55). With the publication of *Adam Bede*, Eliot's reputation was established. Her early fiction, which was drawn largely from a combination of various elements of memory and imagination, became less literally based on figures from the past after the *Scenes* as she began to make rapid progress in her artistic technique. Her early works were also rapidly composed. *Scenes of Clerical Life* was completed in only a little over a year, as was each of the long novels, *Adam Bede* and *The Mill on the Floss*. The short novel, *Silas Marner*, proved to be a transitional work, written as Eliot was beginning to move toward the writing of her more complex novels,

Romola, Felix Holt, Middlemarch, and *Daniel Deronda.* All of these later novels involved more research and took longer to complete.

In the chapters to come, I have limited myself to a discussion of George Eliot's seven novels. These are her major works, and as such, the primary focus of her attention during the twenty years of her creative life. Any attempt to include every work of fiction would result in too ponderous a book, and would not add substantially to my argument. Besides the three *Scenes* and the seven novels, Eliot also published two short stories: "The Lifted Veil," in 1859, between the writing of *Adam Bede* and *The Mill on the Floss,* and "Brother Jacob," written in 1860 after the publication of *The Mill on the Floss* and before the writing of *Silas Marner.* She also wrote *The Spanish Gypsy,* begun as a play in 1864 after the publication of *Romola* and completed as a poem in 1868, after the publication of *Felix Holt.* She wrote other works of poetry, including the "Brother and Sister Sonnets" in 1869 and "The Legend of Jubal" in 1870, before the writing of *Middlemarch;* a collection of her poetry was published later, in 1874. After her last novel *Daniel Deronda,* her only published work was a collection of essays, *Impressions of Theophrastus Such,* published in 1878.

    I have continued my presentation of Eliot's development by placing my analysis of each novel in the context of the ongoing events of her life; I have also described briefly in each case some of the details of her writing process. In this way, I hope to show how Eliot's pattern of extraordinary intellectual, creative, and emotional growth continued throughout her fiction-writing career. I have also placed my discussions in the context of each novel's critical reception, both in Eliot's time and ours. My purpose in so doing is to convey something of the scope of each work of fiction, and the extent of the author's success, at the same time that I demonstrate the way in which my psychoanalytic interpretations can help to answer some of the questions raised by critics; I also want to stress that criticisms of George Eliot's work should be seen in the light of her overall achievement.

    I must also add that Eliot's artistic and personal development did not go smoothly, even once she started on the path of fiction writing. Instead of a smooth ascent, her creative path sometimes seems more like a labyrinth. To many modern critics, *Romola* and *Felix Holt* present serious problems; some even consider one or both to be failures. Yet after attempting to work through the difficulties presented by those novels, Eliot was prepared to write her masterpiece, *Middlemarch;* and by the time she finished what some readers believe to be an even greater work, *Daniel Deronda,* she seems to have achieved, in addition to her eminent position as an English novelist, her own inner sense of completion.

I have tried to write this book in such a way that it will interest the general reader as much as the academic reader. Prior knowledge of George Eliot's novels, or of psychoanalytic theory, although helpful, is not necessary. For those who may be unfamiliar with the variety of academic styles of documentation, I want to explain that instead of using footnotes, I have incorporated all references to the list of "Works Cited" in the body of the text, in order to make it easier for readers to locate my sources. In short, I have tried to write the kind of book that I would like to read myself. I hope my readers will find it useful.

ONE

Self-Disorder and Aggression in *Adam Bede*

After the completion of "Janet's Repentance," the third and last story in *Scenes of Clerical Life*, George Eliot wrote her editor, John Blackwood, on September 5, 1857, that "I have a subject in my mind which will not come under the limitations of the title 'Clerical Life,' and I am inclined to take a large canvas for it, and write a novel" (*Letters* 2:381). On October 17 she wrote, "My new story haunts me a good deal, and I shall set about it without delay. It will be a country story—full of the breath of cows and the scent of hay" (387). She began writing on October 22. After she had finished the novel in November 1858, she recorded in her journal her "History of *Adam Bede*," where she explains the germ of her story: an anecdote told her in 1839 by her Methodist aunt, Mrs. Samuel Evans, of a visit to a "condemned criminal, a very ignorant girl who had murdered her child and refused to confess—how she had stayed with her praying, through the night and how the poor creature at last broke out into tears, and confessed her crime." Eliot had begun thinking, shortly after beginning to write the *Scenes*, of blending this story "and some other recollections of my aunt in one story with some points in my father's early life and character" (502).

She carefully researched the background of her novel, which takes place in 1799 in the county of "Loamshire," a symbolic re-creation of Staffordshire, where her father had come from his childhood home in Derbyshire (re-created in the novel as "Stonyshire"), as a young man to begin his career as a carpenter. Eliot gleaned from Southey's *Life of Wesley* the details she needed for her characterization of Dinah, her Methodist preacher, about women's preaching, visions, the divination of God's will, visits to prisons, and preaching in the open air. She also searched the *Gentleman's Magazine* of 1799 for details of vegetation and weather for her setting. As Gordon Haight observes, "her concern for details helps explain the sense of authenticity, the remarkable density of background her realism achieves" (*Biography* 250). Yet she emphasized in her letters after the novel was published that the story had developed out of her imagination: "There is not a single portrait in *Adam Bede*. . . . The whole course of the story—the descriptions of scenery or houses—the characters—the dialogue—*everything* is a combination of widely sundered elements of experience" (3:155). Regarding her accurate rendering of the local dialect, she stresses that she "never knew any Derbyshire people, or Staffordshire either, except my father and his brothers," and that she had visited her paternal relatives only a few times while she was growing up (157).

It would be hard to overstate the success of *Adam Bede*. It was published on February 1, 1859; by the middle of March, Blackwood wrote to congratulate her upon being "a *popular* as well as a great author" (3:33); he added that "the sale is nothing to the ring of applause that I hear in all directions." In June, her friend Barbara Bodichon wrote, "I wish you could hear people talking about *AB*" (108). In July, Charles Dickens wrote to say that "*Adam Bede* has taken its place among the actual experiences of my life. . . . The conception of Hetty's character is so extraordinarily subtle and true, that I laid the book down fifty times, to shut my eyes and think about it. I know nothing so skilful, determined, and uncompromising. The whole country life that the story is set in, is so real, and so droll and genuine, and yet so selected and polished by art, that I cannot praise it enough to you" (114–15). G. H. Lewes wrote his son in March 1860 that Bede "had had greater success than any novel since Scott (except Dickens). I do not mean has *sold* more—for 'Uncle Tom's Cabin' and 'Les Mysteres de Paris' surpass all novels in sale; but in its *influence,* and in obtaining the suffrages of the highest and wisest as well of the ordinary novel reader, nothing equals 'Adam Bede'" (275).

The scope of the novel reaches far beyond its provincial origins. One twentieth-century critic, U. C. Knoepflmacher, has rightly seen the novel as Eliot's reinterpretation of the fallen and redeemed Adam of Milton's epic (*Novels* 91–126). Although the title character is the primary focus of the author's theme of "tragic growth" (Hardy, *Novels* 39), Eliot attempts to show "an enlargement of moral sympathy" (Gregor 24) on the part of all four major characters—Adam, Arthur, Hetty, and

Dinah. Many twentieth-century readers have difficulty accepting Eliot's message, however, because of the treatment of Hetty, the character who is convicted of infanticide and banished from the community of Hayslope. Critics who have puzzled over the author's apparent harshness toward Hetty include Knoepflmacher, who calls Hetty's early disappearance from the novel her "execution by her moralistic creator" (*Novels* 124), and George Creeger, who suggests that Hetty is "the victim" of her creator's own "hardness" (231). Mason Harris, who refers to Eliot's "unforgivable" refusal to portray Hetty's further development after her exile, objects to the novel's ending on the grounds that "the reconstructed, Hetty-less pastoral of the ending seems to refute the whole process of the novel" ("Hetty" 189, 194). Other critics who have objected to the ending of the novel on similar grounds include Michael Edwards, who feels that its power "is diminished by Adam's lack of guilt as regards Hetty" (218), and Murray Krieger, who suggests that "our discomfort with the conclusion is our sense that the transformed pain is not evident enough" (219).

My purpose in this chapter is to show how Heinz Kohut's "self-psychology" illuminates the problems that critics have noted in *Adam Bede*. I will argue that Eliot's portrayal of the inhabitants of the village of Hayslope shows that the community victimizes Hetty; each of the major characters, Arthur, Adam, and even the idealized heroine, Dinah, is shown using Hetty as a scapegoat. At the same time, I will show how Kohut's theory about the relationship between incomplete self-development and rage helps to account for the aggressive behavior of the characters. I will then explain how Eliot's apparent failure to see the extent of the aggression she portrays in her characters constitutes a denial of the aggressive impulses within herself. Finally, I will point to some of the ways in which the patterns in *Adam Bede* are repeated in the later novels.

Kohut's psychology of the self defines psychoanalytic cure as a process of self-structuralization that results in a productive life, rather than simply as the resolution of oedipal conflict (*Cure* 7). His version of the well-known definition of mental health (the ability to work and to love) is "the capacity of a firm self to avail itself of the talents and skills at [its] disposal, enabling [the individual] to love and work successfully" (*Restoration* 284). To Kohut, the role of parents is central in the develop-

Self-Disorder and Aggression in *Adam Bede* 27

ment of a firm self-structure, which he believes depends more upon the effect of the child's total environment, than on "gross events," such as the deaths of parents (187–91). One step in the formation of the "bipolar self" occurs as a result of the infant's early "mirroring," or interaction with a supportive parent figure; this stage is necessary for the development of a healthy self-esteem. Another step occurs as a result of the child's "idealization" of a parent figure—a stage which precedes the successful internalization of values (*Analysis* 40–49, 106–9). When the process of self-structuralization is left incomplete, the result is a "self-disorder," defined by the persistence of archaic self and parent images that have not become integrated into the mature structures of the personality (Russell 140).

Instead of emphasizing the growth from dependence to autonomy, as does traditional psychoanalysis, Kohut emphasizes the changed nature of the relationship between self and "self-objects" (*Cure* 52). He believes that throughout life human beings need healthy attachments to empathic self-objects which replace their infantile self-objects, their parents. Kohut's view of aggression is also different from the traditional view of it as the manifestation of an innate drive. He sees rage as a reaction to the feeling of loss of connection between self and empathic parental object, or, to put it another way, as a reaction to the sense that the integrity of the self has been violated. Rage results from "the breakup of the primary self-experience in which, in the child's perception, the child and the empathic self-object are one" (*Restoration* 91).

In *Adam Bede*, Eliot portrays characters who suffer from varying degrees of disorders of the self, resulting from their lack of the parental and community support that is necessary for the development of a firm sense of identity. Eliot's characters have lost their parent(s), yet at the same time, because of their unresolved need for them, have failed to separate themselves from their infantile parental image(s). In their need to attach themselves to an infantile object, Arthur, Adam, and Dinah choose Hetty, who functions in the community both as a fertility/mother figure and as a child figure. As the characters struggle to grow beyond their childhood attachments and find replacements for them, however, they need to kill off their old parental images as symbolized by Hetty—hence their banishment of her.

Although Eliot seems to blame Hetty for her flaws, her presentation of the harsh family and social conditions that lie underneath the surface of the Eden-like county of Loamshire shows that Hetty has been victimized by its inhabitants. She has been effectively excluded from the community of Hayslope from the time of her arrival. Orphaned at age ten, she has come to live with her aunt and uncle, the Poysers, who are conscientious about the formalities of caring for her, but who treat her differently from their own children. Hetty's grandfather, who is part of the household, also treats her differently from his son's children, because he still resents her mother's marriage to a man beneath the Poysers' status.

Building on Creeger's view of Hetty's "hardness" as "childish . . . egocentricity" (228), Harris sees Hetty not as an "adult sinner," but as a "confused child" ("Hetty" 179), essentially "abandoned" by her relatives. Her relatives' rigid incapacity to accept her as part of their "respectable" world has resulted in her "arrested development" (180). She has not been able to find an appropriate role in her family or community; her status is somewhere between that of the servants and the Poysers' own children. To Harris, Hetty's lack of parental support has prevented her development of the "sense of an inner self" that she needs to be able to assess the values imposed on her by the Hayslope "shame-culture" (193, 184). Extending Harris's analysis, one may note that, as Eliot portrays her, Hetty has not completed the steps in the creation of the constituents of Kohut's bipolar self. Her intense need for mirroring is shown in her Narcissus-like tendency to gaze at length at her reflection, either in a polished surface or a mirror (117, 194, 199, 294–96, 378). Her failure to internalize values is reflected in the way that "shame . . . was poor little Hetty's conscience" and "religious doctrines had taken no hold on [her] mind" (382, 430).

Contrasting the usual view of Hetty as "a temptress" with his own interpretation of her as "a little girl," Harris demonstrates that her feeling for Arthur is not "sensual love," but a "Cinderella-fantasy" (182–83). Hetty's propensity for looking at herself in the mirror, along with her self-defeating involvement with Arthur, who she dreams will provide her with wealth and importance, suggest her need for self-completion. In the scene in her bed-chamber, she gazes at her image while imagining that Arthur is with her: "his arm was around her, and the delicate rose-scent of his hair was with her still" (195). Hetty is searching for her identity by attaching herself to Arthur, who has the established place in Hayslope that she longs for.

Hetty's treatment of babies and children reenacts her own sense of abandonment. She hates children as much as she hates the lambs and the baby chickens on the farm. When Hetty gives birth to her own child after she runs away from home, she is not able to behave as a mother normally would. "I seemed to hate it," she later confesses to Dinah. Earlier in the confession she says, "And then the little baby was born, when I didn't expect it; and the thought came into my mind that I might get rid of it, and go home again. . . . I longed so to go back again." Hetty's already weak sense of self deteriorates further when she leaves Hayslope, the only source of her identity and values. Her primary thought, when she thinks of murdering her child, is to "go home again" (498). In her confusion, however, "by burying the child, but not completely, Hetty tries both to kill it and to let it live" (Harris 187). Hetty is ambivalent, and rather than actively killing the baby, she abandons it in the woods. Thus the murder takes the form of passive aggression.

The characterization of Arthur, whom Harris calls Eliot's "first extensive study of unconscious motivation" ("Misuse" 45), reveals that his inadequate self-development, although less severe than Hetty's, sets him up for his destructive interaction with her. While Arthur feels his future position in Hayslope is secure, his background has some parallels with Hetty's. For one thing, he has no parents. His mother has died only three months after his christening, and his father is missing. All we know about his father is that Arthur's godmother, Mrs. Irwine, has a low opinion of him (108), just as Hetty's relatives have a low opinion of her father. Like Hetty, Arthur's lack of adequate parent figures creates his ongoing need for the firm support that would enable him to complete the process of his self-structuralization.

Just as Hetty is treated with indifference by her grandfather, so Arthur feels at times "positively hate[d]" by his (302). He also feels controlled by him. As he says to Mr. Irwine, "My grandfather will never let me have any power while he lives" (215). In the same conversation Irwine tells him that his mother (Mrs. Irwine) has prophesied that Arthur's "lady-love will rule [him] as the moon rules the tides" (216). Arthur replies after a narrative interlude, "A man may be very firm in other matters and yet be under a sort of witchery from a woman" (216). Arthur's sense of being controlled is easily transferable to other relationships; he is susceptible to "woman's witchery." Furthermore, like Hetty, his lack of family support has resulted in his failure to internalize firm values. Eliot comments that Arthur "lived a great deal in other people's opinions and feelings concerning himself" (216). As Harris says, Arthur "depends on the approbation of others rather than an inner sense of self [and has] a moral sense based mainly on shame" ("Misuse" 53, 54). He shares to a lesser degree Hetty's need for self-completion, yet also like Hetty, chooses a self-defeating relationship.

Arthur is described as having a "loving nature," but Eliot's irony becomes clear in the subsequent description of his treatment of the "old gardener." When Arthur was seven, he impulsively kicked over the old man's pitcher of broth. Finally realizing that it was the man's dinner, he "took his favorite pencil-case and a silver-hafted knife out of his pocket and offered them as compensation. He had been the same Arthur ever since, trying to make all offences forgotten in benefits" (356).

Although Arthur is too concerned about other people's opinions to be openly aggressive, he evidences a pattern of behaving aggressively and then seeking atonement by giving up something he possesses. In the incident with the old gardener Arthur takes out his aggression on someone whose social status is beneath his own. His relationship with Hetty follows the same pattern: it is an assertion of his power over the lower classes. The sequence of events that occurs at the time just before Arthur becomes involved with Hetty suggests that although his actions with Hetty appear to be impulsive, they are actually a reaction to his sense of being controlled by his grandfather. Arthur is disgruntled because "there was no having his own way in the stables; everything was managed in the stingiest fashion" (172). Then he learns that his horse is lame and feels "thoroughly disappointed and annoyed" (173). He goes out for a ride on the other horse that is available to him, and by the time he returns is unable to resist breaking his resolution not to see Hetty. In his dressing room after lunch, he feels that "the desire to see [her] had rushed back like an ill-stemmed current." He rationalizes that he will "amuse himself" by seeing Hetty that day "and get rid of the whole thing from his mind." Then he goes to see Hetty in the wood (174–75).

The affair is not simply a matter of Arthur's failure to recognize his own frustrated sex drive, which Harris asserts has been "sublimated" into "sentimental musing over Hetty" ("Misuse" 45). Sexual fantasy and behavior can also serve as a defense, for example, against "hostile aggression" (Coen 895). Arthur, feeling controlled and therefore angry at his grandfather, expresses his frustration and need for power in the involvement with Hetty. Yet he also feels he is under her power, or "witchery." As often as he determines to do so, he is not able to end the affair and separate himself from Hetty, who is as much an extension of his fantasies as he is of hers. Just as Hetty's fantasies are about the luxuries of the social position that would be hers as Arthur's wife (144, 181, 199, 296), so Arthur's are about his life as squire after his grandfather's death (170, 483). Arthur's inadequate sense of his own identity, which depends to such an extent on his future inheritance from his grandfather, makes him susceptible to the need for completing himself in the relationship with Hetty, in which he can act out his fantasy of being loved by the lower classes for his philanthropic works after he takes over his grandfather's position in the community.

Arthur does finally suffer from the pain he has caused Hetty. His atonement, however, follows the pattern of his atonement with the old gardener: an attempt to rectify aggressive action by giving up possessions. He gives up his position as squire and goes away. Yet his exile is only temporary. He is eventually able to return and find a place in Hayslope. Hetty, by virtue of her position in the community, is the one who must bear the full weight of the consequences of their behavior.

Eliot attempts to show her title character Adam undergoing a transformation from an inner "hardness" to a capacity for sympathy for others (Creeger 234–35). The description of Adam's family life points to the source of his hardness as his lost "sense of distinction" as "Thias Bede's lad" since the onset of his father's alcoholism during his late teenage years. Adam's "shame and anguish" (92) had caused him to run away from home, but he had returned because he did not want to leave his mother and brother Seth with the burden of enduring the situation without him. Kohut explains that shame results in rage, and in the shamed individual's ongoing readiness to seek revenge ("Thoughts" 380–81)—a reaction that Eliot similarly depicts. By the time Adam's story opens, his shame has turned to rage, which shows itself in his propensity for fighting (211) and in his severity toward his father (86). Adam focuses all his anger about his family situation on his father, although it is clear that his mother Lisbeth has her own problem of "idolatrous love" (87) for Adam and her obvious preference for him over Seth.

Adam's anger toward his father culminates in his actions on the night of his father's death. He is furious because his father is out drinking when he should have been working on the job of making a coffin for a man in a neighboring village. While Adam stays up to finish the job himself, he thinks of his father's continuously "worsening" behavior (92), but feels determined not to run away from the situation again, although he feels his father will be a "sore cross" to him for years to come. At that moment he hears a rap "as if with a willow wand" on the house door, goes to the door to look out, sees that no one seems to be there, and thinks of the superstition that the sound of a willow wand rapping on the door means that someone is dying (93). After he hears the sound again and still sees no sign of his father, he reasons that Thias is probably "sleeping off his drunkenness at the [tavern]." Not wanting to succumb to superstitious thinking, he determines not to open the door again, and for the rest of the night hears no more knocking. The next morning, however, Seth discovers that Thias has drowned during the night, "not far from his own door," as Mr. Irwine says later (137).

Carol Christ notes that Thias's death "occurs as a magical fulfillment of Adam's anger" (131); Krieger suggests that "the resentfulness Adam feels . . . brings him close to wishing his father dead" (211). It is possible to interpret Adam's hearing the sound of the willow wand not only as a manifestation of his sense of foreboding, but as his wish for his father's death. It is also possible to interpret Adam's decision not to open the door again despite his father's expected arrival as a form of passive aggression, and as an indirect contribution to his father's death. In any case, Thias's death causes Adam to repent his "severity" toward him (97). And this repentance, in Eliot's view, turns out to be the first step of the process "in which Adam learns to overcome his angry severity toward others" (Christ 131).

Adam's attitude toward Arthur and Hetty repeats the pattern of his attitude toward his parents. Even before he realizes they are actually having an affair, he is openly outraged at Arthur's involvement with Hetty and provokes him into a fight. Yet he has trouble seeing any wrong in Hetty even after it becomes clear that she has abandoned her baby. Adam's reluctance to feel hostile toward Hetty is related to his reluctance to be angry with his mother. His dream, which recounts the events in the Bede household shortly after Thias's death, shows Adam's close identification of Hetty with his mother. When his mother approaches, accidentally waking him, he is not startled to see her because she had been present "with her fretful grief" throughout his feverish reliving of the day's events. Yet Hetty, too, had "continually" appeared in the dream, "mingling . . . in scenes with which she had nothing to do"; and "wherever Hetty came, his mother was sure to follow soon" (152). Adam's dream suggests that he has transferred his attachment to his mother, who has always loved him with "idolatrous love," to his "preoccupying fancy" with Hetty (161–62).

When Adam learns of Hetty's interest in Arthur, he does not express anger toward her openly. Instead, his aggressiveness takes the form of an intrusion on her relationship with Arthur. By insisting that Arthur not see Hetty again and that he write her a letter breaking off the relationship, he is cutting off all possibility that Arthur will be able to help her. At the time of the intrusion, Adam is not aware that Hetty is pregnant, nor is he aware that Arthur really does care for her more than he has let Adam know. His intrusiveness, however, is inappropriate and ends up making the situation worse. It is perhaps Adam's bitter jealousy (370), more than an interest in Hetty's welfare, that makes him insist on the letter, which he gives to Hetty himself after he tells her that Arthur "care[s] nothing about [her] as a man ought to care" (367). As Bruce K. Martin argues, "Adam thus indirectly contributes to the child-killing" by "remov[ing] from Hetty's mind the possibility of consulting Arthur until it is too late" (759).

Adam's inner struggles center on his inability to see Hetty realistically. Even before he sees her with Arthur in the woods, her locket (a gift from Arthur) drops to the floor in front of Adam; he fears she has a lover, but then rationalizes that she "might have bought the thing herself" (333). After he delivers Arthur's letter to her, he still hopes that she will become interested in him: "She may turn round the other way, when she finds he's made light of her all the while" (370). He continues to hope for her love by "creat[ing] the mind he believed in out of his own" (400). When he learns that Hetty has been accused of infanticide, he finds it impossible to believe: "'It's his doing,' he said; 'if there's been any crime, it's at his door, not at hers. . . . I *can't* bear it. . . . it's too hard to think she's wicked'" (455). At the trial, when it becomes clear that Hetty is guilty, "It was the supreme moment of his suffering: Hetty was guilty, and he was silently calling to God for help" (481). Later, in the "upper room" scene with Bartle Massey, Adam is still having trouble accepting the truth about her: "I thought she was loving and tender-hearted, and wouldn't tell a lie, or act deceitful. . . . And if he'd never come near her, and I'd married her, and been loving to her, and took care of her, she might never ha' done anything bad" (503–4). Adam is struggling to separate himself from his fantasy of Hetty, who symbolizes his lingering parental image of the loving young woman who belongs only to him.

When Adam is forced to face the truth about Hetty's affair and infanticide, and when he finally forgives her and Arthur, he becomes free of her (and his mother's) hold on his mind. The sign of his transformation is his participation in "a kind of Lord's Supper" (Creeger 234) with Bartle Massey in the "upper room" before Hetty's trial. Just before he takes the bread and wine, Adam agrees to go see Hetty in the prison and says, "I'll never be hard again" (475). Finally, in the chapter entitled "Another Meeting in the Wood," he even repents of his "hardness" toward Arthur: "I've no right to be hard towards them as have done wrong and repent" (514).

His own suffering after his father's death, and his vicarious participation in Hetty's suffering after the infanticide, have extended his capacity for "sympathy," which in Eliot's novels must be preceded by "the recognition of difference: between oneself and another" (Ermarth, "Sympathy" 25), as in the case of Adam's changed view of Hetty. Adam's participation in Hetty's guilt causes him to "look upon every sufferer, regardless of guilt, as worthy of sympathy" (Martin 750). In psychoanalytic terms, his identification with Hetty and her suffering is apparently therapeutic because at the same time that he separates himself from his childhood image of his mother, he also transfers his wish for his father's death onto Hetty's murderous act. Through Hetty's suffering, he is cleansed of his own guilt; Hetty is the sacrificial lamb whose suffering makes Adam's redemption possible. Eliot calls his "deep, unspeakable suffering" a "baptism, a regeneration, the initiation into a new state" (471). She tries to suggest that he has become a more complete human being, ready for a mature love for Dinah. Yet in her portrayal, Adam's growth occurs at the expense of Hetty, whose murderous act and subsequent punishment are in part a consequence of his aggressive intrusion on her relationship with Arthur; thus Eliot's attempt, in her reworking of the themes of Milton's epic, to show Adam's transformation in terms of the nineteenth-century "religion of humanity," as Knoepflmacher explains the scene (*Novels* 112), becomes a perversion, rather than a reinterpretation, of the idea of baptism.

In a scene in his mother's cottage shortly after his father's death, Adam hears a foot on the stairs and imagines it is Hetty; but instead, Dinah, the "reality contrasted with a preoccupying fancy," enters (161–62). This is the first hint that Dinah will be able to replace Hetty in Adam's affections. His love for her becomes "the outgrowth of that fuller life which had come to him from his acquaintance with deep sorrow" (574). He and Dinah marry and find their place in Hayslope. Painful memories remain, but in Eliot's view Adam has regained his Paradise.

Although Eliot attempts to idealize Dinah, she emerges as a character with unresolved needs expressed in destructive interactions with Hetty. Like Hetty and Arthur, Dinah has lost both her parents. She has been raised by her Aunt Judith, Mrs. Poyser's sister. When Dinah visits the Bedes' home early in the novel, she tells Lisbeth about her orphaned background and "how she had been brought up to work hard, and what sort of place Snowfield (in Stonyshire) was, and how many people had a hard life there" (157). Yet Dinah does not appear to suffer any ill-effects from her hard life. Lisbeth tells her, "[Y]e look as if ye'd ne'er been angered i' your life" (156). She is referring to Dinah's apparently compliant nature, which Lisbeth thinks must at least have made the aunt's task of bringing up a child a little easier.

The possibility that Dinah's calm exterior is in part a cover for anger is born out in her preaching and other aspects of her ministry. During her sermon, her voice is all calm and compassion until "she had thoroughly arrested her hearers" (71). Then "her utterance" becomes more "rapid and agitated," as she emphasizes the listeners' "guilt . . . wilful darkness, [and] state of disobedience to God" (72). She begins to single out individuals, focusing in particular on Bessy Cranage, who "had always been considered a naughty girl . . . [and] was conscious of it" (73). She accuses Bessy of paying more attention to her earrings and clothes than to her "Saviour" and warns her that when she is old, she will "begin to feel that [her] soul is not saved" and "will have to stand before God dressed in [her] sins." Toward the end of Dinah's pointed message, which, as Christopher Herbert suggests, amounts to "an attack" on her (415), Bessy bursts into tears; finally, "a great terror [came] upon her," and she threw her earrings "down before her, sobbing aloud" (75).

Dinah repeats the pattern of her attack on Bessy when she "intrude[s]" (Krieger 205) on Hetty in "The Two Bed-Chambers," a chapter intended to show the striking contrasts between Hetty, who is "strutting about decked in her scarf and earrings" in front of her mirror (201), and Dinah, who is looking out the window of her room at a "wide view over the fields" (202). Dinah closes her eyes in prayer, is interrupted by a sound from Hetty's room, and begins to think about her. Feeling "pity" for Hetty's lack of "warm, self-devoting love" and "a deep longing to go now and pour into Hetty's ear all the words of tender warning and appeal that rushed into her mind" (203), Dinah goes to her room and with very little introduction says, "It has been borne in upon my mind tonight that you may some day be in trouble" (205). She offers to help in any future time of need, and in her homiletic style reminds Hetty to seek strength from God, who will support her "in the evil day." When Dinah sees that Hetty is reacting "with a chill fear" to her prophecy, her "tender anxious pleading" becomes "the more earnest" until Hetty, "full of a vague fear that something evil was sometime to befall her, began to cry." Interpreting Hetty's reaction as "the stirring of a divine impulse," Dinah begins to "cry with her for grateful joy," but Hetty becomes "irritated under Dinah's caress," and pushing her away impatiently, sobs, "Don't talk to me so, Dinah. Why do you come to frighten me? I've never done anything to you. Why can't you let me be?" (206).

Dinah's style of ministry is in sharp contrast to Mr. Irwine's, who has more a "live and let live" (103) attitude toward his flock. When Arthur comes to see him about Hetty, Irwine refrains from giving him advice because he has already warned Arthur not to get involved with Hetty. Moreover, Irwine has no idea how close he is to an involvement, and is trying to let Arthur take the initiative in any confession or request for advice. Conversely, he very firmly takes the initiative in advising Adam, who he knows has a propensity for violence, not to get into another fight with Arthur. Irwine speaks to him in a rational tone about the consequences of acting out of blind fury and then leaves him to his own thoughts. His behavior indicates that he believes that Arthur and Adam have the capacity to make the right decision. Dinah's behavior toward

Bessy and Hetty indicates that she thinks they are lost souls incapable of any right behavior without her help.

Dinah does not actually see Hetty again until the prison scene, where Hetty's "hardness" is melted (497) as she finally makes her confession to Dinah. Although Eliot tries to show Dinah as facilitating Hetty's breakthrough in this scene, her earlier departure from Hayslope is another indication of Dinah's (in this case, passive) aggressiveness toward Hetty. Dinah repeatedly expresses interest in helping Hetty, but she goes away without leaving an address, and by the time she reappears, it is too late to help, except by listening to her final confession in the prison cell.

Dinah tells Seth she feels "called" to return to Snowfield, although "[her] heart yearns" over her aunt's family "and that poor wandering lamb, Hetty Sorrel" (78). When she is almost ready to leave, Dinah again expresses interest in Hetty, who she says will be in her intercessions (187), and in "The Two Bed-Chambers" scene, Dinah expresses her fear that Hetty "may someday be in trouble" (205). While Dinah is away, Seth receives a letter from her, which refers to her sense of foreboding about her aunt's household (375). When Adam goes to look for Hetty, however, although he believes she is visiting Dinah in Snowfield, he finds that Dinah is out of town and learns that she has not left any address. After Hetty is accused of infanticide, Dinah is still missing and no one knows for certain where she is. The family tries to send her a letter, but they have no idea whether she receives it. Dinah does not reappear until Hetty has already been sentenced, when she visits her in the prison. Dinah's departure and failure to leave an address at a time when she senses that something might be wrong belie the expressions of concern for her aunt's household. Eliot's idealized Dinah thus expresses aggression indirectly both in the form of intrusiveness and passivity.

Dinah's anger is not acknowledged, but it is evident in her words and actions. Hetty, like Bessy, is a likely target for Dinah's aggressions because the community already looks down on her, her self-esteem is low, and she is the least capable of fighting back. Yet perhaps more importantly, Hetty represents the side of herself that Dinah is unwilling to acknowledge: the sexual (the affair with Arthur) and the aggressive (the murder of the baby). In attacking Hetty, Dinah is attacking the threatening forces in her own nature. Several times Mrs. Poyser refers angrily to Dinah's asceticism (121, 236, 518), as though she is aware that there is something wrong with Dinah's failure to acknowledge any normal physical needs. Dinah's denial of natural needs suggests that she is "lacking in self," or in a "sense of human identity"; her "fear of accepting full maturity" (Creeger 236, 237) is reflected, in psychoanalytic terminology, in her persistent archaic idealized self-image, and is a sign of defective self-development (Russell 139, 144). Dinah identifies only with her "ideal self" as she splits off and projects her unacceptable traits onto others. Hetty answers Dinah's need to get rid of her "bad self."

After Adam's proposal, Dinah goes away again to think it over. A few weeks later, when Adam goes to see her, Dinah, apparently having undergone a transformation that enables her to accept her feelings for Adam, finally declares her love: "It is the Divine Will. My soul is so knit with yours that it is but a divided life I live without you" (576). Like Adam, who has gone away and returned, she comes back to Hayslope and finds her place in the community. Like Adam's, however, her new life comes at Hetty's expense. It is only after Hetty's guilt is made clear to the community and she is exiled that Dinah finally replaces her in Adam's affections.

Kohut's view that rage is the reaction to the sense of loss of connection to parental figures is thus well illustrated in the story of Arthur's, Adam's, and Dinah's treatment of Hetty. Their scapegoating of her is a transference of anger felt toward missing or disappointing parent (figure)s. Hetty as fallen mother and child murderer becomes the symbol of failed parenthood who must be banished to make way for her replacements as the characters grow beyond their infantile self and parental images. At the same time, Hetty is the symbol of the abandoned and murdered child, whose suffering enacts the characters' sense of abandonment, along with their unacknowledged murderous wishes toward missing or inadequate parents. Reliving and working through unresolved childhood feelings, as in psychoanalytic therapy, is a way of integrating parental images in the mind. In Kohut's terms, the characters have attempted to complete their self-structuralization through a transference, in order to rework the process of "transmuting internalization" (*Analysis* 49) that should normally have occurred in childhood.

Critics have wondered why Eliot seems unable to see her favored characters in *Adam Bede* and other novels as they come across to the reader. F. R. Leavis is among those who have pointed to a "distinctive moral preoccupation" (28) which, as Barbara Hardy suggests, leads Eliot to idealize certain "charmless" characters in order to provide her readers with a "moral example" (*Novels* 39). Dinah, Dorothea, Romola, and Daniel Deronda are examples in her fiction of idealized hero(ines) portrayed in sharp contrast to an extremely self-centered and/or immature character: Hetty, Rosamond, Tito and Tessa, and Gwendolen Harleth. Such contrasting of idealized and villainous characters is in part Victorian literary convention, and in part Eliot's deliberate attempt "to illustrate the moral truths of her religion of humanity" (Fulmer 28). Eliot's blind spots, however, can perhaps best be explained by the psychoanalytic concept of splitting, defined by Otto F. Kernberg, the object relations theorist, as a "central defensive operation of the ego at regressed levels" which occurs when the neutralization of aggression in the mind "does not take place sufficiently" (6, 29). Kernberg explains that "probably the best known manifestation of splitting is the division of external objects into 'all good' ones and 'all bad' ones" (29). Splitting is manifest in Eliot's art not only in her contrasting characters, but also in their development: although her story is abruptly cut off, Hetty is portrayed in more convincing detail than Dinah, a shadowy ideal who is more often than not offstage. Eliot's failure to see the aggression in her idealized character—in this case, Dinah, and to a lesser degree, Adam (whose aggression is in part acknowledged, in part denied)—is an aspect of the phenomenon of psychic splitting and, as such, constitutes a denial of the aggressive impulses in herself. In Kernberg's terms, Dinah and Hetty represent two conflicting, or "unintegrated" self-images. Hetty, the split-off, bad side of the author's self is banished from Hayslope, and banished from the novel. The failure of the ending of *Adam Bede* (Hetty's disappearance and the marriage of Adam and Dinah) thus reflects the author's fear of the aggressive impulses coming from within herself.

Carol Christ has shown how Eliot's concern with the repression of anger is evident in her repeated use of providential death in her fiction both "to avoid . . . and prohibit aggression . . . in her characters" (132). This chapter has extended such critical insights by showing how Kohut's self-psychology illuminates the patterns of indirect expression of aggression in the characters in *Adam Bede*, explains some of the problems noted by critics, and suggests their connection to the author's fear of her own aggressive impulses. In the chapters to come, I will argue that the author's aggression, like that of the characters in this novel, derives from her sense of disconnection from parent figures, beginning with the sense of separation from her mother following the deaths of the twins, and reinforced later by each of her parents' deaths. Moreover, because the novel was begun only a few months after the estrangement from her remaining family, in May of 1857, when she had informed her brother Isaac of her liaison with Lewes, I believe that her aggression was intensified by her more recent sense of disconnection from them.

Eliot's first novel establishes the patterns that will be repeated in the later novels. The aggression that is evident but denied in the characters in *Adam Bede* follows from their lost sense of connection to parent figures. Hetty's and Arthur's weak sense of self, Dinah's repression of feelings, and Adam's guilt over his murderous anger will reappear in other characters in the fiction. Moreover, Kohut's idea that the development of a firm self-structure depends more on the effect of a child's total environment than on such major events as the deaths of parents is also illustrated in *Adam Bede*. The failed development that has resulted from missing or destructive elements in family environments is seen in a larger social context. Eliot's portrayal of character extends beyond the nuclear family; it demonstrates the way in which social expectations and/or social position may affect self-esteem, and may either enhance or inhibit growth. Finally, the application of Kohut's self-psychology to a study of *Adam Bede* also shows how narcissistic rage, a "dangerous feature of individual psychopathology," may be transformed into an "equally malignant social phenomenon" ("Thoughts" 382), whereby family and social groups turn innocent victims into scapegoats in order to compensate for their own sense of inadequacy.

TWO

Narcissistic Rage in *The Mill on the Floss*

George Eliot began *The Mill on the Floss* in January 1859, shortly after the completion of *Adam Bede*. Her first reference to it is a journal entry on the twelfth: "We went into town today and looked in the Annual Register for cases of *inundation*." According to Gordon Haight, she "copied . . . several passages, mostly of 1771, describing ships driven on to flooded fields, bridges washed away, and a family rescued from the upper storey of their house—all of which appear in the final pages of the novel" (*Biography* 302). By the end of March, she described the novel to her editor John Blackwood as one "as long as *Adam Bede*, and a sort of companion picture of provincial life" (*Letters* 3:41). Dorlcote Mill was drawn from her memory of Arbury Mill near her birthplace, but it took some searching to find a suitable river (one capable of a catastrophic flood) on which to base her story. After a search in Weymouth in early September, she and Lewes finally decided on the Trent, in Lincolnshire, during a later trip out of Gainsborough (Haight, *Biography* 305). Besides the details for the setting of her mill and river, Eliot found it necessary to consult a lawyer for details for her characters' lawsuit (*Letters* 3:180). As in the case of *Adam Bede*, however, the novel grew primarily out of a combination of memory and imagination: "My stories grow in me like plants," as she expressed it early in the process of writing her second novel (3:133).

Eliot tells the story of her leading character Maggie Tulliver in the context of a presentation of her provincial family life, with particular emphasis on her relationship with her brother Tom. One twentieth-century critic, Jerome Thale, referring to Eliot's use of "the sociologist's way of looking at things," observes that unlike earlier novelists who presented details "incidentally, as part of the realistic picture," she presents them as "causally connected to the formation of the characters." He praises the "rich surface texture" and "abundance" of concrete detail that "convinces us that this world must be real" ("Sociology" 128, 129). U. C. Knoepflmacher emphasizes the scope of Eliot's novel, which he calls "unquestionably the most ambitious of the seven works of fiction belonging to George Eliot's first phase of development." He writes that "within three years, [the author] had moved from her rustic 'scenes' to a pastoral epic, and now she hoped to achieve an even greater scope and depth by writing a new kind of novel, a tragedy for her times in which she would try to relate the fate of individual characters to the forces of historical change" (*Novels* 162, 163).

As in the case of *Adam Bede*, *The Mill on the Floss* was enormously successful. It was published on April 4, 1860; Blackwood wrote Eliot before the end of May that "all the reviews and notices of the book with exception of those of one or two obscure newspapers have been most favourable" and that the sales were "highly satisfactory" (*Letters* 3:296, 297). Despite the general acceptance of *The Mill on the Floss*, however, there were some notable criticisms, which foreshadow the criticisms of many twentieth-century critics. Although E. S. Dallas's review in the *Times* was on the whole positive, his reference to the portrayal of the "odious Dodson family" (Maggie's maternal relatives) in their world of "pride, vain-glory, and hypocrisy, envy, hatred and malice, and all uncharitableness" (Draper 57) provoked Eliot to respond that "I have certainly fulfilled my intention very badly if I have made the Dodson honesty appear 'mean and uninteresting'. . . . So far as my own feeling and intention are concerned, no one class of persons or form of character is held up to reprobation or to exclusive admiration. Tom is painted with as much love and pity as Maggie, and I am so far from hating the Dodsons myself, that I am rather aghast to find them ticketed with such very ugly adjectives" (*Letters* 3:299). Edward Bulwer Lytton's April 1860 letter to Blackwood, also predominantly positive, contains criticism of the portrayal of Maggie's "position" toward her suitors Phillip and Stephen as not following from Eliot's characterization of her. Bulwer sees Maggie as treacherous to Phillip in allowing Tom to humiliate him in the scene in the "Red Deeps." Moreover, he believes that the involvement with Stephen is "a position at variance with all that had before been Heroic about [Maggie]. The *indulgence* of such a sentiment for the affianced of a friend under whose roof she was, was a treachery and a meanness according to the Ethics of Art, and nothing can afterwards lift the character into the same hold on us" (8:262). His remarks caused Eliot to respond through Blackwood that while she could accept as just the criticism that Maggie is too passive in relation to Phillip in the scene with Tom in the "Red Deeps," she held that "Maggie's position toward Stephen is too vital a part of my whole conception and purpose for me to be converted to the condemnation of it. . . . If the ethics of art do not admit the truthful presentation of a character essentially noble but liable to great error—error that is anguish to its own nobleness—*then*, it seems to me, the ethics of art are too narrow, and must be widened to correspond with a widening psychology" (3:317–18). These early criticisms, taken together with Eliot's responses, suggest a disparity, increasingly noted by modern critics, between what Eliot intended to portray, and what actually comes across to the reader.

I will argue that the pattern of indirect expression of aggression that I have observed in the characters in *Adam Bede* also emerges in the actions of the protagonist of *The Mill on the Floss*. In Eliot's portrayal, Maggie's unresolved childhood rage, which results from her sense that she is devalued by her family and society, is transformed into her adult misuse of sexual power in her relationships with the male characters, Philip, Stephen, and Dr. Kenn. The author also rationalizes Maggie's behavior with men, at the same time that she turns her into an idealized heroine in the last section of the book. Eliot's apparent inability to see the aggression in her character's actions seems to derive from her identification with her autobiographical heroine, and very likely reflects the patterns of her own relationships with men in her life as a young adult. Eliot's portrayal also shows how childhood interactions with immediate family members can shape lifelong interactions between an individual and her society.

Psychoanalytic literary critics have discussed the closeness between Maggie and her brother Tom, who, as Laura Comer Emery suggests, serves as a substitute in Maggie's life for her rejecting mother and her weak father (17, 23). Emery's Freudian analysis stresses Maggie's need to identify with Tom, a male, in a family which devalues females. Bernard Paris's Horneyan analysis emphasizes Maggie's morbid dependence on Tom: Maggie, the "self-effacing person," is drawn to Tom, the "arrogant-vindictive person . . . because [she] needs to be protected by and to live vicariously through someone who can master life aggressively" (170). Both Paris and Emery emphasize Maggie's childhood fear of being openly aggressive toward Tom because she needs him so much. Paris observes that "[Maggie] suppresses awareness of her vindictive drives and acts them out only in indirect or disguised ways" (171). Emery notes further that Eliot portrays as accidental some of Maggie's aggressive actions toward Tom: letting his rabbits die when she has promised to take care of them while he is away at school (*Mill* 82), and upsetting his pagoda and knocking against his wine (147, 155) during a visit with their relatives (Emery 25–26).

Maggie's excessively close attachment to Tom reflects her underlying need to be accepted by her parents; yet at the same time, her recurring aggression toward him enacts her anger at her parents' rejection. Emery explains that because Maggie feels rejected by her mother, she "remains 'hungry' for love, and . . . her loving retains the quality of narcissistic need" (16). The intensity of her attachment to Tom, along with her repeated expressions of aggression toward him, reflect this hunger for love. Maggie's later relationships with other men also combine the need for attachment with the need to express aggression, as she attempts to revive her childhood sense of closeness to Tom. Yet her involvements with Philip, Stephen, and Dr. Kenn only cause Tom's rejection of her and cannot satisfy her voracious need for his love.

Maggie's expression of aggression follows the pattern of the Prodigal Son story, which is told in a series of pictures on the wall at Luke's (the head miller's) cottage nearby, where she has gone for comfort after she learns that Tom's rabbits are dead. Maggie's behavior follows a cyclical pattern of impulsive and/or aggressive action and flight, followed by guilt and reparation. After she lets the rabbits die, she tries to persuade Tom to forgive her, but he rebuffs her, and she runs upstairs to the attic. When the family notices that Maggie is missing, Mr. Tulliver sends Tom to look for her. Maggie, seeking reparation, "rushe[s] to him and [clings] round his neck," and Tom finally kisses her and offers her a piece of cake (91). On another occasion, when Mrs. Tulliver's visiting relatives make negative comments about Maggie's skin and hair, she seeks revenge by running upstairs and cutting her hair (120). She soon feels sorry for what she has done, and when she returns to face her relatives' inevitable reactions, she seeks reparation by running to her father: she "hid her face on his shoulder and burst out into loud sobbing" (125). When

Maggie pushes the family's model female, Lucy, in the "cow-trodden mud" (164) as a way of getting back at Tom, Lucy, her mother, and her aunts, she runs off to the gypsies. One of the gypsies finally takes her home, and Mr. Tulliver once again rescues and comforts her (180). Thus Maggie's aggression in all three incidents follows the pattern of aggressive action and flight, followed by guilt and finally, reparation with the father (figure).

The cyclical pattern of Maggie's expression of aggression reflects the underlying low self-esteem that results from her family's ongoing devaluation of her. Maggie's is a "narcissistic rage": a chronic and disproportionate anger in response to any incident perceived as a narcissistic injury—any incident that attacks her already weak sense of self, or that repeats the pattern of rejection by her parents and society. When Tom goes away to school, Maggie, the female, stays at home, receives inferior educational opportunities despite her superior intelligence, and is even expected to care for Tom's rabbits. When Maggie is with her relatives, they criticize her and look upon Lucy as an example of femininity; even her beloved Tom ignores her in favor of Lucy. These situations provoke her underlying sense of outrage and result in her aggressive actions.

According to Heinz Kohut, mature aggression is direct, proportionate, and under the control of the ego; it dissipates as soon as the cause of the provocation is removed. Narcissistic rage, however, is not dissipated by aggressive action; the rage continues to return until the underlying problem of low self-esteem is resolved (Kohut, "Thoughts" 388)—hence Maggie's continuing cycles of rage and reparation. Kohut refers to an early work on aggression (Alexander, 1938) which, by way of explaining human aggressive responses, presents the "schema of a self-perpetuating cycle of psychological phenomena." The paper describes "the dynamic cycle of hostility—guilt—submission—reactive aggression—guilt, etc." (Kohut, "Thoughts" 380). This cycle can be applied to Maggie: she behaves aggressively, she feels guilty, she submits to her father or Tom; then she gets angry at her inferior status and reacts aggressively again. Kohut also describes the fight/flight pattern of narcissistic rage: "The narcissistically vulnerable individual responds to actual (or anticipated) narcissistic injury either with shamefaced withdrawal (flight) or with narcissistic rage (fight)" (379). In all three of the above examples, Maggie, ambivalent about expressing hostility, responds with both "fight" and "flight": after she lets the rabbits die, she runs to Luke's house, and then upstairs to the attic when Tom refuses to forgive her; when her relatives criticize her, she runs upstairs to cut her hair; after she pushes Lucy in the mud, she runs to the gypsies. Later in life she repeats the pattern when she goes away from her family and "ostentatious[ly]," as Emery puts it (25), refuses to let Tom support her after her father dies, and finally, when she runs away with Stephen. Her pattern of running away is bound up with her pattern of expressing aggression.

Elizabeth Ermarth, Michael Steig, and Wendy Woodward are among the critics who have discussed the effects on Maggie of her rigid, provincial society. Ermarth discusses the sexist social norms that Maggie has internalized and which have caused her to be "self-effacing and dependent, buying her identity at the price of her autonomy" ("Maggie" 592). Steig shows how the anal traits of the society, represented by the older generation of Dodsons (Mrs. Tulliver's relatives), have affected Maggie's "shame," "self-doubt," and "fantasy of dominance" (49). Woodward shows how Maggie is ostracized from the rigid community of women at St. Ogg's because she is "bold and 'unwomanly'" (47). Among such critics, however, none seems to have fully considered the effect of the family's status in the community on Maggie's self-esteem. The sense of personal disgrace that marks Mr. and Mrs. Tulliver's lives at the outset becomes self-fulfilling in them as they move toward their financial fall and later in Maggie as she finds ways to disgrace herself.

Mrs. Tulliver begins with a low position in her own family: she is compared unfavorably to her sisters, and "is always on the defensive towards [them]" (227). There are many references to Mrs. Tulliver's inferiority: Mr. Tulliver has picked his wife because she is "a bit weak" (68); he is proud to have "a buxom wife conspicuously his inferior in intellect" (73); she is the "feeblest" member of the Dodson family (97). Mrs. Tulliver's own sibling rivalry comes out in her worries that Maggie cannot compare to her sister's daughter Lucy: "It seems hard as my sister Deane should have that pretty child" (61). She is always concerned about the impression Maggie will make on her sisters. When Maggie dips her head in a basin of water "in the vindictive determination that there should be no more chance of curls that day," Mrs. Tulliver warns Maggie that the aunts won't love her, and then adds her fears for herself: "Folks 'ull think it's a judgment on me as I've got such a child—they'll think I've done summat wicked" (78).

Maggie is said to resemble Mr. Tulliver's sister, who suffers the disgrace of marriage to a poor man and has the burden of raising eight children in poverty. Both she and Maggie are said to take after Mr. Tulliver's mother. Mr. Tulliver wants to take care of his sister, just as he wants Tom to take care of Maggie (116). The implication is perhaps that her aunt's existence is what awaits Maggie: marriage to a poor man. As the unappealing daughter of the lowest in status in the family, she could not expect more. One important source of Maggie's rage, then, in addition to that which she feels toward the rejecting members of her nuclear family, is her low position in a rigid society which allows very little room for upward mobility, especially for women.

Maggie's low position in society is made worse by her father's financial fall. Eliot emphasizes the Tullivers' sense of disgrace following the loss of the lawsuit to Wakem. Mr. Tulliver suffers a physical collapse, and Maggie and Tom are devastated: "Tom had never dreamed that his father would 'fail:' that was a form of misfortune which he had always heard spoken of as a deep disgrace, and disgrace was an idea that he could not associate with any of his relations, least of all with his father. A proud sense of family respectability was part of the very air Tom had been born and brought up in" (267). The Dodson family proves to be unsupportive and judgmental. They, like Tom, feel disgraced because "one of the family [has] married a man [who] has brought her to beggary" (294). Both Tom and Maggie are angry with their relatives' reactions, but since Tom shares some of their feeling of blame toward his father, "he felt nothing like Maggie's violent resentment against them for showing no eager tenderness and generosity" (308). Maggie is openly angry with her mother and Tom whenever they seem to be joining the relatives in blaming her father. She "hated blame" and only wants to remember how her father "had always defended and excused her" (284).

Maggie's "Valley of Humiliation" (Book IV), however, her own reaction to the family's fall, sets the stage for the beginning of a new cycle. During the monotonous period of time when Tom is working to pay off the family debt and Maggie is at home taking care of her sick father, she falls into the despair which is described in the three chapters of Book IV. Chapter 1 provides the context for her despair by emphasizing the oppressiveness of life in a society which holds up respectability as its chief virtue. In chapter 2, Maggie, unable to count on her ailing father's customary warmth to distract her from her predicament, is becoming weighed down by her family's disgrace. Her father is unresponsive to "her little caresses" (371) and seems preoccupied with Maggie's "poor chance for marrying, down in the world as they were" (372). In chapter 3, Maggie turns to books for comfort, although she is easily distracted by her sorrow. She has fits of anger and hatred "towards her father and mother who were so unlike what she would have them to be—towards Tom, who checked her and met her thought or feeling always by some thwarting difference" (380). Then she reacts to her own anger with "wild romances of a flight from home in search of something less sordid and dreary:—she would go to some great man—Walter Scott, perhaps, and tell him how wretched and how clever she was, and he would surely do something for her" (381). Her real father would inevitably interrupt her fantasy and complain, for example, that she had failed to bring his slippers. In desperation, Maggie finally discovers Thomas à Kempis and begins to try to apply his ideas to her situation: "Renunciation seemed to her the entrance into that satisfaction which she had so long been craving in vain" (384). As time goes on, her mother notices and approves her new submissiveness; her father, also approving the change, but still worrying about her prospects for marriage, shifts his plaint to: "There'll be nobody to marry her as is fit for her" (388). Thus in chapter 3 Maggie repeats her pattern: she feels angry toward her family for her inferior position in society, she flees (in fantasy), she feels guilty (when her father interrupts her fantasy) and then regains her parents' approval with her newfound submissiveness, brought on by her misguided attempts to apply Thomas à Kempis to her life.

After the Thomas à Kempis incident, there is little mention of Maggie's anger, and there are no accounts of overtly aggressive action on her part. At this point in the story Maggie begins to act out her rage in her relationships with men. Her childhood aggression is transformed into her young-adult misuse of sexual power. Neither Philip nor Stephen is a suitable or appealing choice for Maggie, but she becomes involved with them as a means of hurting them and others around her. Yet just as Eliot portrays Maggie's aggressive actions toward Tom as accidental, so she portrays her heroine's actions toward other men as innocent. Furthermore, by the end of the novel, Eliot idealizes Maggie on the grounds of her struggles of conscience over her involvements with the two men.

Maggie's long period of renunciation has prepared her for a new cycle: her sense of inferiority, exacerbated by her father's financial fall, his illness, and her own self-deprivation and recent growth into "early womanhood" (393), are motivating factors in the action that follows. Maggie's expression of aggression takes the form of pursuing a relationship with Wakem's son, Philip. By becoming involved with him, Maggie expresses her anger toward her family for their inadequacies, and toward Tom, who has forbidden her to speak to Philip (279). Moreover, although she has never acknowledged any feelings of anger toward Philip for his father's role in Mr. Tulliver's failure, she typically acts out her resentment indirectly.

The foundation for the friendship is laid when Maggie meets Philip as a child on a visit to Tom's school. Maggie feels "growing interest" in Philip, despite his and Tom's antagonism toward each other, because he is so "clever," and because she has "rather a tenderness for deformed things" (252). During the visit, Philip becomes Maggie's replacement for Tom, whose troubles with his studies had "made him more like a girl than he had ever been in his life before": his "boyish self-satisfaction" had been replaced by "something of the girl's susceptibility" (210). When Philip becomes a student at the school, his academic successes add to Tom's ongoing need to prove himself as a fighter. Finally Tom bribes the school drillmaster into lending him his sword, which he plans to "tie around his waist" and show off to Maggie as his own. But when the time comes, "his wrist trembles" as he lowers the sword, drops it on his foot, and wounds himself (255)—a symbolic castration, as Emery suggests (19), which reveals his sense of inadequacy. Soon after, Maggie, needing a male to complete her sense of identity, "turns toward Philip, and identifies not with what she would like to be, but with something that resembles her own need" (Emery 19). His humpback represents her own low self-image. In chapter 6, "A Love Scene," which immediately follows the scene in which Tom is injured, Maggie expresses her feelings toward Philip in relation to her need to be loved by Tom: first she tells him that she doesn't think she could love him better than Tom, "But I should be so sorry . . . for you" (259); then she corrects her allusion to his deformity by saying that she wishes he were her brother; finally she concludes, "I think you're fonder of me than Tom is" (260). The relationship that develops later in their young-adult years follows from Maggie's ongoing need to be loved by Tom at the same time that she needs to express aggression toward him.

Maggie meets Philip again a few years later on one of her solitary walks in the "Red Deeps." Although Philip initiates their conversation, Maggie, glad to see him despite the rift between their families, responds warmly. Yet although Eliot assures her readers of Maggie's innocence, her behavior toward Philip is actually flirtatious. When Maggie, who has grown into "early womanhood" (393), asks Philip if she is like what he expected, Eliot comments, "The words might have been those of a coquette, but the full bright glance Maggie turned on Philip was not that of a coquette. She really did hope he liked her face as it was now, but it was simply the rising again of her innate delight in admiration and love" (395). Philip tells her she is much more beautiful than he expected, which Eliot intimates is a surprise to Maggie, who, during her renunciation, has "abstain[ed] from the looking-glass" (396). Maggie then tells Philip that she must not see him again (396), but Philip plays on her sympathies and finally says, "I should be contented to live, if you would let me see you sometimes" (398). Maggie, beginning to wonder whether she might do him some good in seeing him, wavers, and then postpones the decision by submitting to his suggestion that he come to the woods as often as he can until he meets her again on one of her walks. By failing to prevent his meeting her again, she chooses to pursue the relationship. She lets Philip appear to make the decision in which she actually participates. Meanwhile, she inwardly plans to tell him the next time they meet of her determination not to keep seeing him.

Maggie's aggression is not only evident in the choice of Philip against her family's wishes, but also in the portrayals of her interactions with him. Her cycles of giving Philip hope and then rejecting him reveal the latent cruelty in her behavior. For example, in the passage in Book V, chapter 3, "The Wavering Balance," Maggie tells Philip that they cannot meet again (425); Philip responds by asking her to talk for half an hour before they part. Then when he takes her hand, "Maggie felt no reason to withdraw it" (425). Thus she declares that she will not see him again, but then immediately gives in to his advances. Then Philip flatters her by asking to study her face one last time so that he can finish her portrait; he elicits her sympathy and her own discontent about her lot by expressing bitterness about his deformity (426); finally, he argues vehemently against her practice of self-deprivation (427). Maggie, still seeing the relationship in terms of her need for Tom, says, "What a dear, good brother you would have been" (427). By the end of the conversation, in which Philip continues to argue against her determination to renounce him, Maggie finally gives in to his suggestion that he continue to walk in the woods and meet her "by chance" (429). It is clear in this passage that Maggie wants to continue seeing Philip ("her heart leap[t] at this subterfuge of Philip's" [429]), yet "even to Maggie he was an exception: it was clear that the thought of his being her lover had never entered her mind" (430)—that is, his deformity stands in the way of his attractiveness to Maggie. Although Philip's interest in Maggie is clear to the reader, Eliot claims Maggie's innocence of his intentions; so Maggie continues to lead him on, although her rejection of him is inevitable.

A year later they are still meeting. Philip finally declares his love and asks Maggie whether she loves him. She replies, "I think I could hardly love any one better: there is nothing but what I love you for" (435). Later in the conversation when Philip asks if she is forcing herself to say she loves him, she repeats the thought: "I don't think I could love any one better than I love you. I should like always to live with you—to make you happy" (437). But she also says she will never do anything to wound her father, and adds that it is impossible for them ever to be more than friends. Philip continues to try to get her to clarify her feelings, but by this time Maggie is feeling that she must return home: "The sense that their parting was near, made her more anxious lest she should have unintentionally left some painful impression on Philip's mind. It was one of those dangerous moments when speech is at once sincere and deceptive—when feeling, rising high above its average depth, leaves floodmarks which are never reached again" (437). Philip asks, "We do belong to each other—for always—whether we are apart or together?" And Maggie responds, "Yes, Philip: I should like never to part: I should like to make your life very happy" (437). Philip, however, aware of the ambiguity of her answer, is "waiting for something else—I wonder whether it will come" (438). Maggie stoops to kiss him and has "a moment of belief that if there were sacrifice in this love [because of Philip's deformity]—it was all the richer and more satisfying" (438). Her feeling for Philip is more a need to be "worshipped" (426) than the kind of love that Philip wants.

Tom inevitably discovers their meetings, and Maggie promises not to see Philip again without Tom's knowledge (446). He confronts and insults Philip (447–48). After they leave Philip, Tom asks her, "Pray, how have you shown your love that you talk of either to me or my father? By disobeying and deceiving us. I have a different way of showing my affection." Maggie's response, "Because you are a man, Tom, and have power, and can do something in the world" (450), reveals a motive for pursuing the friendship: her sense of powerlessness as a female. Shortly after the discussion with Tom, Maggie inwardly acknowledges her relief that the relationship is over (451). The implication in this passage and those cited above is that she does not want to be seriously involved with Philip. After she becomes involved with Stephen, she quickly loses interest in Philip: she "shivers" at Lucy's offer to contrive a way for her to marry Philip (498); she is "touched not thrilled" when Philip sings to her in the presence of Lucy and Stephen (533). Although Maggie and Philip share many interests, her feeling for him never gets beyond her need to be admired; he plays on her sympathies when he persuades her to see him, and she continues to submit to his suggestions to meet. Yet despite Philip's declarations of love, she never actually declares hers. Relieved when Tom breaks up the relationship, she lets him verbalize what she represses. Through her brother, she vicariously lives out her own unacknowledged feelings of aggression toward Philip, whose father has ruined hers.

The relationship is not all Maggie's fault; Philip has sought her out and pressured her into declaring her love. His motives interact with hers. He feels bitter about his deformity (398, 430), discouraged about his painting, and "had never been soothed by [a] mother's love" (431). Perhaps a relationship with Maggie could also be seen as an expression of his (and his father's) power over the Tullivers. In any case, the story of the relationship between Maggie and Philip is suspended when Mr. Tulliver dies and Maggie and Tom are reconciled. When Maggie asks Tom's forgiveness, "they clung and wept together" (465). Maggie completes her cycle: by becoming involved with Philip she takes revenge on Tom, her family, and the Wakems; "weary of her home" (436), she flees her family by habitually meeting him at the Red Deeps; she feels guilty afterward, especially after her father's death; finally, she is reconciled to Tom.

Maggie's next period of submissiveness follows during her lonely, monotonous two years as a teacher after her father's death. By the time she visits Lucy in Book VI, she is ready for a new cycle. She meets Stephen, Lucy's intended fiancé, and soon finds herself tempted to run away with him. Although he seems to many critics to be an unlikely object of her affections, the reasons for her involvement with him become clear if the relationship is seen in the context of Maggie's recurring cycles of submission and rage.

Book VI, which traces the relationship with Stephen, emphasizes Maggie's low position in the society at St. Ogg's, especially in contrast to Stephen, who represents the established society, or, as Suzanne Graver puts it in her sociological study of Eliot's novels, the "good society." Unlike Maggie, the daughter of a failure, Stephen is in the privileged position of being the son of the owner of "the largest oil-mill and the most extensive wharf in St. Ogg's" (469). Lucy's father and Tom both work for him. Stephen feels superior to all the people around him: he speaks with "supercilious indifference" of Mr. Tulliver (471); he makes fun of Mrs. Tulliver's "conversational qualities" (472); he refers to Tom as "not a brilliant companion" (473); he has even chosen Lucy "because she did not strike him as a remarkable rarity" (477). He is conscious of her inferior position as "the daughter of his father's subordinate partner; . . . he had had to defy and overcome a slight unwillingness and disappointment in his father and sisters—a circumstance which gives a young man an agreeable consciousness of his own dignity" (478). Stephen's sisters, too, "associated chiefly on terms of condescension with the families of St. Ogg's, and were the glass of fashion there" (512). For Maggie, it is supposed to be "a great opportunity" (512) to be included in the parties of such a group.

One of the earlier conversations between Maggie and Philip reveals the motivation for her later involvement with Stephen. When Maggie tells Philip she would like to read a book in which the dark-haired lady triumphs, Philip jokes, "Perhaps you will avenge the dark women in your own person, and carry away all the love from your cousin Lucy." Maggie, insulted, denies that she is "odious and base enough to wish to be her rival" (433), and insists that "it's because I always care the most about the unhappy people. . . . I always take the side of the rejected lover in the stories." Then when Philip asks her if she would ever have the heart to reject a lover, she responds: "I think perhaps I could if he were very conceited; and yet, if he got extremely humiliated afterwards, I should relent" (434). Stephen is the kind of conceited person that Maggie tells Philip she would be able to reject. The infatuation for Stephen is bound up with her hostility toward him and others around her. By running away with him, she repeats the pattern of the gypsy incident: angry with her family and jealous of Lucy, she pushes her in the mud, runs away to the gypsies, where she fantasizes that she is queen—"in Lucy's form" (Emery 38), and then returns to be rescued by her father.

The nature of infatuation has been explored by psychoanalysts, although according to a review by David S. Werman and Theodore J. Jacobs, there is relatively little literature on the subject. One study stresses that such an attraction is "based on resemblance to a fantasy which, for both sexes, derives from the 'original love object'—the mother" (447). Another asserts that "falling in love represents an attempt to undo the original separation from mother, as well as subsequent separations" (448). A third says that "people who become infatuated have an incapacity for establishing [constant relationships with others]: infatuation is a repetition compulsion whose origins are in developmental failures" (448). Werman and Jacobs build on these and other studies in stating their belief that infatuation has its roots in the earliest years of life. Its "shifting and inconstant nature reflects the experience of the child prior to the formation of [love] object constancy" (453) and suggests "the existence of difficulties in the mother-infant relationship that contribute to the development of critically important aggressive conflicts in the child"; this accounts for the latent hostility in infatuations. They can occur normatively during adolescence, a time when oedipal conflicts are revived at the same time that the individual is struggling for a sense of identity. They can also occur repeatedly during a person's life, or in some people, only during a particularly stressful time: "[An infatuation] may come about when an individual is in a crisis of defensive regression, subsequent to severe stress, intense anxiety, or during times of depression" (455). An infatuation "typically condenses both narcissistic and oedipal wishes" (456).

Maggie's infatuation for Stephen comes about as a cyclical reaction to her underlying narcissistic rage against her family and society; it also comes about during a time of special stress and depression: Maggie has suffered the death of her father, has grown bored with her teaching position, and is suddenly in a social setting in which she is continually reminded of her low status.

In a conversation with Lucy in chapter 2 of Book VI, Maggie expresses her discontent by comparing herself to a bear confined in a cage. She says she often hates herself "because I get angry sometimes at the sight of happy people" (481). She feels that she has slipped back "into desire and longing" (482). When she goes for a ride in the boat with Stephen and Lucy, "She felt lonely, cut off from Philip—the only person who had ever seemed to love her devotedly, as she had always longed to be loved" (491). Renewed anger at her relatives adds to her feelings of discontent. When her mother and aunt make remarks about her brown skin, Maggie laughs, but feels "impatient" (493). When Tom expresses his distrust of her, "she rebelled and was humiliated at the same time." She tries to be reconciled to him at the end of the conversation, and he does kiss her, but has to rush off to a consultation with his uncle Deane (504–6). Her anger appears in flashes in her relationship with Stephen: after he takes her for a walk in the garden (521) and after he kisses her arm at the dance (561).

Maggie's first meeting with Stephen recalls the first meeting with Philip in the Red Deeps. Maggie is aware that Stephen thinks her attractive; in this case she pretends to rebuff his compliment. Once again, Eliot denies her heroine's flirtatious behavior: when Maggie mentions that she has had to earn money by plain sewing, Eliot comments, "but if Maggie had been the queen of coquettes she could hardly have invented a means of giving greater piquancy to her beauty in Stephen's eyes" (487).

True to the pattern established in her relationship with Philip, Maggie makes her choices about Stephen indirectly—by allowing Stephen to appear to be making the decisions. When it becomes clear that neither Lucy nor Philip will be able to go along on the planned boat ride, Maggie says to Stephen, "We must not go" (588). Yet when she asks Stephen to tell the man who is waiting for them with the boat cushions, Stephen says, "What shall I tell him?" And "Maggie made no answer." Stephen then says, "Let us go" at the same time he rises and takes her hand, thus relieving her of the burden of openly making the decision for herself.

Maggie's feeling for Stephen, however, is different from what she had experienced with Philip. The relationship with Stephen satisfies her underlying need to feel attached to a stronger person. When she and Stephen return from the first boat ride, Maggie's foot "slips," "but happily Mr. Stephen Guest held her hand and kept her up with a firm grasp. . . . It was very charming to be taken care of in that kind graceful manner by some one taller and stronger than oneself. Maggie had never felt just in the same way before" (492). Again, just before the last boat ride, Maggie feels "that she was being led down the garden . . . by this stronger presence that seemed to bear her along without any act of her own will" (588). Maggie experiences the sense of union with a powerful love object that is part of the fantasy of infatuation.

Werman and Jacobs emphasize the "intense, irrational, and dreamlike" state of infatuation (450). After the first evening with Stephen, Maggie feels "the half-remote presence of a world of love and beauty and delight, made up of vague, mingled images from all the poetry and romance she had ever read, or had ever woven in her dreamy reveries" (495). When they walk in the garden, they are "in the same dreamy state as they had been in a quarter of an hour before" (521). At the dance, Maggie says that the flowers seem to be part of "an enchanted land" (560). When they go away in the rowboat, they are enveloped in an "enchanted haze" (589). Finally, on the Dutch vessel, "Stephen's passionate words made the vision of such a life more fully present to her than it had ever been before; and the vision for the time excluded all realities" (594).

Infatuation is a condensation of the narcissistic wish for the infant's blissful sense of union with the mother and the oedipal wish to marry the parent of the opposite sex; it thus provides for a female a means of being united in fantasy with both parents at the same time. Maggie's fantasies when she is with Stephen recall her blissful childhood moments with Tom, her substitute for both parents, at the "Round Pool" when they would imagine that "they would always live together and be fond of each other." As a child Maggie thought of sitting by the pool as "a very nice heaven." She would "look dreamily at the glassy water" and feel as though nothing could "mar her delight in the whispers and the dreamy silences" (93). The scene at the Round Pool, "deep . . . almost a perfect round, framed in with willows and tall reeds," a symbolic womb (Emery 10), suggests Tom's and Maggie's ongoing need to be together with their lost love object, their mother—a need temporarily met for Maggie later in the dreamlike infatuation for Stephen. And because the "triangle between Stephen, Lucy, and Maggie is a recasting of the Oedipal triangle" (Emery 37), Maggie is also able to be temporarily united in fantasy with her father when she and Stephen elope.

Maggie's interactions with Stephen repeat the pattern of her cruelty to Philip. She encourages and rejects him in cycles. At the dance in Book VI, chapter 10, Maggie and Stephen walk together feeling "that long grave mutual gaze which has the solemnity belonging to all deep human passion." When they pause to look at some flowers, Stephen, overwhelmed by the strength of their feelings, suddenly takes Maggie's arm and "shower[s] kisses on it." Maggie, reacting with "rage and humiliation," refuses to have anything to do with him for the rest of the evening because she feels "Stephen thought more lightly of her than he did of Lucy" (561–62). In their next scene (chapter 11), Stephen comes to see her while she is staying at her aunt's house and tries to persuade her to marry him. Maggie seems on the verge of giving in to her impulses, but just as "his lips are very near hers," Maggie "opened her eyes full on his for an instant, like a lovely wild animal timid and struggling under caresses, and then turned sharp round towards home again" (569–70). When they are alone in the boat together, Maggie fails to notice that they have drifted past the village where they had planned to stop. When Stephen tries to persuade her to marry him before they return home, Maggie feels "angry resistance." She accuses him of wanting "to deprive me of any choice. You knew we were come too far—you have dared to take advantage of my thoughtlessness. It is unmanly to bring me into such a position" (591). The pattern repeats itself again after they board the "Dutch vessel," where Maggie paces "up and down the deck leaning on Stephen," yet soon realizes "that the condition was a transient one, and that the morrow must bring back the old life struggle" (594–95). The next day she tells Stephen she cannot marry him, and finally Stephen, worn out and exasperated, says, "Go, then—leave me—don't torture me any longer—I can't bear it." Even then, Maggie "involuntarily . . . leaned towards him and put out her hand to touch his," but this time Stephen, not wanting to be hurt again, "[shrinks] from it as if it had been burning iron" (606).

Maggie's low self-esteem prevents her from disentangling herself from her old patterns of behavior. She is at the mercy of a repetition-compulsion which causes her to reenact her sense of injury by repeatedly injuring others. By getting involved with Stephen, Maggie hurts everyone around her—Stephen, by repeatedly encouraging and rejecting him; Lucy, her long-term rival, by taking away her intended fiancé just when Lucy is being kind to her; Philip, by failing to be clear about "the position they must hold towards each other," thus continuing to lead him on (527); Wakem, who finally consents to let Philip marry her, and then suffers embarrassment when she goes away with Stephen (632); Tom, whose happiness over regaining the mill is destroyed by her flight with Stephen, and who, it is implied, is already hurting from his own loss of Lucy to Stephen (501). Finally, she hurts all her other relatives, who will suffer from the disgrace she brings on the family.

Yet Eliot's portrayal of the flight with Stephen emphasizes the nobility of Maggie's decision not to marry him. Maggie is implicitly praised as she parts from Stephen for not thinking about "what others would say and think of her conduct" on the grounds that "love and deep pity and remorseful anguish left no room for that" (606). Maggie's superiority to the rest of the community is implied through the words of Dr. Kenn, who lets her know after her return how harshly the community is judging her: "The persons who are the most incapable of a conscientious struggle such as yours, are precisely those who will be likely to shrink from you; because they will not believe in your struggle" (626). At the end of the conversation with Dr. Kenn, his thoughts shift to the narrator's commentary in the last two paragraphs of chapter 2, Book VII, in a defense of Maggie's struggle: "Moral judgments must remain false and hollow, unless they are checked and enlightened by a perpetual reference to the special circumstances that mark the individual lot" (628).

The relationship with Stephen, like the one with Philip, is not all Maggie's fault. Stephen repeatedly seeks her out and finally pressures her into leaving with him. His "inward vision of her which perpetually made part of his consciousness" (559) is evidence that he is suffering from infatuation himself. Like Philip, Stephen's motives interact with Maggie's. His involvement with her can be seen as an outgrowth of his feelings of superiority over those around him—an expression of power over the Tullivers, Lucy, Philip, and even his own father.

Book VII opens with Tom as master at Dorlcote Mill: he has fulfilled the family's wish to own it again; but his success is spoiled by Maggie's disgrace upon her return from the failed elopement with Stephen. From Tom's point of view, it is a disgrace worse than death (611): "You have disgraced us all—you have disgraced my father's name. You have been a curse to your best friends" (612). Maggie attempts to repent and be reconciled to him, but Tom's refusal is final: he does not even want her under his roof. Mrs. Tulliver comes to her rescue, however, and they go to Bob Jakin's house together. Maggie goes through a period of extreme guilt in the form of (belated) anxiety for Stephen, Lucy, and Philip (621). While she claims a desire for financial independence (622), she thinks of Dr. Kenn, the Anglican clergyman she met at Lucy's bazaar, and "the momentary feeling of reliance that had sprung in her when he was talking with her." She determines to see him, despite her knowledge that he is grieving over the recent death of his wife (623). She attempts reparation through her confession to him, a new father figure.

Maggie's Aunt Glegg offers her shelter at her house, but Maggie, insisting on her "independence," takes a position with Dr. Kenn instead, thus again establishing a connection with a strong male. But in chapter 5, "The Last Conflict," Dr. Kenn, who has grown sensitive to the local gossip and feels he should avoid even the "appearance of evil," has asked her to leave and offered to find her a position in another town. Maggie suffers an overwhelming sense of abandonment: "There was no home, no help for the erring" (646).

On the third day of her despair she receives another letter from Stephen, who is still pleading for her love. She wavers, and then burns the letter, but puts off writing him "the last word of parting" until the next day (649). Maggie is caught in a cycle which only death can bring to an end. Conveniently, just as she wishes for death, she feels the flood water at her feet.

The flood ending has been the primary focus of the large quantity of modern literary criticism on *The Mill on the Floss*. Bulwer Lytton anticipated later critics by suggesting in his 1860 letter to Blackwood that "the Tragic should be prepared for and seem to come step by step as if unavoidable. But that is not the case here" (*Letters* 8:262). Eliot herself acknowledged in response to Bulwer's criticism that she also felt that "the tragedy is not adequately prepared"—a "defect" which she felt resulted from her "love of my subject in the two first volumes," which "caused a want of proportionate fullness in the treatment of the third," and "which I shall always regret" (3:317). Rosemary Mundhenk is among the modern critics who have suggested that the problem with the flood scene is that it does not resolve Maggie's internal struggle; the ending is a repetition rather than a resolution of what has preceded it (20–30). Barbara Hardy describes the ending of the novel as too abrupt a movement from "particularity" to "fantasy" (*Mill* 172), and Peter Garrett as an inappropriate shift from a "realistic" to a "symbolic" mode (45).

Psychoanalytic interpretations of the ending of the novel, where Maggie and Tom drown together in a final embrace, emphasize Maggie's need to be reunited with Tom, whom no other man can replace. David

Smith, describing the relationship between Maggie and Tom as incestuous, sees the flood scene as the symbolic consummation of their passion. Emery sees many levels of meaning: the flood represents the outpouring of Maggie's repressed rage toward Tom at the same time it fulfills oedipal and oral wishes (to be reunited with both father and mother, for whom Tom is a substitute), and finally, the wish to return to the womb (to be at one with her mother and Tom), which is simultaneously a wish for death (23). Tom is the focus of Maggie's infantile attachments, from whom she is unable to separate. Her unmet need to be accepted by her parents creates her hunger to be attached to symbols of them (first Tom, and then other men) in later life.

Kohut explains that narcissistic rage is "aggression mobilized in the service of an archaic grandiose self and that it is deployed within the framework of an archaic perception of reality" ("Thoughts" 385). In other words, in the person who suffers narcissistic rage, the self-image is inflated, at the same time it is merged with one or more images of others. The most violent forms of narcissistic rage, Kohut writes, arise in individuals in whom "the maintenance of self-esteem—and indeed of the self—depends on the unconditional availability of the approving-mirroring functions of an admiring self-object, or on the ever-present opportunity for a merger with an idealized one" (386). Maggie's sense of self depends on her perception of herself as attached to Tom, the symbolic substitute for her parents—hence her ongoing need to seek reparation with him. The flood ending brings Maggie and Tom permanently back together through death.

Eliot's friend Sara Hennell thought *The Mill on the Floss* "unfinished" because of "[Eliot]'s intense sympathy with Maggie. . . . In every word of the book . . . she could hear [Eliot]'s voice of ten years before" (Haight, *Biography* 335). Many twentieth-century critics have also seen Eliot's overidentification with Maggie as a flaw in the novel. Leavis refers to "a tendency toward the direct presence of the author" (33) and to Maggie's "lack of self-knowledge shared by George Eliot" (43). Paris, essentially agreeing with Leavis (165–66), writes that Eliot "succeeds brilliantly" in the characterization of Maggie, but "fails to interpret her correctly" (186). Hardy refers to the problem of "underdistance" of the narration toward the ending (*Mill* 173) and to the relationship between personal need and artistic shaping at each stage of the novel (179). Emery refers to a particular point at the beginning of chapter 13 in Book VI, when Maggie and Stephen drift off together, where "the narrator's point of view [merges] with Maggie's" (49).

The autobiographical nature of the novel is well known. Jane McDonnell is among the critics who have noted parallels between the Maggie-Tom relationship and the relationship between Eliot and her brother Isaac (381), who, although close in early childhood, had grown increasingly distant and finally cut off all communication with her in 1857, when she had finally told him of her liaison with G. H. Lewes. I would add that there are also parallels in the patterns of Maggie's and Mary Ann Evans's young-adult relationships with other men—relationships which involved dependence on men unavailable for marriage.

Following the March 1841 move with her father to Coventry before Isaac's marriage, Mary Ann seems to have replaced her evangelical enthusiasm, including her enthusiasm for her friendship with her former teacher, Maria Lewis, with a new enthusiasm for scientific studies and a different group of friends, along with a heightened susceptibility to infatuations for men. Judging from her letters at the time, she had suffered anxiety over Isaac's approaching marriage because of her fear that a new sister-in-law might supersede her as housekeeper at Griff. She wrote Lewis in May 1840 that "there seems a probability of my being an unoccupied damsel" (*Letters* 1:50); in October she was still in a state of uncertainty about what would happen to her when Isaac married (68). Once the decision to leave Griff with her father was made, however, she seemed to regard the move itself with mild annoyance. She wrote at the time that "we are undergoing one of the chief among the minor disagreeables of life—moving" (85). Yet afterward, she felt something more like grief. Besides missing her "lack of a free range for walking which I so enjoyed at Griff," she found "what I did not fully anticipate, a considerable disturbance of the usual flow of thought and feeling on being severed from the objects so long accustomed to call it forth. There is the same cope . . . clouds . . . verdure . . . but I have never yet enjoyed that communion with them, viewed from my present position, that long familiarity rendered spontaneous in my early home" (93). Perhaps the move from her childhood home at Griff, occurring in conjunction with Isaac's marriage, came to symbolize the loss of her childhood, and created in her a need for new attachments to which she could transfer the strong feelings of her childhood. In any case, she responded with alacrity to a new set of friends, particularly including Charles Bray, whom she met with his wife in November 1841. Bray's abandonment of the evangelical enthusiasm of his youth and current interest in scientific matters seems to have fueled her own increasing doubts about her faith—although, as Haight observes, "the change in her religious views . . . would have [happened] in any case" (*Biography* 39). Haight also writes that "it is impossible to overestimate the importance of Mary Ann's introduction to the Brays, which led quickly to a warm, life-long friendship" (44). Mary Ann's enthusiasm for Charles was observed by her old friend Maria Lewis, who, according to Marghanita Laski, "was shocked to see them walking arm in arm, 'like lovers' she said" (28). Ina Taylor, viewing Charles Bray as the "Don Juan of Coventry," also writes that Mary Ann "was completely enamoured of [him]" (46).

Another instance of Mary Ann's shifting attachments occurred during this stage of her life, in 1843, following the "Holy War" with her own father. She was invited to the home of the sixty-two-year-old scholarly Dr. Robert Brabant after his daughter Rufa's marriage to Charles Hennell, one of her Coventry group of friends. While Mary Ann, who "was to be a second daughter to him," was visiting at his home, the two became involved in an intimate friendship, characterized on Mary Ann's side by rapturous devotion: "We read and walk and talk together, and I am never weary of his company," she wrote Cara Bray (Haight, *Biography* 49). Dr. Brabant's wife, however, possibly urged on by her sister, who also lived with the family, soon became jealous and insisted that she be put out of the house before the previously agreed upon end of her stay (50).

While she was working on the Strauss translation in 1845, Mary Ann took a trip to Scotland with the Brays, but had to return home almost immediately because her father had broken his leg the night of her departure. From that point on, his health seems to have declined; it became increasingly necessary during the years until his death in 1849 for Mary Ann to focus her attention on caring for him and the household, although she did contribute articles to the Coventry *Herald* during this time (61). During the last year of her father's life, as Cara wrote to Sara Hennell, "poor [Mary Ann], alone with him, has the whole care and fatigue of nursing him night and day with . . . constant nervous expectation [of his death]" (*Letters* 1:272). During this time her moods vacillated widely: at times she seemed extremely depressed (264, 265) and at times almost elated at the opportunity to be with him in his suffering (283, 284). Yet more than anything she dreaded losing him. The strain showed in a letter she wrote to the Brays shortly before his death: "What shall I be without my Father? It will seem as if a part of my moral nature were gone. I had a horrid vision of myself last night becoming earthly sensual and devilish for want of that purifying restraining influence" (284).

After Mary Ann's father's death in May 1849, the Brays suggested a trip to the Continent, where they helped her get settled in a pension in Switzerland. On her own she found a home for the winter in Geneva, in the household of François D'Albert Durade, a forty-five-year-old painter. Although Mary Ann formed what turned out to be a another lifelong friendship with both him and his wife, she seems to have been especially attached to him. She wrote the Brays in October that she had already come to love him "as a father and brother" (*Letters* 1:316–17). Her description of his "deformed spine—the result of an accident in his boyhood," calls to mind Philip Wakem, whom the character Maggie also loved as a brother. Mary Ann also became fond of Mme. d'Albert, whom she called "Maman," and by February of 1850 described as "just the creature one loves to lean on and be petted by." As Haight remarks, however, "she leaned even more on Maman's little husband" (*Biography* 77). When the time came for Mary Ann to return to England in March, Durade accompanied her to London, although he could "ill afford it," as Laski observes (34).

Her return to England to be reunited with her relatives was less happy than expected. Apparently she felt unwelcome at Isaac's: "It was some envious demon that drove me across the Jura to come and see people who don't want me" (*Letters* 1:335), she wrote to Sara; and although she felt Chrissey "much kinder than any one else in the family," she also felt "delighted that I am of no importance to any of [my relatives], and have no motive for living amongst them" (336). For several months she lived with the Brays. It was during this time that she wrote her first article for John Chapman, the publisher of the *Westminster Review*. In mid-November of 1850 she delivered the article to his house (and publishing business) in London, where she then stayed on for two weeks as a boarder.

Marian's experience at the Chapmans' home repeats, perhaps with added intensity, the pattern of her earlier emotional involvements with married men. The fact that Chapman, a "notorious philanderer," to use Haight's words, already had not only a wife, but a mistress in his household, created a conflict between Marian and the other two women which precipitated her premature departure (*Biography* 85, 86). The relationship between Chapman and Marian has been the subject of much speculation among gossips and biographers, but most agree that at the very least, it involved a mutual infatuation; whether or not the infatuation actually developed into a sexual relationship is unknown. Devoting a whole volume to the story of their relationship, Haight concludes that "there is little question that she was guilty of some indiscretion [during her initial stay at his house], which was probably magnified by the exacerbated feelings of the other ladies" (*GE & JC* 22). Although she returned to his household at the end of 1851 to work for him as assistant editor for the *Westminster Review*, it was only possible because they had agreed earlier to a "solemn and holy vow which henceforth will bind us to the right," as Chapman expresses it in his June 5 entry in his diary (*GE & JC* 175). McDonnell is among the critics who suggest that the infatuation for Chapman "may have influenced [Eliot's] depiction of Stephen Guest" (381).

While Marian was working for Chapman, she met Herbert Spencer, with whom she established another lifelong friendship. Biographers have emphasized all that the two friends had in common. They were the same age and had both come to London from the Midlands to earn their living as writers. Furthermore, as Haight explains, "Both were engaged as assistant editors of liberal periodicals and lived with their employers, exactly opposite each other in the Strand" (*GE & JC* 48). They also shared many common interests, and began frequently to attend concerts and go on walks together. No doubt because they were such good friends, and because they were both single, people began to think of them as engaged. Marian wrote the Brays in April 1852, however, that "We have agreed that we are not in love with each other" (*Letters* 2:22), although she also wrote in May that "my brightest spot next to my love of *old* friends, is the deliciously calm *new* friendship that Herbert Spencer gives me. We see each other every day and have a delightful *camaraderie* in everything" (29). Apparently Spencer had no interest in marriage, although biographers believe that Marian pursued him. Her letter to him in July (written, according to Haight, after his rejection of her love) reveals the intensity of her feeling for him at the time: "I want to know if you can assure me that you will not forsake me, that you will always be with me as much as you can and share your thoughts and feelings with me. If you become attached to some one else, then I must die, but until then I could gather courage to work and make life valuable, if only I had you near me" (8:56–57). Two weeks later, however, she was able to write, "It would be ungenerous in me to allow you to suffer even a slight uneasiness on my account which I am able to remove. I ought at once to tell you, since I can do so with truth, that I am not unhappy. . . . If, as you intimated in your last letter, you feel that my friendship is of value to you for its own sake—mind on no other ground—it is yours" (8:61). Although one biographer, Ruby Redinger, questions the idea that Mary Ann could have "swung with such intensity from man to man to man [Chapman to Spencer to Lewes] (210)," it fits her ongoing pattern (no doubt exacerbated by the death of her father and her sense of homelessness upon her return to England from the Continent) of susceptibility to infatuations, which can indeed shift easily and rapidly from one temporarily idealized love object to another.

Marian also met G. H. Lewes while she was working for Chapman at the *Westminster Review*. Lewes was a good friend of Herbert Spencer's, and the two sometimes stopped in together to visit Marian. Haight records that "on one of these visits [apparently in the fall of 1852], when Spencer rose to leave, Lewes signified that he was going to stay; this, said Spencer [in a letter in 1884], was the beginning of their intimacy" (*Biography* 128). By November 1852, she referred to one of Lewes's chats in a letter to the Brays. At the same time that she was getting to know Lewes, she was becoming increasingly discontented with her work at the *Review*; she longed to free herself of the burden of working with Chapman, whose business was struggling. By October 1853 she had changed her lodgings—a move which most biographers believe marked the beginning of her union with Lewes. Although Lewes had been happily married to Agnes Jervis, with whom he had had four sons, the couple eventually suffered the consequences of their belief in free love. They had been estranged since October 1851, after Agnes had born his friend Thornton Hunt's child and become pregnant with a second. The fact that Lewes had accepted the first illegitimate child as his own (thus condoning his wife's adultery) prevented him, according to the limitations of English law at the time, from obtaining a divorce later (132). In July 1854, when he and Marian decided to take a trip to the Continent together, the couple left for Germany by boat, where, in Haight's words, "Like Maggie and Stephen Guest aboard the Dutch vessel, Marian paced up and down the deck, leaning on George's arm" (148). Marian's series of infatuations with married men had culminated in her choice of Lewes, with whom an elopement would inevitably precipitate a scandal. The sequence of relationships suggests that Eliot's "dependence on the arm of man" (Haight, *Biography* 52, quoting Edith Simcox) was combined with aggression in the form of defiance toward society's values.

Eliot's choice of the forbidden Lewes can be seen as a self-perpetuation of her childhood and adolescent sense of alienation from family and society. Although Eliot did not often allude directly in writing to such feelings, a few references in letters of her friends to mutual acquaintances reveal that she had talked with them about her unhappiness with her family. In March 1842, during the Evans's "Holy War," Cara Bray wrote Sara Hennell that "poor Miss Evans . . . says not one of her family seems to care what becomes of her" (*Letters* 1:130n). In December 1854, shortly after the elopement with Lewes, Charles Bray wrote George Combe that "[Marian's] own relations . . . have never noticed her—never appreciated her" (8:131). Years later, in 1869, Emily Davies recorded a conversation with Eliot about *The Mill on the Floss:* "I asked if she had known actual people like the Dodsons, and she said 'Oh, so much worse.'. . . She considers that in the Mill on the Floss, everything is softened, as compared with real-life. Her own experience she said was worse" (8:465). Eliot's earlier denial of any intention of portraying either the Dodsons or Tom negatively in her statement to Dallas that "no one class of persons [in *The Mill*] . . . is held up to reprobation or to exclusive admiration," probably reflects the depths of her own unacknowledged negative feelings toward her own relatives, on whom her characters were based. Her real-life love for Lewes, however, seems to have successfully replaced her disappointing childhood attachments. Moreover, the relationship seems to have provided the mutually reinforcing, nurturing environment that Eliot needed for her creative gifts to unfold.

Eliot's failure to see Maggie as readers see her seems to derive from her own faulty self-perception. I would suggest that in *The Mill on the Floss*, George Eliot projects the idealized self-image of her youth onto her character Maggie Tulliver. By rationalizing Maggie's behavior with

Philip, Stephen, and Dr. Kenn, Eliot justifies her own pattern of behavior, including her choice of Lewes, and defends herself against her family's and society's judgment. Her failure to separate her own life from her heroine's results in a work of art flawed by decreasing control over the narrative as the novel approaches its deus ex machina ending.

THREE

Loss, Anxiety, and Cure: Mourning and Creativity in *Silas Marner*

After the completion of *The Mill on the Floss* in March 1860, Eliot and Lewes took a trip to the Continent, which Eliot described afterward in a letter as "one of those journies that seem to divide one's life in two by the new ideas they suggest and the new veins of interest they open" (*Letters* 3:311). It was on this trip that Lewes suggested the idea of writing a historical novel based on Savonarola's life in medieval Florence. Eliot responded with alacrity and immediately began her research there, in preparation for the writing of *Romola* (Haight, *Biography* 326). She and Lewes had particularly looked forward to the time alone together away from England because of an imminent change in their personal lives: Lewes's son Charles, who had finished his schooling in Switzerland, was to come live with them; thus Eliot was to become a parent for the first time. Upon their return from the Continent, Charles moved into their home at Holly Lodge in Wandsworth. He soon obtained a civil service job at the Post Office—a circumstance that necessitated the family's household move into London, so that he could be closer to his office. The decision to live in London constituted something of a sacrifice for Eliot, who disliked urban life; but she wanted to provide a home for Charles at this stage. In the process of finding a suitable house, the family moved first, on September 24, to Harewood Square; three months later they finally settled in a house in Blandford Square, "which we have taken for three years, hoping by the end of that time to have so far done our duty by the boys as to be free to live where we list," as Eliot wrote in her journal in December (qtd. in Haight, *Biography* 334).

Eliot explains in her journal that the idea of writing *Silas Marner* "thrust itself" upon her shortly after the September move, during the time when she was preparing to write *Romola* (*Letters* 3:360). She wrote her editor, John Blackwood, that the story "came to me, quite suddenly, as a sort of legendary tale, suggested by my recollection of having once, in my early childhood, seen a linen weaver with a bag on his back" (382). The writing advanced "slowly and interruptedly" (360), however, until the move to Blandford Square. As Eliot noted in her journal on December 31, once *The Mill on the Floss* was finished, 1860 had not been a productive year: "Distractions about our change of residence have run away with many days, and since I have been in London my state of health has been depressing to all effort" (368). Gordon Haight, stressing Eliot's malaise, languor, and "intense sadness" during this time, attributes her frame of mind to her "equivocal marital state" (*Biography* 338). Indeed, Lewes had investigated the possibility of obtaining a divorce abroad, but to no avail. Eliot insisted in a letter to a friend that "I am not sorry. I think the boys will not suffer, and for myself I prefer excommunication" anyway, for its "freedom from petty worldly torments" (*Letters* 3:366–67). Despite her social ostracism, she nonetheless "held [herself] under all the responsibilities of a married woman," taking her role as stepmother to Lewes's sons seriously. She wrote to one friend in January 1861, "I begin, you know, to consider myself an experienced matron, knowing a great deal about parental joys and anxieties" (373).

Once the family was settled in London, Eliot's writing went very quickly, and *Silas Marner* was completed by March 4, 1861. Like her first two novels, it was a financial success, and as Haight reports, nearly all the reviews at the time were favorable (*Biography* 342), although critics in the twentieth century have tended to underestimate the importance of the work. Perhaps in view of Eliot's account of its sudden inspiration, which had interrupted her work on *Romola*, and in view of the novel's brevity, modern critics have tended to regard *Silas Marner* as "uncharacteristic," as Rosemary Ashton expresses it (*GE* 49), and have typically treated it as an interruption on the path toward the writing of her major works. From a psychoanalytic perspective, however, the very fact that this novel seems to be a departure from Eliot's usual practice is a compelling reason for giving it attention. My purpose in this chapter is to examine the personal factors that surrounded Eliot's composition of the work and to account for the novel's genesis by relating its concern with the theme of betrayal to the pain of losses that Eliot had repressed.

In so doing, I will draw on the writings of Sigmund Freud, the studies of contemporary psychologists on obsessive-compulsive behavior, and the research of John Bowlby and Margaret S. Mahler on early child development, as well as the work of George H. Pollock and others on anniversary reactions as manifestations of unresolved mourning. In the process, I will demonstrate the way in which Eliot's fiction writing constituted her constructive response to her sense of loss.

In *Silas Marner*, the isolated life-style of the protagonist is presented as a long-term reaction to a series of painful losses that had occurred fifteen years earlier. As a result of his betrayal by his best friend, William Dane, Silas had been unjustly accused of theft, cast out of his religious sect, and rejected by his fiancée, Sarah, who then married William. Having left the urban community of Lantern Yard, Silas came to live alone as a weaver in the rural village of Raveloe. Emery's Freudian study of *Silas Marner* focuses on the "repression of feelings associated with a disguised or revived Oedipal conflict" (58) in the love triangle involving Silas, Sarah, and William. My own study extends Emery's insights by illuminating, in the light of contemporary psychoanalytic findings, the pre-oedipal dimension of Silas's relationship with his loved ones. My use of Bowlby's and Mahler's studies of the behavior of children under age three in relation to their mothers thus reflects the shift in emphasis in psychoanalytic theory since Freud.

In Raveloe, without a sense of connection to family, friends, or community, Silas's work has lost its purpose. His weaving becomes "an end in itself . . . [a] bridge over the loveless chasms of his life," which is reduced to the "unquestioning activity of a spinning insect." His money, formerly "the symbol of earthly good," also becomes important for its own sake. Feeling the gold coins "in his palm" and looking at "their bright faces" every evening becomes his greatest pleasure (64, 65).

After he is robbed of the gold coins that had come to mean so much to him, Silas develops the habit of opening the door and "looking out from time to time," as though he hoped to see or hear of his money: "It was chiefly at night, when he was not occupied in his loom, that he fell into this repetition of an act for which he could have assigned no definite purpose, and which can hardly be understood except by those who have undergone a bewildering separation from a supremely loved object."

Silas would look out "not with hope, but with mere yearning and unrest" (166).

Eliot's presentation of repetition as Silas's reaction to the loss of a "supremely loved object" anticipates Freud's elaboration of the concept of the repetition-compulsion. In *Beyond the Pleasure Principle,* Freud describes the repetitive game of "disappearance and return" invented by a toddler, age one and a half, in response to separations from his mother. Freud then explains the connection between the toddler's repetitive game and an adult's compulsion to repeat, which is a response to "narcissistic injury," or to painful experience which the mind interprets as loss of love. The aim of the repetition is to make the passive experience active, or, in other words, to "master" it (18:12–22).

Freud had come to see the child's separation from the mother as a primary factor in the origin of anxiety (16:406–7). In one of his late works, *Inhibitions, Symptoms, and Anxiety* (1926), he explains his view that anxiety is the reaction to the danger of loss; that the pain of mourning is the reaction to actual loss; and that defense is a mode of dealing with both anxiety and pain (20:128, 136–45, 153). John Bowlby, the contemporary British psychoanalyst, takes these insights from the last stage of Freud's career as his point of departure in his own three-volume work on *Attachment and Loss.* Following Freud's idea that childhood trauma causes disturbances in later life, Bowlby regards the young child's separation from the mother as traumatic within the definition proposed by Freud (1:10, 11). He also explains in his discussion of separation anxiety in young children that when the mother, or attachment figure, is missing, not only fear and anxiety, but also anger, are aroused (2:25–30). A vicious circle can thus be set in motion when the child feels hostility as a result of separation from the attachment figure, and then feels afraid of losing the attachment figure as a result of this hostility (254).

Eliot's portrayal of Silas as feeling "no resentment, but only pain" at William's accusatory behavior, quickly followed by his feeling of "anxiety" over the possible loss of Sarah's love (58), suggests the close connection between anxiety over impending loss and the defensive process of repressing anger. Silas's fear of losing attachments renders him unable to assert himself against William, who had played the dominating role in their friendship. In the account of the events leading up to his departure from Lantern Yard, Silas's "impressible self-doubting nature" and "trusting simplicity" are contrasted with William's "over-severity towards weaker brethren" and self-assurance (57). Unwilling to admit any hostility toward his close friend, Silas complies too easily with William's theft of his fiancée. Throughout the novel, Silas is portrayed as a gentle person, incapable of hurting others. After Eppie, the orphaned toddler, enters his life, "he trembled at a moment's contention with her, lest she should love him the less for it" (186). His decision to rear her "without punishment" (189) is part of his pattern of disallowing any negative feelings toward loved ones for fear of losing them. In an ongoing circle, the fear of loss of love, or separation anxiety, itself provokes the aggressive impulses that must then be denied.

Fear of aggressive impulses is a prominent feature of what psychologists now call the obsessive-compulsive disorder—an anxiety disorder characterized by the sustained experience of repetitive actions and/or thoughts (Insel ix). According to a phenomenological analysis of the disorder, the most common forms of compulsions are washing, cleaning, counting, and checking. Among the many forms of obsessions are repetitive thoughts, doubts, impulses, or images, typically about subjects like dirt and/or contamination, aggression, sex, or religion (Akhtar 342–48).

In *Silas Marner*, Eliot vividly portrays her character's compulsive behavior. She writes that Silas's "first movement after the shock [of being cast out of the congregation] had been to work at his loom; and he went on with this unremittingly" (64). She then goes on to delineate the connection between Silas's compulsive weaving and the development of his obsession for gold. She compares him to men "shut up in solitary imprisonment" who keep track of intervals of time with marks on the wall, "until the growth of the sum of straight strokes, arranged in triangles, has become a mastering purpose." "That will help us to understand," she goes on, "how the love of accumulating money grows an absorbing passion in men whose imaginations, even in the very beginning of their hoard, showed them no purpose beyond it." His "money had come to mark off his weaving into periods, and the money not only grew, but it remained with him" (67). His compulsive actions ("unremitting" weaving during the day and ritualistic counting every night) and his obsession for gold seem to form a tightly bound circuit in which each continually reinforces the other.

In his classic case study, *Notes Upon a Case of Obsessional Neurosis*

(1909), Freud observed that compulsive actions, felt by a person to be out of his control, represent a "conflict between two opposing impulses" of approximately equal strength, namely love and hate (10:192). He also explains that the precipitating trauma in the obsessional neurosis is remembered but "deprived of its affective cathexis" (10:196); in other words, the traumatic event may be remembered, but strong emotions felt in connection with it are repressed. Contemporary studies of obsessive-compulsive behavior have confirmed Freud's later (1926) insight into the connection between fear of loss and symptoms of anxiety. In his recent psychoanalytic case study of compulsive symptoms that developed during a therapeutic transference, Richard L. Munich concludes that "the timing of each onset and the content of the material served to defend against material associated with separation and loss" (526).

In Eliot's portrayal, it is Silas's sense of abandonment that drives him to turn the gold into a replacement for prior attachments. The coins become his companions: "He handled them, he counted them, till their form and colour were like the satisfaction of a thirst to him." Eliot writes that Silas "*clung* with all the force of his nature to his work and his money" (68; emphasis mine). The more Silas devotes himself to work and money, the more he takes on their qualities. Becoming like an inanimate object himself, he develops a "monotonous craving" for the "monotonous response" of the loom: "His gold, as he hung over it and saw it grow, gathered his power of loving together into a hard isolation like its own (92)." The gold becomes a symbol that contains both the longing and the aggression (Freud's love-hate) felt toward a lost love.

Eliot's portrayal of Silas's cure, in turn, is in keeping with the psychoanalytic model advanced by Otto Fenichel, who explains that "upsetting" and "unforeseen" events can break through the obsessive-compulsive system, and serve as the source of "traumatic cure" of a "compulsive character" (307). In *Silas Marner*, the theft of Silas's bag of gold coins is the unforeseen event that precipitates his cure. At first he cannot believe the gold is really gone; he can feel "only terror, and the eager effort to put an end to the terror" (92). Then, after a search of his cottage convinces him of the reality, he "put his trembling hands to his head, and gave a wild ringing scream, the cry of desolation. For a few moments after, he stood motionless; but the cry had relieved him from the first maddening pressure of the truth" (93). Later, in a reflective passage elaborating the change in Silas, Eliot writes that Silas's "disposition to hoard" was "utterly crushed" by his "sense of bereavement" (190). He had lost the symbol which had satisfied his "need for clinging. . . . Now the support was snatched away," and he was forced to feel all the pain of loss that had earlier been repressed: "He filled up the blank with grief" (129).

The theft of the gold serves as a cure because, as a symbol for prior attachments, it provides Silas with a means of reexperiencing and ultimately resolving earlier losses. The loss of his fiancée had created the need to repeat its pattern in order to resolve it: by leaving his front door unlocked, Silas allows the thief to steal his coins, much as he had earlier allowed William to steal his fiancée. This time, however, he finds a more constructive way to respond to his pain. Instead of isolating himself, he goes out into the community and asks for help. Through talking with others, particularly with Dolly Winthrop, the neighbor who serves the function of a supportive therapist, he slowly reestablishes his sense of connection with others and with his own past. The sense of emptiness felt after the theft of the gold is finally filled by emotional ties, in particular by his relationship with his adopted daughter Eppie. When Marner first discovers Eppie, he thinks, "The child was come instead of the gold . . . the gold had turned into the child" (180). Eliot goes on to elaborate, "The gold had kept his thoughts in an ever-repeat[ing] circle, leading to nothing beyond itself; but Eppie was an object compacted of changes and hopes that forced his thoughts onward" (184).

Through his connection to the child, Silas also rediscovers his own childhood. His involvement with the strict religious sect at Lantern Yard had caused him to lose sight of his legacy from his mother: "Some acquaintance with medicinal herbs and their preparation—a little store of wisdom which she had imparted to him as a solemn bequest." He had come to have "doubts about the lawfulness of applying this knowledge . . . so that his inherited delight to wander through the fields in search of foxglove and dandelion and coltsfoot, began to wear to him the character of a temptation" (57). Through Eppie, Silas recovers what Brian Swann calls his "true past" as his "childlike vision" is restored ("Mythus" 110, 113). Silas, whose sense of self had depended to a great extent on his environment, finally grows into "a new sense of wholeness"

(Cohen 419), or "into the community and into a sense of continuity with the past" (Shuttleworth 280).

Biographical evidence, along with evidence derived from the patterns in her early fiction, suggests that through writing *Silas Marner*, Eliot was working through losses of her own. Her "intense sadness" before and during the writing of the short novel went beyond any discomfort over her "equivocal marital state," and beyond any sense of dislocation brought on by her household moves. A more serious (albeit related) matter was her estrangement from her family. Since May 1857, when she had finally notified her brother Isaac of her living arrangement with Lewes, she had been a "complete outcast" from her relatives. Refusing to respond to her letter himself, Isaac had communicated his displeasure through a family lawyer; at the same time, he pressured their half-sister Fanny and their sister Chrissey to send letters breaking off all communication (Haight, *Biography* 233).

Many writers have emphasized the strength of Eliot's childhood attachment to her brother Isaac—a relationship which, as I suggested earlier, has often been compared to Maggie's with Tom in *The Mill on the Floss*. Yet judging from the references to her family in her letters, both as an adolescent and as an adult Eliot felt closer to her sister Chrissey, who had recently died, in March 1859. In letters to friends up to that point, she frequently mentions her sister, whereas references to Isaac are relatively rare.

Chrissey had been a beautiful child, and, according to Haight, her mother's favorite (along with Isaac), whereas her mother "had never been very close to Mary Anne" (10, 21). Nonetheless, Eliot's letters from her adolescent and young-adult years reflect her ongoing attachment to Chrissey during the period of her life when she frequently had conflicts with Isaac. When Chrissey married in May 1837, a little over a year after their mother's death, Mary Ann, as she began to spell her name at this time (22), became the housekeeper at Griff. Her references to Chrissey during the early years of her marriage to a struggling "medical officer" (*Letters* 1:4) show the gradual decline of her sister's life. In her letters, Mary Ann mentions with joy the births of Chrissey's children in 1838, 1839, and 1841 (1:4, 12, 15, 27, 79). Yet by June 1841, she refers to her sister's domestic life as "one continued endurance" (95). In October she expresses sympathy for her troubles: "My dear Sister is rather an object of solicitude on many accounts—the troubles of married life seem more conspicuously the ordinance of God, in the case of one so meek and passive than in that of women who may fairly be suspected of creating half their own difficulties" (117).

Over the years Chrissey's losses accumulated. In May 1842, her third child, only a little over a year old, died. A few years later, in February 1848, a nine-month-old baby boy died of "Hooping Cough and Convulsions" (*Letters* 1:249n). Her father, Robert Evans, died in May 1849. The following August, while Mary Ann was away recovering in Switzerland, Chrissey lost her seven-year-old daughter. Mary Ann wrote that "my heart aches to think of Chrissey with her children ill of scarlet fever—her husband almost frantic with grief and her own heart rent by the loss of this eldest little daughter" (301). Upon her return to England, where Mary Ann reported she felt more like an "outcast" than she had in Geneva (333), she wrote her friend Cara Bray that "dear Chrissey is much kinder than any one else in the family and I am happiest with her. She is generous and sympathizing and really cares for my happiness" (336).

In December 1852, Chrissey's husband died, leaving her by this time with six remaining children, "the eldest not yet fifteen years old, the youngest not fifteen months, and with little to support them" (Haight, *Biography* 125). Marian became increasingly concerned about her sister's welfare, and more than once expressed her desire to help her financially. During the following years, as Chrissey struggled to raise her children and find suitable positions for them, she lost another son, "drowned at sea," in 1855 (*Letters* 2:204). In April 1857, she lost another daughter to typhoid fever (314). At that point, Eliot asked Isaac to give Chrissey fifteen pounds of her own income "to spend taking a change of air as soon as she is able to do so"; but in early May, she learned that Chrissey herself was very ill. Later that month, after she had informed her family of her life with Lewes, she wrote her friend Sara Hennell that she cared the most about staying in touch with Chrissey so that she would be able to help her (342), although at the time her financial capacity to help her was very limited (Haight, *Biography* 230).

In February 1859, "in the midst of . . . [the] gratifying reception of *Adam Bede*" (277), she finally received a letter from Chrissey, who was very ill, and who expressed regret that she had "ever ceased to write . . .

one who under all circumstances was kind to me and mine" (*Letters* 3:26). When Chrissey died shortly after, Eliot, who had already written Sara Hennell that "the past is abolished from my mind—I only want [Chrissey] to feel that I love her and care for her" (3:26), wrote: "Chrissey's death has taken from the possibility of many things toward which I looked with some hope and yearning in the future. I had a very special feeling towards her, stronger than any third person would think likely" (38).

During the years that Chrissey's life seemed to be steadily declining, Eliot was slowly finding her way to success. It seems ironic that just at the point when the publication of *Adam Bede* had established her reputation as a writer, her sister's life ended. Chrissey died on March 15, 1859, when Eliot was beginning work on *The Mill on the Floss*, and just as she was approaching the tenth anniversary of her father's death, which had occurred in May 1849. In the light of Bowlby's explanation of the way in which a recent loss, or the anniversary of a loss, or both, can activate repressed feelings of grief for an earlier one (3:152–60), I would argue that Eliot's sense of estrangement from her family intensified her grief (and, especially in light of her own current success, perhaps guilt) over her sister's misfortunes and death—a death which, because of its timing, revived feelings, however long repressed, associated with her parent's death. The intensity of Eliot's sadness during this period, then, could be said to derive not only from her current losses, but from the reexperiencing of unresolved feelings about past losses—the "anniversary reaction" that Pollock describes in his work on mourning (183ff). The return of Eliot's repressed feelings from the past is the "time-specific variant of the repetition-compulsion" that manifests the human mind's unconscious sense of time. Extending Marie Bonaparte's idea that the mind may associate the passing of time with death (442), Mintz explains that the unconscious sense of time emerging in the anniversary reaction may be crystallized out of the anxieties about death (722).

The sibling attachment that is elaborated in *The Mill on the Floss* is only alluded to in *Silas Marner*, but is still at the core of the central character's psychological situation. Moreover, the sibling attachment in both novels is tied to earlier loss. As I have noted in my study of the earlier novel, Maggie finds in Tom a symbolic replacement for both mother and father, who have proven to be disappointing parent figures. In *Silas Marner*, Silas finds in the golden-haired toddler a replacement for "his little sister [Eppie] whom he had carried about in his arms for a year before she died, when he was a small boy" (168). He tells Dolly in a later conversation that his little sister had been named after his mother, Hephzibah (183). Thus his new love for his adopted child Eppie is linked not only to his lost sister, but to his mother, although it is the sibling attachment that is most clearly remembered.

Eliot's childhood attachment to her older brother has led critics and biographers to ask questions about her relationship with her mother. In his early *Life* of Eliot, John Walter Cross explains that although Mrs. Evans had been "a very active hard-working woman," she "became ailing in health," "shortly after her last child's birth"; consequently, Chrissey, her oldest child, was sent a short distance away to a school in Attleboro, and Mary Anne and Isaac spent part of every day at a "Dame's school close to Griff gates" (7). Haight intimates that Eliot experienced a poor relationship with her mother, but he provides no support for his contentions that "her mother's favorites were Isaac and Chrissey," and "her mother had never been very close to Mary Anne" (*Biography* 10, 21). It seems that nothing is actually known of her early interactions with her mother. Cross emphasizes the adolescent Mary Anne's grief over her mother's death; he makes the statement that "Many references will be found in the subsequent correspondence to what she suffered at this time" (15). Yet Ruby Redinger, explaining that the "letters for the two years following the mother's death are missing," concludes that "there is no objective evidence about George Eliot's memory of her mother" (37, 38). Haight's discussion of her reaction to her mother's death notes Eliot's general "paucity of comment about her mother," and suggests the possibility of a psychological explanation, although the point is not elaborated (*Biography* 22). I would argue that Eliot's notable silence on the subject of her mother is the silence of repression of painful affect in response to the loss of her mother—a loss which she associated with the deaths of siblings.

When Eliot was about sixteen months old, her mother gave birth, on March 16, 1821, to twin boys, who died when they were ten days old. After that, her mother "had not been well"—a circumstance which probably explains the development of her intense attachment to her older brother Isaac, "the dominating passion of her childhood," as Haight describes it (6, 5). Eliot's mother, who, as it seems to me, was virtually missing in her daughter's life after that time, then died when she was sixteen. The timing of the deaths was such that they occurred during critical stages in Eliot's development: the deaths of the twins occurred during a time when a child is still dependent on her mother's reliable presence for her own developing sense of her self; the death of her mother, during Mary Anne's adolescence, occurred at a time when early childhood stages are revived as part of the process of working toward adult identity.

Like Bowlby, Margaret S. Mahler has studied the behavior of infants and young children in the context of their interactions with their mothers. She is best known for her ground-breaking work, *The Psychological Birth of the Human Infant*, which describes in detail what she calls the "separation-individuation process"—a process, as explained by Paul Stepansky in his introduction to Mahler's memoirs that "denotes the series of stages marking the infant's gradual intrapsychic 'separation' from the mother and correlative understanding of himself as a distinct individual in a world composed of other equally distinct individuals" (xvii). Mahler's use of the term "separation" is thus different from Bowlby's. Whereas Bowlby emphasizes the negative effects of the child's too early and/or prolonged physical separations from the mother, Mahler's "separation" refers to the normal intrapsychic developmental process that is prerequisite to identity formation in all humans, both male and female.

Mahler characterizes the separation-individuation process, which she says begins during the fourth or fifth month and continues to the thirtieth or thirty-sixth month, as involving four subphases: the first, a "hatching" process of differentiation and the development of body image; the second, a "practicing" process of learning to move away from the mother by crawling and walking; the third, "rapprochement," beginning about the middle of the second year, involving the development of language and the beginning of gender identity; and the fourth, the consolidation of individuality and the beginnings of emotional object constancy (*Birth* 52, 65, 76, 109). Thus it can be argued that it was toward the end of the second, or "practicing" subphase, that circumstances caused Eliot's mother to withdraw from her—a possibility that is also suggested by Bowlby's studies of the adverse effects on the surviving children of mothers who have lost babies: sometimes there is a failure to respond to one or more surviving children, and sometimes outright rejection (3:123).

Mahler emphasizes the importance of the "rapprochement crisis," which she believes occurs at 18–20 or 24 months and beyond (in Eliot's life, the period immediately following the deaths of the twins), and which may result in an unfavorable fixation that interferes with later development (*Birth* 95, 107). It is a crisis "made more poignant by the coming together of the three main anxieties of childhood: namely, fear of abandonment (fear of object loss), fear of loss of love, and, in particular, castration [or mutilation] anxiety" (144).

If Eliot's early childhood after the twins' deaths was indeed "dominated" by her passion for her brother, then the fact that she was sent to a boarding school at age five involved a double loss—of both mother and brother. Haight writes of this time in 1824 that "Mary Anne never forgot her suffering . . . and her fears at night" (*Biography* 6). Although there seems to be little information regarding the period of her life that immediately followed, Haight mentions that her brother, who was attending a different school, began to grow away from her, and that Mary Anne was forced to turn to books for solace (7). He then describes the way others saw her by 1827: as "a very serious child" whose "unusual gravity" prompted the older girls to call her "little Mamma"; a child who did not like to be "made untidy," who suffered from "night terrors," who was "sensitive" and "easily reduced to passionate tears," and who came to be known for her preference for adults over children (8).

These traits are very much in keeping with Mahler's descriptions of pre-oedipal children who show signs of longing for their absent mothers. Mahler describes the "low-keyedness," a solemnity approaching depression, of children during the second subphase, when their mothers are absent from the room—a condition that can extend "beyond its normal place in the practicing subphase" (*Birth* 74, 161). She mentions one child who, identifying with his older brother (apparently as a substitute for the mother), would feel lost and stare into space when the brother was absent (174). She also describes children whose sign of longing for the mother takes the form of a preference for adults, and others whose symptoms include sleep disturbances. Finally, she writes of one child whose combined separation and castration anxieties were reflected in his need to have everything "in place, in order, and complete" (179).

In *Beyond the Pleasure Principle,* Freud gives examples of how the compulsion to repeat operates in the lives of adults —like "the man whose friendships all end in betrayal by his friend" or "the lover each of whose love affairs . . . passes through the same phases and reaches the same conclusion" (24). The adult compulsion to repeat also seems to characterize the pattern of Eliot's response to losses in her family. Haight records that when Eliot's mother died in 1836, her adolescent religious zeal "increased," and was accompanied by a determined self-denial (*Biography* 22). Her response to her father's death thirteen years later repeated the pattern, although in the latter case it involved an intense interest in Thomas à Kempis, whom she admired for his emphasis on "renunciation" (67). Eliot seems to have reenacted the loss of her parents by temporarily identifying with an ideal that would then necessitate further loss.

A similar compulsion to repeat links Eliot's fiction to her reaction to Chrissey's death. Eliot's creation of the golden-haired toddler Eppie reflects her mind's attempt to rework the period of her childhood when she first experienced the loss of her mother that followed the deaths of her twin siblings. The idealized Eppie, who represents both sibling and mother to Silas, can also be seen as a symbol of Eliot's idealized self, reunited with mother, father, and siblings, all represented by Silas. As Eppie brings back to Silas "a dreamy feeling, [with] . . . old quiverings of tenderness—old impressions of awe at the presentiment of some Power presiding over his life" (168), so she provides for Eliot a means of re-creating the symbiosis with the lost mother that Mahler believes it is part of the human condition to crave (*Birth* 227).

Yet at the same time, in *Silas Marner* (which was completed in March 1861, the anniversary month and year of the deaths of the twins in 1821), the need to leave the mother and the past is also dramatized. When Eppie's mother, a drug addict with no remaining capacity to care for her child, dies, the child shows no sign of fear. With "the ready transition of infancy" (like Mahler's infants in the second subphase, practicing to move away from the mother by crawling and walking), Eppie turns easily from her dead mother's body; starting out on "all fours," she rises to her feet and toddles toward the light gleaming from the door of Silas's cottage (165). She is soon discovered by Silas, who cares for her, is allowed by the villagers to keep her, and then raises her "without punishment." Eppie and Silas continue to maintain their close attachment even after she grows up and marries a young man from the village. Thus, at the same time that *Silas Marner* expresses Eliot's wish to be reunited with her family, it also expresses her wish to separate painlessly from her deceased mother (in the sense of leaving behind her grief over her loss), and to find a new, lasting love.

In *The Mill on the Floss,* George Eliot shows Maggie repeating—in her relationship with her brother Tom, and then with other men—her sense that she is rejected by her parents and society. Although Eliot apparently intends to arouse sympathy for Maggie when Tom casts her out for stealing their cousin Lucy's fiancé, what comes through is Maggie's ongoing provocation of him. Contrary to Eliot's conscious intentions, the text shows that Maggie, like Silas, brings about her own exile. The same could be said for Eliot herself, whose choice of Lewes was bound to provoke the wrath of her relatives. She foresaw their reaction well enough; she had waited nearly three years after the fact before telling her family of her decision to live with Lewes, because "their views of life differ in many respects from my own" (*Letters* 2:349).

Eliot's ambivalence toward her family is expressed in letters long before Lewes came into her life. As early as the letter to Cara Bray written after her return from her trip to the Continent following her father's death, she adds to the expression of her preference for Chrissey, "But I am delighted to feel that I am of no importance to any of them, and have no motive for living amongst them" (1:336). After the break with Isaac, she wrote Sara Hennell that "I dare say I shall never have any further correspondence with my brother, which will be a great relief to me" (2:364). Such comments belie her later assertions that "I cling strongly to kith and kin though they reject *me*" (5:74). Even some ambivalence toward Chrissey is suggested by the timing of the disclosure of her liaison to her family: she learned of Chrissey's serious illness in early May 1857 (8:169); her letter to Isaac was dated shortly after, on May 26, at a time when she knew so little about Chrissey's condition that she had to ask Isaac "whether she is strong enough to make it desirable for me to write her" (2:332)—hardly a time to risk losing touch with her. Moreover, the letter was written very close to the twentieth anniversary of Chrissey's wedding date, May 30, 1837, and close to the anniversary of their father's death twelve years later, on May 31, 1849. Although (judging from the written record), Eliot's poor timing was not deliberate, it may well have reflected unacknowledged resentment felt at the effect her sister's marriage had had on the course of her own young single life, as she became solely responsible for her father's care.

Certainly Eliot's new life with Lewes had allowed her to find her identity as a fiction writer—a vocation which flourished under "the inspiriting influence of his constant encouragement" (Haight, *Biography* 369, quoting Edith Simcox). Moreover, her life of alienation from family and society simply allowed her the time she needed to write. Perhaps *Silas Marner* expresses Eliot's own "ready transition" from familial attachments to her new relationship with Lewes. It may also express her positive reaction to her new role as adoptive mother to Lewes's stepson, Charles—who perhaps like Eppie might serve as "an object compacted of changes and hopes that forced [her] thoughts onward" (184). By contrast, as seems evident in the tragic course of her life, her sister Chrissey did not find a way out of her apparent identification with the mother who lost babies, became ill, and died. As Chrissey observed in a letter to Isaac only two months before her own death, "I was 45 Monday—only 2 years younger than my Mother when she died" (*Letters* 8:222). Bowlby's studies of adults who have lost parents in adolescence and who suffer illness or breakdown as they approach the age of the parent's death (3:158) suggest that the timing of Chrissey's own death may have been influenced by her state of unresolved mourning over the loss of her mother; and by implication, that it was Eliot's use of her intellectual and creative gifts that defended her against the possibility of her own early demise.

Toward the end of *Silas Marner*, Silas returns to Lantern Yard to try to talk to the minister of his old congregation. He wants to ask some questions about the past, in particular about the "drawing of the lots" [the method the congregation had used to determine his guilt], and tell him "about the religion o' this countryside, for I partly think he doesn't know on it" (238). When he arrives in town and looks around, he discovers that "Lantern Yard's gone." As he tells Dolly Winthrop upon his return to Raveloe, "The old home's gone; I've no home but this now. I shall never know whether they got at the truth o' the robbery, nor whether Mr. Paston could ha' given me any light about the drawing o' the lots. It's dark to me, Mrs. Winthrop, that is; I doubt it'll be dark to the last" (240–41). Silas feels that he has been wronged in some way that he will never understand. His sense of loss, more than simple grief, is a mix of feelings, even including moral outrage. Yet he concludes that from now on, Eppie's presence will give him "light enough to trusten by."

Silas and Eppie, as unlike each other as they appear to be, are characters who mirror one another. The change in Silas's psychological state is dramatized not only in his story, but in hers. Eppie, the idealized character, does easily what Silas, the realistically portrayed character, accomplishes only with great pain; she acts out literally what Silas must do indirectly, through a process of symbolization. Eppie readily turns away from her dead mother, while Silas is forced, only when his gold coins are stolen, to turn away from the "dead disrupted thing" which had satisfied his need for "clinging" (129). The scene in which Eppie walks away from her mother is juxtaposed with the scene in which Silas repeatedly goes to the door to look for his lost gold, his "supremely loved object"; thus the two characters are brought together on the basis of their shared loss. Moreover, just as Eppie acts out what Silas needs to do, so Silas feels the pain that Eppie denies. Through the interaction of the mirroring characters, the novel makes the connection between the act of separation and the pain of loss. *Silas Marner* is among other things, then, a story about the pain of separating from maternal attachment.

If it is true, as I have argued, that Eliot was engaged in her own struggle to work through a too early and abrupt loss of maternal closeness, then her own mind, in "thrusting" upon her a story which would enact the process she needed to relive, provided her with an indirect, symbolic means of getting at painful material from her past. According to Freud, the repetition-compulsion that is observable in children's play can also be observed in artistic creation. "Artistic play" is a means of "making what is in itself unpleasurable into a subject to be recollected and worked over in the mind" (18:17). Like Freud's toddler, dramatizing his mother's departure and return by flinging his toy out of sight and pulling it back again, Eliot could attempt to master her pain of loss by writing a story that would dramatize her mother's disappearance (the theft of Silas's gold and the death of Eppie's mother) as well as her return (the attachment between Silas and Eppie).

Eliot is also like Freud's "patient" who "cannot remember the whole of what is repressed" and "must *repeat* the repressed material as a contemporary experience" (18:18). Through writing a work of fiction, Eliot could, like the patient in a therapeutic transference, enter into a fantasy in which she could reenact repressed feelings toward prior attachments. Through the interconnecting stories of her mirroring characters, Eppie and Silas (whose psychological situation is in turn mirrored by the leading characters in the Cass family subplot), the painful feelings that had previously been denied could be reconnected to the traumatic loss; thus the repressed pain could be confronted indirectly. When Silas returned to Lantern Yard to ask questions about his past, he came to realize that some things would remain "dark"; similarly, in her own descent into the "unrememberable and unforgettable realm" of her mind (Mahler, *Birth* 226), Eliot could not recover lost details of her infancy. She could, however, repeat the process of losing and regaining her mother indirectly, through the writing of her fiction, as often as necessary to master her sense of loss. In the inspiration to write *Silas Marner*, her mind had thrust upon her a work of art that illuminates as it enacts its own progress toward self-healing.

FOUR

Pathological Narcissism in *Romola*

Literary critics of *Romola*, whatever their persuasion, agree that the novel represents a turning point in George Eliot's career. *Romola* is a very different kind of novel from *Adam Bede, The Mill on the Floss*, and *Silas Marner*, each of which takes place in provincial England during the generation before its creation. By contrast, *Romola* is set in medieval Italy. Eliot began her research for her historical novel during her stay with Lewes in Florence in 1860, after the completion of *The Mill on the Floss*. Although the writing of *Silas Marner* interrupted her plans for *Romola*, she returned to Florence to do research in April 1861—for "thirty-four days of precious time spent there" (GE Journal, qtd. in Haight, *Biography* 348). Upon her return to England she settled into "prolonged study [of medieval history, literature and art] for the background of the novel" (349). She began to write in October, but almost gave up in despair in November. Beginning again in January 1862, she finally completed the novel in June 1863; it was published in parts, in the *Cornhill Magazine*, beginning in July 1862 and ending in August 1863, and as a three-volume book in July 1863, by Smith, Elder and Company.

Eliot's interest in writing a novel about Savonarola's life in medieval Florence should be seen in the context of mid-Victorian enthusiasm for historical fiction, and in particular, for the medieval period. In *The Victorian Historical Novel*, Andrew Sanders attributes this enthusiasm to the pervasive influence on nineteenth-century literature of Sir Walter Scott's Waverley novels; he also makes the point that Scott's influence on the nineteenth century was actually based more on his development of the novel into a "morally and socially serious" literary form (5) than on his interest in history. In a chapter on *Romola*, Sanders stresses Eliot's particularly "profound and pervasive debt to Scott." As her biographers attest, she began reading Scott at age seven, and as an adult, when she was living with her aging father, read aloud Scott's novels to him at night. Sanders asserts that Eliot's appreciation of the Waverley novels "was a vital shaping influence on the nature, form and intent of her own fiction" (168). Scott's influence can be felt in her portrayal of the provincial communities of her early novels, "and in the way in which all of her novels consider the relationship between a particular place and a particular time. Both novelists were fascinated by a sense of human community and by the links between the responsive individual and the society around him" (169).

Eliot experienced much anxiety over the accuracy of her use of details of the period. Critics and biographers often mention her conscientious labor over the research, and her difficulties, for fear of insufficient knowledge, in getting started on the writing. In addition, she herself often mentioned in letters to friends before and during the writing of the book her recurring depressions and illnesses, as well as Lewes's frequent and sometimes severe illnesses. Yet she felt later that writing the book had transformed her. She told John Cross toward the end of her life that "she could put her finger on it as marking a well-defined transition in her life. 'I began it a young woman,—I finished it an old woman,'" she said. She also told her editor, John Blackwood, in 1877, that "there is no book of mine about which I more thoroughly feel that I could swear by every sentence as having been written with my best blood, such as it is, and with the most ardent care for veracity of which my nature is capable" (Haight, *Biography* 362).

Critics have appreciated the novel's complexity. Henry James saw *Romola* as the "most important" of Eliot's novels—"not the most entertaining nor the most readable, but the one in which the largest things are attempted and grasped" (Haight, *Century* 52). Many modern critics, too, like Jerome Thale, recognize in *Romola* an attempt to develop a new kind of novel with more "weight" and "depth" than her early fiction (*Novels* 75). George Levine sees the novel as anticipating her last work, *Daniel Deronda*, by virtue of its movement in the direction of a more complex vision than exists in her earlier novels (81). Felicia Bonaparte's book-length study of the novel, *The Triptych and the Cross: The Central Myths of George Eliot's Poetic Imagination*, confirms Eliot's own statement that "there is scarcely a phrase, an incident, an allusion that did not gather its value to me from its supposed subservience to my main artistic purpose" (*Letters* 4:97). Bonaparte concludes herself that *Romola* is "a symbolic narrative in which every character, every event, every detail—every word, in fact—is an image in an intricate symbolic pattern" (10). Sanders, assessing the novel's value as historical fiction, calls it "one of the major monuments . . . in its period, . . . a masterpiece integral to the entire cultural achievement of the nineteenth century" (196).

The story of *Romola* begins in 1492 in Florence, toward the end of the life of Savonarola, a Roman Catholic friar (1452–98) who became famous as a religious reformer. Concerned early in his life with the humanistic paganism that he perceived as corrupting every aspect of life in Italy, including religion, he finally renounced the world to enter the Dominican order. He became a lecturer in the convent of San Marco, where he gained a reputation for his learning and asceticism. Nine years after becoming a friar, he experienced a sudden revelation which inspired him to begin his prophetic sermons. During lent in 1485 and 1486, he put forward his well-known propositions that the Church needed reforming, and that it would be scourged, and then renewed. Popular enthusiasm for his preaching increased when his prophecy that the Medici rule would be overthrown by the invasion of Charles VIII of France proved true. By that time, according to Donald Weinstein's account of the period (1494–98), Savonarola dominated the Florentine scene. He succeeded in establishing a democratic government which he hoped might initiate the reform of Italy and of the Church (274–77). Unfortunately for him, however, his sudden rise to power provoked opposition in the form of a political party, the Arrabiati, which formed an alliance with foreign powers, including the pope. In 1495 the pope took the step of forbidding Savonarola, who was critical of the corrupt clergy, to preach. Although Savonarola continued preaching, his popularity waned, as Florence began to experience economic difficulties. He was excommunicated in 1497 for disobeying the pope's order, and was eventually tried and condemned by an ecclesiastical court, which then turned him over to the civil authorities for punishment. He was hanged and his body burned in 1498.

Historical interpretations of Savonarola have varied greatly; in the nineteenth century, he was admired by some historians as a prophet and vilified by others as a self-deluded fantast (Weinstein 4, 5). Although

Eliot shares Pasquale Villari's interpretation [*Life and Times of Girolamo Savonarola* 1859, 1861], which accepts "the liberal and moral tendencies in the Frate's program," yet "rejects the vestiges of medievalism which encumbered effective political and moral action" (Santangelo 119), her reading of history was extensive, and it would be a mistake to point to one source as defining her perspective on Savonarola's life. Her analysis of him as a charismatic preacher whose visions and oratory were fueled by his anger at the corruption he perceived in society, and whose influence over others derived from an "innate need to dominate" (621), seems to be entirely her own, based on her reading of the sources, including Savonarola's own writings.

Eliot's conception of her historical novel was influenced by Bulwer Lytton's *Rienzi*, a Victorian novel about a medieval Roman patriot who became tyrannical after he gained political power. According to Hugh Witemeyer, Eliot shared with Bulwer, who was "the foremost theorist and one of the foremost practitioners of the genre," the mid-Victorian emphasis on factual accuracy in historical fiction—a departure from Scott's practice of "violating known chronology and inventing fictitious incidents" for dramatic purposes (*Studies* 62). At the same time, she shared Bulwer's belief that the "inner history" of a person, "when it is unknown, may be imagined or invented in keeping with the traditional license of romance" (63). Unlike Bulwer, however, Eliot does not make her historical figure the title character of her story. By making a fictitious character, Romola, the protagonist, and showing how that individual's life is affected by historical events, Eliot thus "reverts to [the practice of] Scott in his Waverley novels" (68). Moreover, Eliot's account of her character is more complex than Bulwer's; she brought to historical romance her "vision of society as a complex structure or tissue of interdependent elements, dynamically changing through time under the influence of multiple and interacting causes, and gradually ameliorating the lives of its individual members" (70).

Eliot's portrayal of the growth of a young woman into adulthood in the context of the political events of fifteenth-century Florence has much in common with her English novels; Romola shares traits with Dinah and Maggie, and with Dorothea, the heroine of Eliot's later novel, *Middlemarch*. Romola is "a tall maiden of seventeen or eighteen" (93), the daughter of an obsessive blind scholar, Bardo. Her father has provided her with an education, with the result that she is able to be a substantial help to him in his work of organizing and preserving his library. She patiently endures his ongoing demands, which have intensified with old age; nonetheless, the two have a loving, if ambivalent, relationship. Unfortunately, Romola soon marries an opportunist, a Greek newcomer to Florence, the handsome and charming Tito, who has posed as a scholar willing to help her father. Tito proves to be Eliot's greatest villain. Not only does he betray his stepfather, his father-in-law, and his wife Romola during the course of the story, but he also becomes a spy and counterspy for each of the warring political factions; in the process he helps to bring about the execution of Romola's godfather, Bernardo, as well as that of Savonarola.

Romola first meets Savonarola on a visit to see her brother Dino, who is also a friar, before her marriage. Later, when she tries to run away from her husband after she learns he has sold her father's library for his own gain, Savonarola convinces her of her duty as a wife to return. As the story progresses, however, not only does Romola's personal life become intolerable, but she becomes disenchanted with Savonarola because of his refusal to help prevent the execution of her godfather: Bernardo, although innocent of intrigue, is associated with the opposing political party. In despair, Romola runs away from Florence. By the time she returns, she has recovered from her anger at Tito and Savonarola, both of whom have died violent deaths in the meantime, and she is transformed by her creator into a saintly figure, a veritable Madonna, caring for the sick and dying in the plague-stricken city, and finally even willingly taking responsibility for the care of her husband's mistress, Tessa, and her two children.

Eliot's excessive idealization of Romola has been criticized by Victorians and moderns alike. One contemporary critic, Dorothea Barrett, refers to the ending of the novel as "embarrassing," because of the author's attempt to suppress "the dark side" of her heroine (88–91). Yet Romola's dark side is suggested by "the extraordinary violence with which images of the father are treated [in the novel]," as Gillian Beer expresses it (121). Emery, seeing Romola and Tito as "opposing aspects of one psyche" (85), suggests that Tito acts out Romola's hostility toward fathers (103). My own psychoanalytic interpretation will extend such discussions of Eliot's portrayal of aggression in *Romola*, first by examining Tito's characterization from the perspective of Otto F. Kernberg's study of pathological narcissism. Previous critical views of Tito have ranged from those like Levine, who finds him uninteresting (91), and Thale, who sees the characters in Romola as less well developed than those in other novels (*Novels* 82), to critics like Ashton, Bonaparte, and Barbara Hardy, who see in Tito's characterization a "fine piece of psychological analysis" (Ashton, *GE* 54; see also Bonaparte, *Will* 181; Hardy, *Novels* 74). My application of Kernberg's ideas to a study of Tito will, I believe, demonstrate to a much greater extent than has been done before the depth of psychological insight that Eliot achieved in her portrayal of him. I will then discuss more briefly the characterizations of Baldassarre, Savonarola, Tessa, and Romola, also in the light of Kernberg's theory, to show not only the "essential unity" (Emery 85) of Tito and Romola, but also the interconnections among all the major characters, who together form a psychological unity; in so doing, I will point to the source of the author's excessive idealization of Romola. Finally, I will show how the characterizations and other aspects of the novel, including the improbable ending, are related to the past and current events in Eliot's life at the time of writing.

The term "narcissism" as originally used by psychoanalysts and currently used popularly has a pejorative connotation that is unfortunate in light of the current thinking of both object relations theorists and self-psychologists. Whereas early Freudians thought of narcissism as the concentration of the libido on the self at the expense of object love, contemporary psychoanalytic theorists see healthy self-love and healthy object love as closely related. Kernberg, making a distinction between normal and pathological narcissism, describes normal narcissism as "the libidinal investment of the self." He explains that in a healthy person, "when there is an increase of narcissistic investment, there is a parallel increase in the capacity to love and to give, to experience and express gratitude, to have concern for others, and for an increase in sexual love, sublimation, and creativity" (320). Attempting to avoid either the overuse or too general use of the term, Kernberg limits his definition of pathological narcissism to a group of patients in whom "the main problem appears to be the disturbance of their self-regard in connection with specific disturbances in their object relationships" (17). Pathological narcissism, as he defines it, is characterized by the simultaneous development of pathological forms of self-love and pathological forms of object love (230). Whereas the normal self-structure consists of multiple, integrated (good and bad) self-images, Kernberg's "narcissistic personality" has a pathological self-structure, in which the self-concept is a confusion of realistic and idealized self-images, merged with an idealized object image; at the same time, unacceptable self-images are "repressed and projected onto external objects" (231–32).

Kernberg emphasizes a particular set of traits that characterizes the adult narcissistic personality. One is a surface adaptation that "masks . . . the absence of deep object relationships . . . [as well as the] severe pathology of their internalized object relationships" (146). Underneath the surface adaptation and "relatively good social functioning" (229), however, the narcissistic personality experiences a sense of inner emptiness (217, 220, 237) that accompanies an observable quality of shallowness in relationships, achievements, and convictions. The sense of inner emptiness also results in a feeling of boredom when tributes from others are not forthcoming. Thus activities are performed for the sake of outside rewards rather than for the sake of an inner sense of satisfaction. The narcissistic personality is also deficient in the capacity for genuine feelings of sadness (229) or guilt (307)—an incapacity which enables the narcissist to exploit others without remorse (228). Indeed, Kernberg stresses the narcissistic personality's need to manipulate and/or control others, a trait which, as Richard D. Chessick observes, may only appear when the person attains a position of power (8). More than any other trait, however, Kernberg emphasizes the central importance of the narcissistic personality's basic dread of attack and destruction (234)—a dread which is actually a projection of his own aggression (257). Kernberg explains that the person's unconscious fear of his own envy and rage arises from his fantasy that his aggression will destroy his needed love object (287–88). All the traits of the narcissistic personality are interrelated and reflect, in Kernberg's words, "the serious deterioration of all internalized object relationships" which the narcissistic personality attempts to replace with his or her pathological grandiose self. Narcissistic personalities have not succeeded in internalizing and integrating good and bad parent images; nor have they succeeded in completing the process of super-ego integration, because "the pathological fusion between ideal self, ideal object, and actual self images prevents such integration of the superego" (232). The felt sense of emptiness, then, reflects the reality of the narcissistic person's lack of essential internal self-structures.

In *Romola*, Eliot portrays Tito as possessing the qualities that Kernberg describes. Through his "distinct self-conscious adaptation of a part in life" (279), he finds it easy to become a success in Florence. Yet he is deficient both in genuine accomplishments, either as a scholar or a political leader, and in genuine feelings—of appreciation, attachment, love, guilt, or sorrow. Tito's exploitativeness follows from his incapacity for such feelings; he relates to others only to satisfy his own needs. In his view, the purpose of life is "to extract the utmost sum of pleasure" (167).

In order to live the carefree life that he desires, Tito must deny or put off any unpleasantness. He is unable to be honest with his mistress Tessa about his marriage to Romola because "it would have been brutal to leave her, and Tito's nature was all gentleness" (156). He cannot bear expressions of sadness: "It was enough for Tito if [Tessa] did not cry while he was present. The softness of his nature required that all sorrow should be hidden away from him" (162). Nor can he bear any open expression of anger. Romola notices early in their relationship that "nothing makes [Tito] angry" (189); but she soon learns that his seeming lack of anger is not a positive trait. When she confronts him with her knowledge of the sale of her father's library, Tito is, typically, "not angry; he only felt the moment was eminently unpleasant," although at the same time, his underlying aggression is evident in his determination to display his "masculine predominance" (356). Later on, his feeling toward Romola, as she confronts him about the plot against Savonarola, turns to "that cold dislike which is the anger of unimpassioned beings" (482). He withdraws from his relationship with her because, as Eliot puts it, "From all relations that were not easy and agreeable, we know that Tito shrank" (495). Avoiding painful situations of all kinds, he is not present at Bernardo's execution despite having participated indirectly in the plot to kill him, because "he had a native repugnance to death and pain" (582).

At the same time that Eliot portrays Tito's incapacity for authentic feelings, she emphasizes, more than any other trait, his paralyzing sense of dread—a dread that originates in his fear of his stepfather Baldassarre's revenge for his abandonment of him after their shipwreck. Like Kernberg's narcissistic personality projecting his aggression onto others and feeling only paranoid fear in himself, Tito does not think of committing murder himself: "All other possibilities passed through his mind, even to his own flight from Florence; but he never thought of any scheme for removing his enemy. His dread generated no active malignity, and he would still have been glad not to give pain to any mortal" (288). Yet the strength of his fear, which seems out of proportion to the danger as it would be perceived by others, surprises him: "Why should he, a young man, be afraid of an old one? a young man with armour on, of an old man without a weapon" (377). Slowly he comes to associate his fear of Baldassarre with his dread of Romola's judgment, after she learns he has betrayed his stepfather and begins to see into the depths of his capacity for duplicity. Tito becomes aware that "a crisis was come in his married life. The husband's determination to mastery, which lay deep below all blandness and beseechingness, had risen permanently to the surface now, and seemed to alter his face" (489–90). The gradual "hardening of cheeks and mouth" (600) is reminiscent of the change in Hetty's face as she approaches her trial and banishment in *Adam Bede*.

In order to appreciate the "fine piece of psychological analysis" in Eliot's characterization of Tito, it is necessary to understand her use of the technique of literary pictorialism. In *George Eliot and the Visual Arts*, Witemeyer explains that Eliot learned from Nathanial Hawthorne's *The Marble Faun* how to use "*ecphrasis,* or the verbal imitation of works of visual art, as a technique of psychological revelation and prophecy. . . . In *Romola* and her later novels, she regularly juxtaposes her characters with morally significant art works located inside the story" (55–56). In the scene when the artist Piero di Cosimo enters Nello's barber shop, where Tito has come shortly after his arrival in Florence, he makes the abrupt remark, after briefly fixing his eye on Tito, that he would like to use his face for "a picture of Sinon deceiving old Priam" (87)—a reference to the story of the betrayal of the Trojan king by the young Greek son of Sisyphus. In contrast to Nello, who assesses Tito on the basis of his surface beauty, Piero, with his "direct" and "comprehensive" artist's vision and his commitment to "truthful representation," sees "the complexity of things" almost immediately, as William J. Sullivan observes in his essay on Eliot's characterization of the artist (393–94). Piero answers Nello's protest by saying that Tito makes the "perfect traitor," with his "face which vice can write no marks on—lips that will lie with a dimpled smile—eyes of such agate-like brightness and depth that no infamy can dull them—cheeks that will rise from a murder and not look haggard" (87). His remarks occur just before Cennini, another patron of the shop, notices Tito's ring—the gift from his stepfather which, as Joseph Weisenfarth explains in his essay on antique gems, was intended to symbolize the bond between them (58). Thus Piero's perception that Tito has the face of a traitor is linked ironically with the fact of his possession of the ring. As Witemeyer notes, Piero's "intuition is prophetic: Tito will betray virtually every major character in the novel" (*Visual* 56).

The difference between Tito's distorted self-image and Piero's visionary perception of him is conveyed pictorially throughout the novel. After Tito sells his father's ring, he goes to Piero's residence to request a portrait of himself and Romola in a mythological scene. He asks for a "miniature device ... painted on a wooden case ... in the form of a triptych" with a scene of "the triumph of Bacchus and Ariadne." He explains that he wants the subject treated "in a new way," that is, with Bacchus seated in a ship with "the fair-haired Ariadne with him, made immortal with her golden crown—that is not in Ovid's story" (244). Thus Tito expresses his grandiose self-concept in the form of a description of a portrait of himself and Romola as god and princess in a Greek myth.

The scene on the ship that Tito wants depicted occurs in Ovid's poem, "Pentheus and Bacchus" (73–80), in which Bacchus, as the son of Zeus, has triumphed over the pirates who tried to kidnap him, and turned them into wild animals; he is seated in the ship amidst symbols of luxuriance. By asking for Ariadne to be placed with him in the painting, however, Tito includes elements of another mythological story of Bacchus, in which he rescues Ariadne, the princess of Crete, on the island of Naxos after she had been abandoned by Theseus, the Athenian prince whose life she had saved. By putting together the two stories, Tito thus rearranges the images of himself, his bride, and his missing stepfather in such a way that he presents himself in the painting as the rescuer of someone who has been abandoned. The portrait he requests, then, consists of an "all good" unrealistic self-image which denies the failure of his real self to rescue his stepfather, whose existence is not acknowledged. Instead, Tito is presented as the triumphant son of a Greek god.

Eliot's pervasive allusions to the mythological Bacchus, about whom she did considerable research (Bonaparte, *Triptych* 63–64), convey Tito's psychological situation. Two elements in the Bacchic tradition seem especially pertinent in this regard. The first is the account of Bacchus's origin. According to Edith Hamilton's summary of the stories of Bacchus (54–62), the only god whose parents were not both divine, he was the son of Zeus and the Theban princess Semele, who had died before he was born; Zeus had hidden the child in his side until he was ready for birth. Thus he had never known his mother. According to the story, Bacchus longed for her so much that he defied the power of death to rescue her from the underworld and took her to Olympus, where, as the mother of a god, she was deemed fit to live with the immortals. I would suggest that when Tito refers to making Ariadne "immortal with her golden crown," he is merging yet another image in the portrait of himself and Romola—the image of his missing mother, whom he had never known, and whom he, like Bacchus, had turned into a goddess. Tito's distorted self-concept thus includes his identification of himself with the triumphant son of Zeus, united with the princess Ariadne, who represents both wife and "immortal," or eternally longed-for, mother, each of whom he has rescued from abandonment. Viewed in this light, Eliot's nineteenth-century pictorial characterization of Tito is a striking illustration of Kernberg's twentieth-century idea that the narcissistic personality's self-concept is a fusion of "ideal self, ideal object, and actual self images as a defense against an intolerable reality in the interpersonal realm" (231).

The second point to be made is that the worship of Bacchus contained two paradoxical ideas: of "freedom and ecstatic joy" and of "savage brutality" (Hamilton 57); "As the god of wine he was both man's benefactor and man's destroyer" (60). The two sides of Tito's nature are thus expressed in the idea of a portrait of him as Bacchus—with his pleasure-loving magnanimity, along with his savage aggression hidden underneath the surface. In keeping with Kernberg's theory of pathological narcissism, Tito's aggression, projected onto others, takes the form of a paranoid fear. Piero, the keenly observant artist, has already noticed this fear in Tito. He has sketched an image of him that contrasts sharply with Tito's self-image as the carefree Bacchus. "I must take the fright out of it for Bacchus," he says. "Yours is a face which expresses fear well," Piero adds, as he shows him the sketch. When Tito looks at it, "He saw himself with his right hand uplifted, holding a wine-cup, in the attitude of triumphant joy, but with his face turned away from the cup with an expression of such intense fear in the dilated eyes and pallid lips, that he felt a cold stream through his veins, as if he were being thrown into sympathy with his imaged self" (247).

Despite this shock to his "usual easy self-command," Tito proceeds with his plan to have the portrait made. When he gives it to Romola on the day of their betrothal, he puts away the crucifix that Savonarola had given her at the time of her brother's death (216–17) and locks it in her cabinet, replacing it with the painting of Bacchus and Ariadne, to be used as a "shrine" instead (259–60). Bonaparte interprets in detail the meaning of Tito's action in her chapter, "Bacchus and Ariadne Betrothed" (86–109). She explains that "just as the hollow triptych is a visual translation of Bernardo del Nero's description of Tito, so the juxtaposition of the two images—of the crucifix locked inside the triptych—is a visual translation of one of the chief moral metaphors in the book" (94). In Kernberg's terms, Tito's inner emptiness is coupled with an incapacity to tolerate mournful feelings. Thus he attempts to "lock away all sadness" (263).

It is the artist Piero who also discerns the source of Tito's fear. In a crowded scene on the piazza, he sees Baldassarre, one of a group of prisoners, clutch Tito's arm (283). Piero, the only person in the crowd who could see Tito's face, takes note of his look of terror. His perception is later expressed by his addition of Baldassarre to his sketch of Tito in his studio. When Romola comes to see him about a portrait to be made of herself and her father, she notices the sketch and begins to wonder about the connection between Tito and Baldassarre, but she is afraid to ask Tito about it. At this point, as Sanders observes, "[Romola] acknowledges the gulf that now divides her from her husband and his secrets" (183).

Eliot's use of Bacchic imagery in her portrayal of both Tito and Baldassarre, whose amnesia and mania are elements of the Bacchic ritual (Bonaparte 157–58), conveys the idea that the two characters are inextricably bound together, although Tito attempts to escape his stepfather's hold on him. He tells Romola's father Bardo that he was raised in Italy by a stepfather who was an accomplished scholar and who was recently lost at sea (107). He remembers well how Baldassarre had "rescued a little boy from a life of beggary, filth, and cruel wrong, had reared him tenderly, and been to him a father." Tito now feels, however, that

"Baldassarre was exacting, and had got stranger as he got older: he was constantly scrutinising Tito's mind to see whether it answered to his own exaggerated expectations" (148–49). Baldassarre appears in the scene with the group of prisoners in the piazza, where Piero di Cosimo notices him clutch Tito's sleeve. Afterward, "Inside the Duomo," Baldassarre suffers a severe emotional reaction to the encounter with Tito: "Images from the past kept urging themselves upon him like delirious visions strangely blended with thirst and anguish. No distinct thought for the future could shape itself in the midst of that fiery passion: the nearest approach to such thought was the bitter sense of enfeebled powers, and a vague determination to universal distrust and suspicion" (290). It is in this frame of mind that Baldassarre suddenly hears Savonarola say in his sermon, "The day of vengeance is at hand" (291), and becomes swept up in the passion of the Frate's oratory. Responding to Savonarola's emphasis on punishment for wrongdoers, he identifies his personal anger with the preacher's religious and political message. He is moved "by the idea of perpetual vengeance" to a "fierce exultant delight" (295).

With his unrelenting desire for revenge and his incapacity to forgive, Baldassarre becomes the novel's incarnation of narcissistic rage. Chessick asserts that human aggression in its most dangerous form arises out of narcissistic rage (136); accompanied by feelings of humiliation, it may arise in an acute episode or with chronic unforgiving relentlessness (179). Eliot elucidates the complex causes, involving both present and past circumstances, that lie behind Baldassarre's rage in chapter 30, "The Avenger's Secret," which occurs after his escape from captivity. One is his reaction to the effects of old age. Baldassarre stops to look at his reflection in a pool and contemplates himself, with "the intense purpose in his eyes" (335). He had lost his previously acquired knowledge (apparently through a stroke), except for brief flashes when his memory seems to return. "What he dreaded of all things now was, that any one should think him a foolish, helpless old man. No one must know that half his memory was gone" (336). In the face of the humiliating loss of his intellectual powers, Baldassarre is like the typical narcissistic personality who cannot come to terms with aging (Chessick 8).

The losses of aging are felt the more keenly because they accompany the loss of Tito. Through Baldassarre's ruminations, however, we learn his real reason for originally rescuing Tito: "I was a loving fool—I worshipped a woman once, and believed she could care for me; and then

I took a helpless child and fostered him; and I watched him as he grew, to see if he would care for me only a little. . . . I have strained to crush out of this hard life one drop of unselfish love. . . . I thought, this boy will surely love me a little: because I give my life to him and strive that he shall know no sorrow" (338). Thus he is like the parents of Kernberg's narcissistic patients who seem to give their children everything, but whose interest in them actually extends only to the gratification of their own needs. When Baldassarre does not get the appreciation that he expects, his "primary need and hope" becomes "to see a slow revenge under the same sky and on the same earth where he himself had been forsaken and had fainted with despair" (339).

Finally, Baldassarre reveals what is perhaps the ultimate source of his rage in an action that repeats the pattern of Tito's sale of his ring: he decides to sell the one memory he has of his mother's love, a tiny sapphire amulet which he finds inside the "breve" she has left him. Then he uses the money to buy a dagger so that he can murder Tito (340–41). Bonaparte explains that "like all the gems in the book, the sapphire has a symbolic significance. Often called the 'holy sapphire,' it is held to have the power to confirm the soul in its good works and to prevent wicked thoughts. . . . when Baldassarre sells the sapphire to buy the dagger, he too, like Tito, exchanges the protection of Christ for a Bacchic weapon" (156). The fact that the amulet is a gift from his mother, however, is also significant, especially when juxtaposed with Tito's sale of his stepfather's gift. One psychoanalytic interpretation suggested by the narrative sequence in "The Avenger's Secret" is that Baldassarre has transferred the hostility originally felt toward the lost mother (perceived as abandoning), first onto the woman who rejects him, and then onto his adopted son Tito, whom he also sees as abandoning him. Thus, seen in the light of Kernberg's theory, Baldassarre perpetuates his cycle of projecting his own aggression onto the unintegrated image of the lost, or "bad" parent. Even when Tito, desperately afraid for his own life, finally asks his forgiveness, Baldassarre is too caught up in his desire for revenge to be able to relent: "I saved you—I nurtured you—I loved you. You forsook me—you robbed me—you denied me. What can you give me? You have made the world bitterness to me; but there is one draught of sweetness left—that you shall know agony" (379). Baldassarre confuses his nurturing of Tito with his own desperate need for a "draught of sweetness." When Tito abandons him, he is left alone with his own need;

his rage at his loss is all that is left to nurture him, and he nurtures it in return. "I am not alone in the world; I shall never be alone, for my revenge is with me," he says before he looks again at his image in the pool "till he identified it with that self from which his revenge seemed to be a thing apart" (338). When he finally kills Tito in chapter 67, "Waiting by the River," he is still so determined that "justice" be done to the abandoner, that he is not able to let go of the dead body. He wants "to die with his hold on this body, and follow the traitor to hell that he might clutch him there" (639). Thus Tito and Baldassarre remain bound together even after death.

Baldassarre is the only character in *Romola* who expresses rage openly; the other major characters, like so many of the characters in Eliot's fiction, express aggression indirectly. Just as Tito projects his rage onto Baldassarre and feels only an acute sense of dread within himself, so Savonarola projects visions of doom, although never for himself, but always for others—for Church and state officials who are perceived as corrupt. His "burning indignation at the sight of wrong" and his "fervent belief" that an "Unseen Justice" would "put an end to the wrong" (272) fuel his sermons. He possesses a charismatic power over the crowds who listen to his sermons and provide him with adulation.

Chessick's observation that the need to control others may only appear when a narcissistic personality is in a position of power (8) is illustrated in the portrayal of Savonarola. Eliot shows how Savonarola, who begins by being so concerned with the corruption of those in power, becomes corrupted by power himself. His need for control finally causes him to contradict the Christian message he had originally espoused. Noting the egoism that links Tito and Savonarola, Bonaparte observes that "as Tito is the chief agent in the disclosure of the Medicean plot against Savonarola's party, so Savonarola is the chief voice that sanctions the execution of the Mediceans—or the chief silence, rather. . . . It is that 'neutrality' so wholly inappropriate in a spokesman for Christ, and so ironically reminiscent of Tito's moral skepticism, that makes it difficult for us now to distinguish in Savonarola's actions between the Bacchic and the Christian visions" (219).

In Kernberg's terms, Savonarola displays the inflated self-concept, the need for adulation, and the sense of his right to control others that characterize a narcissistic personality. In a discussion of group psychology, Chessick describes the unshakable self-confidence and the voicing of opinions with absolute certainty that characterize an individual suitable for group idealization. Referring to Kohut's descriptions of the charismatic individual who identifies with his grandiose self and the messianic individual who identifies with his idealized parent imago, he notes that a group crisis (such as the one caused by the political changes in Florence in Savonarola's day) can create the temporary need for a charismatic leader to mobilize a group during the difficult time (148-49).

Savonarola's temporary influence over Romola reflects the rise and fall of his political power over Florence. It begins immediately after the death of her brother when she accepts Dino's crucifix from him (214). Later, when she attempts to run away from Florence for the first time, Savonarola asserts his authority over her, as he has over the people of Florence, by urging her to return to Tito on the grounds of her duty as a wife (435). When Romola comes to him to plead for the life of her godfather Bernardo, however, he takes a passive course, arguing that others are in charge of the decision to execute him. He rationalizes that his ends justify any sacrifice required of others: "The death of five men—were they less guilty than these—is a light matter weighed against the withstanding of the vicious tyrannies which stifle the life of Italy, and foster the corruption of the Church; a light matter weighed against the furthering of God's kingdom upon earth, the end for which I live and am willing myself to die" (577-78). Savonarola's unwillingness to help Bernardo jolts Romola to reality. As she comes out from under his spell, she sees "all the repulsive and inconsistent details in his teaching with a painful lucidity which exaggerated their proportions." She understands that his concern for Church reform had come to be equated with "the measures that would strengthen his own position in Florence" (587). Romola's reaction reflects Savonarola's waning influence on the people of Florence. Eliot interweaves the story of his downfall with Romola's offstage resolution of her conflicts and her assertion of her own power as the spiritual leader and head of a family at the end of the novel. Romola succeeds in throwing off the power of the controlling father figure in a way that Savonarola, who himself rebelled against his society's controlling authority figures, ultimately failed to do. In the "Epilogue," however, Romola is reconciled to Savonarola's role as temporary father in her life. She recognizes that he had helped her when she "was in great need" (676).

Tessa is linked to Tito throughout the novel, until after his death, when she becomes part of Romola's family. As a character, she seems to be so lacking in an inner sense of self that it is possible to discuss her only in relation to other characters. The emphasis in her opening scene, when Tito notices her asleep in the crowd in the piazza, is on her childlike qualities and her need for protection, which in this case is quickly provided by her mother, Monna Ghita (68–72). The fact that both Tito and Tessa are each discovered sleeping alone in their opening scenes links them together and foreshadows the dreamlike quality of their relationship. Tessa's next scene occurs just after Tito's ruminations about his stepfather, when Tito sees her in the crowd during a "festa" (153) and rescues her from harassment by a "conjuror" (155). In this scene, the dynamics of their relationship are developed. Tito, apparently in reaction to the uncomfortable reality of his failure to rescue his stepfather, responds to Tessa's own childlike need for rescue. It soon becomes clear from what she says to him that, although Tessa seems to lack an inner sense of self, her inner world is populated with unloving object representations, to use Kernberg's terms. Tessa explains that she has lost her mother in the crowd, that she fears both parents, and that she fears her stepfather will beat her (156). Moreover, she tells Tito that her mother scolds her, loves her younger sister better, and thinks Tessa is lazy. She concludes her litany of complaints by stressing that even those outside her family are cruel to her: "Nobody speaks kindly to me. . . . And the men in the Mercato laugh at me and make fun of me" (158). Tessa's situation, underlined by her loss of her mother in the crowd and her fear of her stepfather's punishments, mirrors Tito's. She feels alienated from her family, and by extension, from her society, which is perceived as treating her cruelly.

Tito sees Tessa from a distance from time to time in the city (144, 201, 255–57), but he seeks her out only in reaction to his great fear, first of his stepfather, and later, of Romola. His fear that Romola will learn his secret from Dino, the only person who knows his stepfather has been taken into slavery, provokes his "irresistible desire to go up to her and get her pretty trusting looks and prattle" (201). He reflects that "when all the rest had turned their backs upon him, it would be pleasant to have this little creature adoring him and nestling against him" (203). He yields to the temptation to subject her to a fake marriage ceremony by the same conjuror who had earlier harassed her. Like Arthur with Hetty, Tito acts out his rescue fantasy (as suggested by the Bacchus portrait) in the relationship with Tessa, who in turn acts out her fantasy of attachment to a figure who seems to provide her missing self-esteem. As the story progresses, although Tito finds Tessa's presence comforting, he realizes he does not love her (371). He visits her rarely, and spends as little money on her as possible, even after they have children. He is aware that he had first felt "a real hunger for Tessa's ignorant lovingness and belief in him . . . on the day when he had first seen Baldassarre, and had bought the armor [to protect himself from him]." He remembers how "he had felt an unconquerable shrinking from an immediate encounter with Romola," who, he knows, will disapprove, if she learns of his failure to rescue his stepfather (371). For Tito, the emotionally shallow relationship with Tessa, which he initiates simultaneously with his plans to marry Romola, provides protection against "the arousal of fears of attack by the object becoming important to [him]" (Kernberg 37). Tito's relationship with Tessa enacts the defensive situation of a narcissistic personality, who confuses the fear of the parent image with a potential new love object. His "ideal concept of himself" as rescuer of the childlike Tessa is "a fantasy construction which protects him from . . . dreaded relationships with all other people [because people are perceived as dangerous]." At the same time, as Kernberg notes, this ideal self-concept also contains "a hopeless yearning and love for an ideal mother who would come to his rescue" (257).

Just as Tito is portrayed as bound to his father even in death, so Romola is initially portrayed as bound to hers, although Bardo dies early in the story. She is introduced with him in chapter 5, "The Blind Scholar and his Daughter," in the setting of his library and possessions, which include "a headless statue, with an uplifted muscular arm wielding a bladeless sword; rounded, dimpled, infantine limbs severed from the trunk" (93). Sanders notes that "the broken statues arranged around the room match the two figures and provide a powerful image of the lifelessness of Bardo's philosophy" (191). It could also be said that the "pale and sombre" look of the surroundings, along with the broken statues and

Bardo's "moneyless" state (93, 92), convey the picture of a powerless old man, effectively castrated.

Romola has been motherless since infancy, although she has been cared for by her mother's cousin, Monna Brigida. Her subsequent close attachment to her father comes at the cost of his control over her life. As he ages, he makes increasing demands on her time and energy for the completion of his scholarly work. Their closeness is based on their shared sense of loss: "[Her] young but wintry life . . . had inherited nothing but memories—memories of a dead mother, of a lost brother, of a blind father's happier time." In chapter 18, "The Portrait," the artist Piero tells Tito he wants Romola to pose with Bardo for a painting of Oedipus and Antigone at Colonos. As in the case of Tito and Baldassarre, Piero perceives and depicts pictorially the psychological dynamic underlying the parent-child relationship. The message of the portrait is that Romola and Bardo are exiled together, the father's sense of castration shared by the daughter.

Bardo longs for his son Dino, who has left home to become a friar. Romola struggles to be a good enough scholar to replace her brother, yet she is made to feel inadequate simply because she is a female. Even her father's praise reveals his dissatisfaction with her, when he says that "even in learning thou art not, according to thy measure contemptible. Something perhaps were to be wished in thy capacity of attention and memory, not incompatible even with the feminine mind. But . . . thou hast a ready apprehension, and even a wide-glancing intelligence. And thou hast a man's nobility of soul: thou hast never fretted me with thy petty desires as thy mother did" (100).

Romola's own longing for her brother is described in the context of her first meeting with Tito, which suggests that Tito is a replacement for him: "There was only one masculine face, at once youthful and beautiful, the image of which remained deeply impressed on her mind: it was that of her brother, who long years ago had taken her on his knee, kissed her, and never come back again: a fair face, with sunny hair, like her own" (105). Bardo's longing for a son to help him with his work accounts for his susceptibility to Tito; Romola, sharing her father's longing for Dino, is equally susceptible. When she tells Bardo that she wants to marry Tito, she makes her motivation clear when she adds, "that we may both be your children and never part" (181). Tito's betrothal gift, the triptych of Bacchus and Ariadne, also suggests that he intends to be a replacement for Dino, whose crucifix he locks away, to help Romola forget her brother's ominous deathbed vision of her forthcoming marriage.

Just as Tito replaces Dino, so Savonarola replaces her father. Romola initially subjects herself to his authority, as she had done with her father. The story of Romola's growth to womanhood, then, is the story of her simultaneous separation of herself from her brother (represented by Tito) and her liberation of herself from her father's authority (represented by Savonarola). Yet, as I have suggested earlier, Eliot's portrayal of the change in Romola is not convincing.

Among recent critics, Graver, Ashton, and Bonaparte account for the improbable ending of Romola in terms of Eliot's less than successful attempt to combine historical realism with symbolic elements (139, 54, 240). Eliot herself seems to confirm this view in a letter she wrote in response to Sara Hennell's lavish praise of Romola, whom she had described as a "goddess . . . not a woman": "You are right in saying that Romola is ideal—I feel it acutely in the reproof my own soul is constantly getting from the image it has made. My own books scourge me. I value very much your assurance that you are 'satisfied.' The various *strands* of thought I had to work out forced me into a more ideal treatment of Romola than I had foreseen at the outset—though the 'Drifting away' and the Village with the Plague belonged to my earliest vision of the story and were by deliberate forecast adopted as romantic and symbolic elements" (*Letters* 4:104).

Contemporary critics have increasingly pointed to the author's own conflicts as the ultimate source of the novel's unconvincing resolution. Carole Robinson sees in the novel a Victorian existentialist outlook that its author could not acknowledge; in her view, Romola embodies a "despair beyond what her author intended for her" (30). Robinson sees a "repetitive plot pattern of commitment and disillusion, decision and indecision" that "may be attributed to the novelist's dissatisfaction with the solutions she proposes for the heroine" (31). Susan M. Greenstein's feminist essay also describes "hesitations, denials, and magically achieved resolutions of hidden conflicts," in this case, "about women and work" (489). Such criticisms, added to the observations mentioned earlier regarding the images of violence that subvert the author's message of visionary altruism, echo the critical assessments of the endings of *Adam Bede* and *The Mill on the Floss*.

The failed resolution of *Romola* is comparable to that of *Adam Bede* in that it is related to the author's excessive idealization of the heroine; the reader is expected in each case to idealize a character whose aggression is not acknowledged by the author. Contrary to the author's intention, both Dinah and Romola are actually portrayed as remaining passive in critical circumstances, while other characters act out the hostile feelings they deny. When Baldassarre tells Romola about Tito's infidelity, he tries to take advantage of her anger by persuading her to help him murder Tito. Although she does not agree to help him, she does not try to dissuade him from committing the murder. Instead, she "chose not to answer," reasoning that she "would win time for his excitement to allay itself" (533). Soon after, instead of warning Tito of Baldassarre's intention, she refrains from doing so, rationalizing first that Tito would not listen to her anyway, and second, that there was more danger of Tito hurting Baldassarre than of Baldassarre finding the strength to murder him (540). In the end, in neither novel is the reader persuaded by the author's attempt to convince her audience of the internal change in the protagonist. This is so in part because the protagonist's new life is made possible only by the misfortune of the opposing character: in Adam's and Dinah's case, Hetty's banishment, and in Romola's, Tito's death.

The ending of *Romola* can also be compared to that of *The Mill on the Floss*. After Savonarola's refusal to help save Bernardo, Romola becomes disillusioned and flees Florence in despair. Wishing for death, she recalls Boccaccio's story of "that fair Gostanzo," who committed suicide by getting into a boat and pushing off to sea (588). Romola finds a boat for herself and, lying down inside it, lets it drift down the river toward the sea. The river scene in Romola contains elements of the two river scenes in *The Mill on the Floss:* the first, when Maggie, unaware of the hostility that motivates her, passively allows herself to be abducted by Stephen; the second, when Maggie, unable to resolve her conflicts, finally drowns in the flood. By letting herself drift down the river in the boat, Romola, like Maggie, temporarily "free[s] herself from the burden of choice" (590). While she is away, however, Savonarola is arrested and Tito is murdered. She has not acted on her anger at Tito; nor has she been forced to resolve her conflict about whether or not she is obligated to remain married given the circumstances of Tito's ongoing betrayals. In both novels, passivity remains the solution for hostility and/or inner conflict.

Unlike Kohut, Kernberg stresses that it is essential for narcissistic personalities to confront their rage, which Kernberg regards as central to the psychopathology (228). This is because narcissistic personalities have a tendency to project their own aggression onto others; before cure is possible, they must come to see that the aggression is coming from within themselves. Interestingly, it is Eliot's failure to confront the aggression in her character Romola that results in the novel's greatest flaw, and that causes the reader's disbelief in her growth. It is Romola's "all good," split-off quality, in contrast to Tito's villainy, Baldassarre's rage, Savonarola's corruption, and Tessa's weakness, that the reader cannot accept, because Eliot has not integrated the "all bad" side of human nature into her personality. Romola, the character who longs for her "dead mother, [her] lost brother, and [her] blind father's happier time," herself becomes the idealized, longed-for mother of narcissistic pathology.

Emery writes that when Romola flees Florence in the boat, she runs away "from an intolerable inner tension which now can be relieved only by a further regression" to a "passive oral-receptive mode" in which "she is longing for parents, and dreams of seeking the beloved dead in the tomb" (97–98). I would argue in addition that Eliot's own reaction to her father's death is reenacted in her heroine's situation in *Romola*, a novel which was researched and written during the time (1861–63) that marked the tenth anniversary of the period following her move to London from the Midlands. The period 1851–53 was a time when she had suffered frequent depressions and, judging from her shifting attachments to men, a time spent searching for a replacement for her father. Eliot's words—"What shall I be without my Father? It will seem as if a part of my moral nature were gone. I had a horrid vision of myself last night becoming earthly sensual and devilish for want of that purifying restraining influence" (*Letters* 1:284)—foreshadow her involvement with Chapman in 1851. The friendship with Herbert Spencer developed in 1851–52; the affair with Lewes the summer of 1853 (Taylor 125).

Eliot's reaction to her father's death is embedded not only in her heroine's idealization of her father figure Savonarola, but in her inevitable disillusionment with him. When Romola loses faith in him, the narrative asserts that her "best support" had "slipped away from her. The vision of any great purpose . . . was utterly eclipsed for her now by the sense of a confusion in human things which made all effort a mere dragging at tangled threads" (586). Wishing for death, she gets into the boat and flees Florence by passively floating down the river. The scene is also associated with Romola's decision to break her marriage vows: "The bonds of all strong affection were snapped. In her marriage, the highest bond of all, she had ceased to see the mystic union which is its own guarantee of indissolubleness, had ceased even to see the obligation of a voluntary pledge: had she not proved that the things to which she had pledged herself were impossible?" (586). Bonaparte mentions that "in her readings Eliot was often concerned with discussions of the indissolubility of marriage" (240). It seems likely in light of Eliot's social ostracization that she still felt some lingering discomfort over her role in the Leweses' permanent separation, which had been formally arranged after Eliot and Lewes had eloped to the continent and returned to England (Haight, *Biography* 163, 179); any such feelings would no doubt be intensified by Lewes's recent failure to find a way to obtain a divorce abroad. Such discomfort is reflected in Romola's deliberations over the sacredness of her marriage vows: "She was thrown back again on the conflict between the demands of an outward law, which she recognised as widely-ramifying obligation, and the demands of inner moral facts which were becoming more and more peremptory" (552). Just as Maggie's rationalizations about Stephen in *The Mill on the Floss* seem to reflect Eliot's self-justification for her elopement with Lewes, so Romola's reasoning in the later novel seems to serve as the novelist's rationalization for her part in Lewes's decision to separate from his wife and live permanently with Eliot without obtaining a legal divorce. Moreover, the idealized Romola quite possibly reflects Eliot's self-idealization over her support and stepmothering of the Leweses' children.

Eliot frequently mentions her depressions and illnesses in her letters before and during the writing of *Romola*. She also reports fluctuations in her frame of mind, for example, "despondency and distrust of myself . . . followed by hours of strength when life seems glorious" (*Letters* 3:460)—a mental state that repeats the pattern of her experience during the time when her father was dying. Bowlby emphasizes in his volume on *Loss* the high degree of overlap between depressive disorders of all kinds and states of chronic mourning (3:255). He explains that disordered mourning is more likely to follow the death of someone with whom there has been, until the loss, a close relationship (175), as was the case with Eliot and her father. He also explains that a protracted period of dying maximizes in the survivor any preexisting ambivalence, thus resulting in pronounced feelings of guilt and inadequacy; if a survivor has done the nursing, she may feel left without a role or function after the loss (182). Such had also been the case with Eliot. Moreover, as I suggested in my chapter on *Silas Marner*, Eliot associated the loss of her father with her earlier loss of her mother. According to Ina Taylor's biography, the death of Eliot's mother had symbolized for her "the end of childhood and the orderly world of school"; she had had to give up any hope of furthering her formal education (23). Her brother Isaac, by contrast (like Romola's brother Dino), was free to pursue his vocation. Bowlby reports that many patients who had difficulties with mourning had experienced additional distress following the death, for example, in the form of expectations that the bereaved person fill the deceased parent's role (3:306); he also reports poor outcome when the surviving parent had made strong demands on the children for emotional support or made the child the caregiver (314). Both circumstances occurred in Eliot's life following her mother's death and her sister's marriage: she became her father's housekeeper; and later, as he aged, became ill, and approached death, she served as his sole caretaker.

The characterizations in *Romola* taken together form a psychological unity exhibiting the traits that Kernberg describes as characterizing pathological narcissism. As such, they reflect the defensive processes of splitting and projection against the rage that followed from what I believe to be the author's renewed sense of loss following her family's estrangement, her sister Chrissey's death, and her new family's move into London. Bowlby's conclusion that the anniversary of a loss can activate feelings about an earlier one (152–60) provides support for my view that Eliot's current losses revived feelings associated with the difficult time in her life surrounding her move to London ten years before. Her anxiety over the research and writing of a new kind of novel may also have been associated with her feelings at that earlier time, when she was beginning her new work for Chapman at the *Westminster Review*.

The excessive idealization of Romola serves, as it does in the work of the literary artists in David Aberbach's study, *Surviving Trauma*, "to counterbalance extremes of unconscious hatred and guilt also provoked by . . . loss. [Such extreme idealization] is found with unusual frequency and intensity among writers who . . . lost their mothers early on" (146).

Aberbach also writes that "insofar as creativity derives from loss, the quality of the art reflects the artist's success in mastering it, and in this way he may achieve a measure of symbolic repair" (155). Eliot's feeling that she had grown into a new stage as a result of writing *Romola* is in keeping with the psychoanalytic view of "development as a series of mourning experiences" (Rothstein 226). The "weight" and "depth," as well as the "complex vision" and "intricate symbolic pattern" of this novel are signs of growth in the artist that may also point to a "measure of symbolic repair." Yet Eliot's artistic failure to resolve her heroine's dilemma, reflecting as it does both the intensity and the denial of her own aggression, almost certainly indicates her still incomplete success in mastering her own sense of loss.

FIVE

Fear of the Mob in *Felix Holt*

After *Romola* was published in July 1863, Eliot and Lewes became busy with arrangements for another household move; their lease on their house in Blandford Square was to expire in November. In August they bought their last home, the Priory, at 21 North Bank in London—a large, secluded, comfortable house, where they moved in November. Plans for helping Lewes's younger sons get established in their work had added to their sense of turmoil during the summer. Thornie, in particular, needed guidance. He had failed to pass the final examination for civil service in India, and although his father wanted him to try again, he had "set his mind on going out to Poland to fight the Russians" (GHL Journal, qtd. in Haight, *Biography* 364). Finally, their friend Barbara Bodichon persuaded Thornie to settle in Natal, where she had good friends to whom she could recommend him. He sailed for Durban in October "in excellent spirits" (372). Meanwhile, Bertie had been sent in July to a farm in Lanarkshire, to prepare for a career in agriculture. Lewes summed up the year of 1863 in his journal by writing that "in a domestic sense it has been a chequered year. Much trouble about the two boys; much bother about the new house; continued happiness with the best of women" (370–73).

In May 1864, during a trip to Venice, Eliot conceived the idea for a play, *The Spanish Gypsy*. Her work on it, however, became a struggle with her own depressions and her worries over Lewes's health, to which were added family interruptions, including the festivities surrounding their oldest son Charles's new engagement. She managed to complete three acts, but by February became so discouraged that Lewes persuaded her to put the drama aside. When she tried to begin working on it again after Charles's wedding on March 20, an idea for an "English story" kept intruding on her, as *Silas Marner* had done when she was trying to work on *Romola* (381). By March 29, 1865, she had begun a new novel; her "English story" became her "political novel," *Felix Holt, The Radical*, which she completed by the end of the following May; it was published by Blackwood on June 15, 1866.

In deciding to write *Felix Holt*, Eliot had returned from the medieval Italy of *Romola* to the Midlands of her childhood. The story is based on an election riot that she had witnessed in Nuneaton at age thirteen, in 1832, the year of the passage of the First Reform Bill. To prepare for writing her political novel, she read *The Times* and the *Annual Register* for 1832–33; she also read a number of substantial works on history, politics, and economics. For legal details, she consulted Frederic Harrison, a prominent lawyer who provided her with the information on the law of entail and the statutes of limitations that she needed in order to portray her characters' lawsuit. As in her early fiction, however, "the vivid touches that illuminate the novel were drawn from her childhood memories," in this case, of "Nuneaton at the time of the Reform Bill, when she was a schoolgirl at Mrs. Wallington's" (381–84).

Besides being a political novel, *Felix Holt* seems to be Eliot's conscious attempt at her own version of Dickens's theme in *Bleak House*, much in the way that her historical novel, *Romola*, was an attempt at her own version of Bulwer Lytton's theme in *Rienzi*. A few critics have observed that both Dickens's and Eliot's novels concern an idealized heroine named Esther, who at the conclusion of an extended law case unexpectedly gains the right to an inheritance. The similarities between Lady Dedlock in *Bleak House* and Mrs. Transome in *Felix Holt*, the middle-aged "fallen woman" who must suffer the consequences of her youthful misdeeds, have also been noted (M. H. Dodds, Jerome Meckier, and Robert L. Caserio). I would add that in both novels, society itself can be seen as the protagonist (Carroll, "Protagonist" 237; Donovan 206–37); society is perceived as organic (in the sense of consisting of interconnecting parts that contribute to the good of the whole); and society is in need of reform. As Robert Donovan suggests, "The main theme of *Bleak House* is responsibility" (209). A reflection of the increasing focus on social justice that developed throughout Dickens's fiction-writing career, the 1853 novel is critical of a corrupt and smug mid-Victorian society, in which the privileged fail to take responsibility for the disadvantaged, despite the interconnecting ties that bind them. Sharing Dickens's vision of an organic society, Eliot applies the theme of responsibility in *Felix Holt* to the working man, whom she urges to educate himself before demanding the vote.

Reviews of *Felix Holt*, including those in the *Saturday Review*, the *Spectator*, and *The Times* (Carroll, *Heritage* 255, 258, 263), were positive, although the criticisms of plot development and characterization foreshadow twentieth-century views. While the Victorian "inheritance plot" and the slow unfolding of the "mystery" of Mrs. Transome's past can be said to make *Felix Holt* Eliot's most suspenseful novel (Hardy, *Novels* 5), most modern critics stress the novel's formal flaws. F. R. Leavis criticizes the overuse of legal details (50), W. J. Harvey the "clumsy sequence of coincidences" (*Art* 132), and Barbara Hardy the insufficient character development, which she sees as resulting from the limitation of the short period of time covered in the novel (*Novels* 93). The "weaknesses of the plot" (Coveney 15), including the novel's disunity, are also criticized by Jerome Thale and Fred C. Thomson, who see an "incomplete fusion" of the personal and political sides of the narrative (Thale, *Novels* 89).

Critics have increasingly noted in *Felix Holt* what Basil Willey observed early to be a conflict, as evident in Eliot's writing, between her conservative and liberal (or reforming) tendencies (*Studies* 237). William Myers comments that Eliot reaches a point in the narrative of *Felix Holt*, as she does in *The Mill on the Floss* and *Romola*, at which "the impulse and the need for change" become "incompatible with the impulse and the need for continuity" (85). My purpose in this chapter is to attempt to explain this conflict between the author's conservative and reforming tendencies, as seen in *Felix Holt*; in so doing, I want to show the connection between the author's apparently contradictory political views and her personal conflicts. Arnold Kettle has suggested that Eliot's withdrawal from "the realities of the social situation which [*Felix Holt*] is about" (109) derives from her Victorian fear of the mob (113). I will argue that Eliot's fear, like her character Tito's fear in *Romola*, is a projection of her own aggression; thus her fear of the working man's potential for violence reflects her fear of the possibility of acting on the impulses coming from within herself.

Felix Holt presents a comprehensive view of English society at "a critical moment of transition from aristocratic and agrarian values to the new leadership of the middle class" (Vance 103). In so doing, the novel juxtaposes two sets of characters—those representing the declining old order, who live at the country estate of Transome Court, and those representing the rising working class (including Felix Holt), who live in the village of Treby Magna. The central character at Transome Court is the middle-aged Mrs. Transome, whose incapacity to transcend her past is contrasted with the young villager Esther Lyon's capacity for growth. Esther's development, like Romola's, is portrayed in the context of the political events of her time in history. As David Carroll observes of *Felix Holt*, an analogy is made between the reform of the individual and of society that is sustained throughout the novel ("Protagonist" 238).

When the story opens, Mrs. Transome is waiting for the arrival of her son Harold, whom she has not seen in fifteen years. Her eagerness to see him is mixed with her sense of dread lest he discover the truth about his origin: he is the illegitimate son of the family lawyer, Jermyn, with whom Mrs. Transome had committed adultery years before. Her husband, a frail and "frightened" older man, is still alive, doddering about the house (88). Harold is his mother's only living son. The existence of Durfey, Harold's imbecilic older brother (and heir of the estate), had originally forced Harold to leave home to earn his own living in Smyrna. Now that Durfey is dead, Harold has returned to inherit Transome Court, and to run for Parliament on the radical ticket—a decision which naturally shocks his mother (92).

Felix Holt, Eliot's idealized working man, is presented in contrast to Harold Transome. He is also his mother's only living son; both his father, a "quack doctor" (130) who had begun his working life as a weaver, and his two siblings are deceased. Although his mother wants him to study to be a doctor, he has no interest in rising above the working class; it would have been better, he believes, if his father had remained a weaver (144); he works diligently as a journeyman to a watchmaker. Felix meets Esther when he goes to see her father, Rufus Lyon, the dissenting clergyman, at their home. He immediately forms a negative opinion of Esther; everything about her appearance, manner, and tastes "suggested a fine lady to him, and determined him to notice her as little as possible" (149). Esther's ladylike qualities suggest the truth about her background. She does not yet know that she is an adopted child; Rufus has only told her that her mother was a Frenchwoman, who died when she was about five years old (161). Like Mrs. Transome, Rufus is burdened by the secret of his child's parentage.

Eliot's characterization of her idealized young working man stresses Felix's "danger of getting into a rage" (226); yet at the same time, it also emphasizes his ability to keep his rage under control. His "habitual preoccupation with large thoughts and with purposes independent of everyday casualties" (390) and his work as a watchmaker, which required "the utmost exertion of patience," help to keep him on an even keel. He knows "that he [is] dangerous; and he avoid[s] the conditions that might cause him exasperation" (391). The coming election is presented as a potentially explosive situation for Felix, and he searches for strategies to keep himself from losing his temper. After he becomes angry at one political speech, he avoids the speaker in order to keep from getting into a fight (226, 238). On nomination day he reacts to the dishonest tactics of Harold Transome's agents by "walk[ing] about," and "telling himself that this angry haste of his about evils that could only be remedied slowly, could be nothing else than obstructive, and might some day . . . be obstructive of his own work" (393). Afterward, he decides upon words as his best weapon, because "blows are sarcasms turned stupid: wit is a form of force that leaves the limbs at rest" (394).

Felix finds his opportunity to speak—to a group which has gathered "at the ultra-Liberal quarter of the High Street" following a speech endorsing Harold Transome. The speaker has summed up his arguments for supporting Transome by declaring that "if we working men are ever to get a man's share, we must have universal suffrage, and annual parliaments, and the vote by ballot, and electoral districts" (397). Felix's speech, by contrast, is hardly radical. He actually argues against suffrage for the working man, who, he suggests, is ill-prepared to vote. Arguing for slow change, he says that "I hope we, or the children that come after us, will get plenty of political power some time . . . but . . . votes would never give you political power worth having while things are as they are now" (399). When Felix is asked by "a man in dirty fustian" how "to get the power without votes," he replies that "the greatest power under heaven . . . is public opinion—the ruling belief in society about what is right and what is wrong, what is honourable and what is shameful" (400–1).

Election Day puts Felix's capacity to control his rage to the test. The 1832 election riot in Nuneaton, the event on which the riot in the novel is based, began, according to a local newspaper account at the time, after the supporters of the Radical candidate had taken over the poll and refused to allow others to vote. In response, the town magistrates called in a military force; further reinforcement proved necessary, and the Riot Act was read to the crowd. By the next day, the newspaper reports, "The mob presented an appalling appearance, and but for the forbearance of the soldiery, numerous lives would have fallen a sacrifice. Several of the officers of the Scots Greys were materially hurt in their attempt to quell the riotous proceedings of the mob. . . . Two or three unlucky individuals, drawn from the files of the military on their approach to the poll, were cruelly beaten and stripped literally naked. We regret to add that one life has been sacrificed during the contest and that several misguided individuals have been seriously injured" (qtd. in Cross 14–15).

Gordon Haight's account of the day gives a different perspective on the events, although he does not refer to the discrepancy himself: "The sentiment of the majority of the townspeople was strongly Radical. . . . In a fair election [they] would have won easily. But the Tories, seeing the tide going against them, suspended the poll, and called in a detachment of Scots Greys. . . ; the Riot Act was read, and when the mob did not disperse, horse soldiers with drawn swords rode through the town, charging the people, cutting and trampling them down. One man died of his injuries" (382).

Eliot's portrayal of Election Day in *Felix Holt* shares the conservative perspective of the local newspaper account. Her opening description of the day stresses the sense of impending crisis among the townspeople. One of the town magistrates prepares himself for the occasion by "inwardly rehears[ing] a brief address to a riotous crowd in case it should be wanted" (407). As the day goes on, voters are harassed, and "by stages . . . the fun grew faster, and was in danger of getting rather serious" (413). The account of Felix's behavior on that day emphasizes his self-control; the author carefully distinguishes his motives and actions from the mob's. Before the riot begins, Felix is seen seated at his work, still hoping that violence might be averted, despite the tumultuous noise of the crowd from the street. After checking the safety of the neighborhood and reassuring his mother, he goes out to look after Esther, with whom he shares his fears that the situation might worsen again (415–17).

By the time Felix returns to the heart of town, the mob has added outsiders to its number, and "the majority of the crowd were excited with drink." The poll has been adjourned and military aid has been summoned. The rector reads the Riot Act, a 1715 law which required dispersement of twelve or more persons "tumultuously assembled together to the destruction of the public peace" (669n.). The high constable then reads the Riot Act again in another location, but the crowd, rather than dispersing as ordered, begins to throw raw vegetables at the unpopular speaker; then there is a "rush toward the hardware shop for better weapons." The constables arm themselves, and, as the author puts it, "all the respectable inhabitants who had any courage prepared themselves to struggle for order" (421–24).

The violence begins with the smashing of a window at the inn. Eliot presents Felix as joining the crowd only in order to save the life of Mr. Spratt, "the hated manager of Sproxton Colliery" (391) who has found refuge in the building; Felix pretends to assume the role of mob leader. When the crowd backs off Spratt momentarily and Felix moves forward, a constable, Mr. Tucker, thinking the worst, rushes up in an attempt to keep Felix from killing him. Felix, however, "fell upon [Tucker], and tried to master his weapon." The constable falls, Felix takes his weapon, and the crowd, thinking he is on their side, cheers. When Tucker does not rise immediately, Felix does not check to see that he is all right because, as the author puts it, he "did not imagine that he was much hurt." Instead, Felix tells the crowd not to touch the constable and then leaves with them. The author then explains that "Felix was perfectly conscious that he was in the midst of a tangled business"; but he wants to prevent "the mass of wild chaotic desires and impulses around him" from causing any more destruction. Felix is not worried about how anyone else might interpret his actions: "He believed he had the power, and he was resolved to try, to carry the dangerous mass out of mischief till the military came to awe them" (425–27).

Now, with the constable's sabre in hand, he continues to play the role of the mob's leader. To save Spratt's life, he has him tied up and leaves him on a stone platform. He loses control of his leadership of the mob, however, when a group of "sharp-visaged men who loved the irrationality of riots for something else than its own sake, and who at present were not so much the richer as they desired to be" begins to lead the crowd to Treby Manor. Again, the narrative explains why Felix does not liberate himself from the mob once he has lost control of it: he reasons that others will carry information about the course of the mob to the military, and he wants to help the family at the Manor. The military arrives shortly after the mob gets to the Manor. Felix is shot, and arrested on three counts: "for having assaulted a constable, for having committed manslaughter (Tucker was dead from spinal concussion), and for having led a riotous onslaught on a dwelling-house" (428–32).

Felix's self-defense at his trial is based on his explanation of his conscious motivation during the riot (564), just as Esther's defense of him is based on his conscious intentions as reflected in the conversation with her just before he joined in the riot. She tells the court that "his mind was full of great resolutions that came from his kind feeling towards others. It was the last thing he would have done to join in riot or to hurt any man, if he could have helped. His nature is very noble; he is tender-hearted; he could never have had any intention that was not brave and good" (572). Although he is convicted of manslaughter and sentenced to four years' imprisonment (574), the local magistrates work successfully after the trial to have him pardoned (575, 589, 600).

In the narrative of the election riot, the author denies her character Felix's indirect expression of aggression (his rationalized participation in the violence, and his failure to check on the constable) much as she has earlier denied the aggressive behavior of Adam, Dinah, Maggie, and Romola. Presenting Felix's intentions as entirely noble, the author rationalizes what is actually shown to be his participation in the killing of the constable. Critics like Ruth B. Yeazell and William Myers have also seen Eliot as retreating from the violence of Felix Holt's aggression in the riot scene (137–44, 149–75). Emery, calling the scene a "destructive fantasy," observes that even though Eliot attempts to "separate the rage in the crowd from Felix," the "phallic weapons and the death of an authority-figure are Oedipal elements" (130). Contrary to her intentions, Eliot has portrayed Felix, the angry "quack doctor's son" (130), as acting out his aggression toward the constable, the authoritarian father figure, rather than as exercising the self-control that she is attempting to advocate to the working man.

After the portrayal of the election riot, the author retreats not only from the subject of her protagonist's aggression (which is apparently meant to be resolved by the demonstration of his self-restraint), but also from her political subject. Linda Bamber notes the "constant sense of retreat on the part of the author" (422) which finally results in her abandonment of the effort to write a political novel (425). Yeazell asserts that the idea of violent change is contained by the Victorian love story (of Felix and Esther), as is the case in other Victorian "political novels" (144). Eliot's intention to convey her vision of society as a necessarily "slow-growing system of things" (qtd. in Coveney 609 [Appendix A]) is lost as she focuses on her individual character's growth. The author's ideas about the gradual democratization of society are left behind, distilled in the form of Felix Holt's speech.

Esther is "not much liked by her father's church and congregation," because of her "airs and graces," and because of her questionable contacts with French culture at the school she attended on the Continent. Indeed, Esther is not contented with her present life at her father's house. Although she is able to live with a degree of independence by earning money from her teaching of pupils from town, she has not forgotten that the "best-born and handsomest girls at school had always said that she might be taken for a born lady." She has expensive tastes, on which she spends all her earnings (157–60). Felix, who has become friends with Rufus, makes it clear on one of his early visits to their house that he wants Esther to change. "Of course I am a brute to say so. I ought to say you are perfect. Another man would, perhaps. But I say, I want you to change." He criticizes her failure to join her father's church; he accuses her of not seriously considering "whether life is not as solemn a thing as your father takes it to be"; he says she is discontented only "because you can't get just the small things that suit your pleasure" (211). Afterward, Esther feels for the first time "seriously shaken in her self-contentment. She knew there was a mind to which she appeared trivial, narrow, selfish. Every word Felix had said to her seemed to have burnt itself into her memory" (214). Not long after, she visits Felix to ask to have a watch repaired, but the real reason for her visit is that she wants to let him know she does not hold a grudge against him. At this time, the two get a better impression of each other. Esther begins to sense that "if Felix Holt were to love her, her life would be exalted into something quite new," and Felix feels that "there was a new tie of friendship between them" (327).

Esther experiences the next step in her growth when Rufus finally gains the courage to tell her that he is not her biological father. He has failed to give her any information about her deceased mother, because of "deep sorrows of his life as a Christian minister that were hardly to be told to a girl" (162). He had suffered a crisis at age thirty-six, "a moment in which religious doubt and newly-awakened passion had rushed together in a common flood, and had paralysed his ministerial gifts" (163). One evening on his way home from church he discovered "a young woman with a baby on her lap," in need of help, and brought them both to his house. During the night he experienced "wild visions of an impossible future" which he felt were "irreconcilable with what he was, and must be, as a Christian minister" (165). The next morning he learned the woman's history. A daughter of a high-ranking French military officer, Annette had come from France to England in an attempt to find her husband, a prisoner of war; upon arrival at their meeting place, she had received word that he was dead. Rufus decided to let the apparently helpless woman stay at his house—a decision which was complicated by the power of his unspoken passion for her, and which met with the disapproval of his congregation and thus precipitated his decision to resign his post. Eventually, after an illness during which Annette nursed him back to health, she agreed to marry him, although she had initially refused his proposal. She soon subsided into apathy and died, leaving Rufus with her child, Esther, "as the one visible sign of that four years' break in his life." A year later "he entered the ministry again, and lived with the utmost sparingness that Esther might be so educated as to be able to get her own bread in case of his death" (174).

Although Rufus regards his confession of the long-kept secret as "a revelation . . . of his own miserable weakness and error," Esther reacts positively to her new knowledge. Her "mind seemed suddenly enlarged by a vision of passion and struggle . . . in the lot of beings who had hitherto been a dull enigma to her. And in the act of unfolding to her that he . . . had only striven to cherish her as a father, had only longed to be loved as a father, the odd, wayworn, unworldly man became the object of a new sympathy in which Esther felt herself exalted" (354).

That afternoon, Felix pays a call, and, sensing in Esther the agitation that had accompanied her suddenly changed view of her father, invites her to go for a walk. As they talk, Felix shares with her his determination not to repeat the pattern of his father's fraudulent practice. He had told Rufus earlier of his conversion "by [the] six weeks' debauchery" that had convinced him of the futility of living a life of "easy pleasure" (142–43). Now he tells Esther that instead of seeking "money and position," he aspires to be "a demagogue of a new sort; an honest one, if possible, who will tell the people they are blind and foolish, and neither flatter them nor fatten on them." He also wants to "try to make life less bitter for a few within my reach." Although the scene of their conversation suggests that they are falling in love, "Nothing had been said which was necessarily personal" (362–67). Afterward, Esther feels that "the first religious experience of her life—the first self-questioning, the first voluntary subjection, the first longing to acquire the strength of greater motives and obey the more strenuous rule—had come to her through Felix Holt" (369).

Their next scene occurs as the riot is beginning, when Felix comes by to check on her safety. After their conversation, Felix "could not help seeing that he was very important to her"; yet at the same time, "He felt that they must not marry—that they would ruin each other's lives" (419). After the riot, and before the court scene, Esther feels shut off from Felix when he is in jail (468). During this time away from Felix, she receives the shocking news that, as the result of the completion of an extended lawsuit, her ancestors' claim to the Transome estates is deemed valid, and, as the only living descendant, she is entitled to possession of the property (470).

At first the news of the inheritance seems to be a fulfillment of her wish for an "elevation in rank and fortune" (473). The Transomes, wanting to assure Esther that they "will not contend for what is not our own," soon come to see her to invite her to live at Transome Court while the details of her inheritance are being worked out (480). As she leaves her home to go with them in their carriage, she looks forward to her new life (484). At Transome Court, however, she senses that something is wrong in the family, and she slowly becomes disillusioned, even though Mrs. Transome is kind to her and Harold courts her. On her first visit to her father's house, she is dismayed to learn that Felix assumes she will marry Harold; on her second visit, she asks to go with Rufus to visit Felix; at this point, she feels "divided and oppressed" by the need to make a decision (550)—but the jail visit ends with their declaration of love, in the form of a kiss and an embrace.

After the courtroom scene, Esther is back at Transome Court. She has become increasingly aware of the "joyless, embittered age" that has replaced the "youthful brilliancy" of Mrs. Transome's past, as evident in her portrait as a young woman (585). Harold, meanwhile, has learned the truth about his parentage, and, seeing his life in a new light, offers to "proceed at once to the necessary legal measures for putting [Esther] in possession of [her] own" (588). By this time, however, Esther had undergone "something little short of an inward revolution." At Transome Court, she had come to see herself "in a silken bondage that arrested all motive, and was nothing better than a well-cushioned despair" (592). Thus finally able to make her decision to resign "all claim to the Transome estates," she returns to her father's house (599).

Esther's "inward revolution" is more convincing than Romola's because her growth is presented as a "slow growing system of things," made visible to the reader. Esther's growth begins with Felix's insistence on her change; but first it is necessary for her to get a clear picture of her parents, including her adoptive father, Rufus. Esther had had no clear memory of her mother; she had only "a broken vision of the time before she was five years old" (161). After Rufus tells her the details of her past, she is then able, on the basis of her new knowledge, to begin to appreciate her life with Rufus, as she lets go of her fantasies of "rank and fortune." In Kernberg's terms, she can finally distinguish her realistic self and parent images from her idealized ones. At Transome Court, she confronts "the dimly-suggested tragedy of [Mrs. Transome's] life, the dreary waste of years" and she is "afflicted . . . even to horror." The reality of Mrs. Transome's life is the "last vision to urge her towards the life where the draughts of joy sprang from the unchanging fountains of reverence and devout love" (597); thus she completes the process of her "conversion." Esther is able to use the vision of the "bad" (lost) mother, in the present form of Mrs. Transome, as part of the process of leaving her deceased parents behind (or, of renouncing her inheritance) and making her decision to marry Felix. Esther's decision to leave behind the lost mother is analogous to Eppie's movement away from the deceased mother in *Silas Marner*. The new novel, *Felix Holt*, thus repeats the pattern of the earlier one.

Eliot's own "Address to Working Men," which she was asked to write in the persona of Felix Holt for Blackwood's *Magazine* in January 1868, reinforces the message of her character's speech in the novel. Written after the passage of the Second Reform Bill, the speech emphasizes the responsibilities of working men who are now able to vote, and argues for the preservation of order during a process of inevitably slow change. On the basis of its vision of the interdependence of groups of individuals in society, the address also argues not that class distinctions be abolished, but that each class "perform its particular work under the strong pressure of responsibility to the nation at large" (617). Recalling the 1832 election riot, "which showed . . . what public disorder must always be; and . . . [which] was brought about chiefly by the agency of dishonest men who professed to be on the people's side," the voice of Felix warns against rousing again "the savage beast in the breasts of our generation" (618–19). Finally, the address exhorts parents to educate their children, and voters to "get the chief power into the hands of the wisest" (*FH* 609–27 [Appendix A]).

In 1848, Mary Ann Evans had expressed in a letter to John Sibree, Jr., a young radical's "happiness" over the French Revolution. At the same time, however, she wrote that "our working classes are eminently inferior to the mass of the French people. . . . Here there is so much larger a proportion of selfish radicalism and unsatisfied, brute sensuality (in the agricultural and mining districts especially) than of perception or desire of justice, that a revolutionary movement would be simply destructive—not constructive. Besides, it would be put down. Our military . . . are as mere a brute force as a battering ram and the aristocracy have got firm hold of them. Our little humbug of a queen is more endurable than the rest of her race because she calls forth a chivalrous feeling, and there is nothing in our constitution to obstruct the slow progress of *political* reform. This is all we are fit for at present" (*Letters* 1:254). By the mid-1860s, however, judging from the skepticism of political reform expressed both in *Felix Holt* and in the "Address," George Eliot's views had taken a conservative turn.

The pattern of Eliot's relationship with her conservative family suggests that the radical views of her young-adult years developed in response to her increasing sense of alienation from them, but that as she matured, the conservatism that was an aspect of her nostalgia for the past reasserted itself. Even her earlier adolescent evangelical enthusiasm can be seen as part of her pattern of rebellion against her family. Eliot was introduced to evangelicalism by her boarding-school teacher, Maria Lewis, who, according to Gordon Haight, "gave the bright, eager little girl the sympathetic support and affection" that she had been unable to find at home, "except from her father" (*Biography* 10). By the time she was fifteen, she had experienced a religious "conversion," from which followed "acts of charity . . . performed with greater fervour, and . . . mild abstinences from innocent pleasures." Her "gloomy Calvinism" apparently served the purpose of increasing her distance from her brother Isaac, who had "imbibed High Church views" from his own schooling (19).

At Coventry, Eliot's acquaintance with a new group of friends, her increased time for study and writing, her new interest in the sciences, and her sense of conflict with her family seem to have worked together to foster the development of her liberal tendencies. Biographers agree on the importance of her "Holy War" with her father—the period beginning in January 1842 when she refused to go to church with him because of her changed view of the Christian faith. Ruby Redinger suggests that Mary Ann's behavior reflects her "hostile aggressiveness" toward her father (119), who actually shared with her his own new interest in the evangelical movement within the Anglican Church (Haight, *Biography* 34). It seems to me that her rebellion in Coventry against her father's Christianity was a continuation of the pattern of her adolescent involvement with the evangelicalism that opposed her brother's High Church views. Church attendance was a serious matter to Mr. Evans, who was so upset by Mary Ann's refusal to go with him that he considered sending her away from home. However, according to Haight, Isaac rescued the situation by inviting her to stay at Griff. Two weeks later Eliot and her father arrived at their truce (44). Yet her family continued to disapprove of her, in particular of her friendship with Charles Bray, the Coventry reformer whom Isaac described as "only a leader of mobs . . . [who] can only introduce her to Chartists and Radicals" (Cara Bray, qtd. in Haight, *Biography* 48).

Eliot's increasingly liberal ideas about marriage were another aspect of her rebellion against her family, whose chief concern, as Cara expressed it, seemed to be that she find "a husband and a settlement." Her exposure to the unconventional ideas of the Brays' circle seems to have fostered her notion that "the truth of feeling [is] the only universal bond of union" (qtd. in Taylor 57). Taylor emphasizes the irregularity of the Brays' marriage, during which Charles sired six illegitimate children with a mistress. She concludes that "although these relationships were a revelation to Mary Ann, she so admired the people involved and so completely understood the reasons for their unconventional arrangements that all seemed quite acceptable to her" (58).

After her father's death in 1849, Eliot's life changed dramatically. Her financial situation was such that with only a small trust left to her by her father's will, she was faced with decisions about how to support herself in the future. A decade later she described herself during the period following his death as "very unhappy, and in a state of discord and rebellion towards my own lot" (*Letters* 3:230–31). Upon her return to England from her trip to the Continent, she finally settled down to live with the Brays. Soon she was offered the opportunity to write an article for the *Westminster Review*. As it turned out, her Coventry association of radical ideas with unconventional marriages was reinforced by her experience at the Chapmans' home, where John lived with both a wife and a mistress, and soon also apparently developed an interest in Marian. Within a short time she was to make her own unconventional choice: her lifelong liaison with Lewes, who was at the time known for his radical ideas and life-style. Even as late as the publication date of *Felix Holt* in 1866, Lewes was editor of *The Fortnightly*, which was known to be "open-minded and wide-ranging, with tendencies toward free-thinking and liberalism" (Ashton, *GHL* 225). Eliot's unconventional choice of a liaison with a free-thinking partner thus adds to readers' expectations that the author's views should have been more radical than they prove to be in *Felix Holt*.

The pattern of Eliot's development suggests, however, that her intellectual growth was associated with family loss, and that her stages of rapid intellectual development were therefore accompanied by painful longing for past attachments. The evangelicalism that had served to increase her distance from her brother Isaac, for example, was also accompanied by a significant advance in her education. It was Miss Lewis who recommended to her father that she attend the Franklins' school in Coventry, where she went on to excel in composition, piano, and painting, and where she became acquainted with many English authors, including Shakespeare and Milton (Haight, *Biography* 11–13). After Isaac's marriage, her rapidly developing interest in secular subjects had also served to increase her distance from her father. Eliot's association of intellectual growth with personal loss and family conflict would explain the coexistence in her writing of liberal and conservative tendencies, which can be seen as a displacement of her personal conflict between her desire to grow away from her conservative family and her continuing need for them.

Eliot's political novel, which takes place in 1832, the year of the passage of the First Reform Bill, was written and published during the period of unrest in England leading up to the Second Reform Bill of 1867. The historical setting is intended to suggest the connection between the past events as depicted in the fiction and those of the current political situation. The repetition in *Felix Holt* of the pattern in *Silas Marner* also suggests that the past historical situation that is repeated in the present novel is emblematic of the author's psychological situation. Like *Silas Marner*, *Felix Holt* had intruded on Eliot's attempts to work on something else. On the basis of the psychoanalytic literature on anniversary reactions, I would argue that the timing of the 1866 publication date of *Felix Holt* reflects the author's ongoing unconscious attempt to master earlier traumas through the writing of her fiction. As I explained earlier, the anniversary reaction is a manifestation of the repetition-compulsion which occurs at a time when the mind associates present circumstances with one or more traumatic events of the past. Pollock writes of a type of anniversary reaction in which there is conscious awareness of a date or event, which produces a specific ego response "which is then associatively linked to specific earlier conflict, with its revival via symptoms, behavior, dreams, and so forth" (228, qtg. I. L. Mintz). Freud emphasizes the "liberties that 'unconscious mental activity' takes with numbers" (19:89). He explains how associated traumas can be discerned, for example, in cases of individuals who are obsessive about certain numbers (6:246). In regard to psychoanalytic technique, he explains that "the associations to numbers chosen at random are perhaps the most convincing [of the effectiveness of the technique of word association]; they run off so quickly and proceed with such incredible certainty to a hidden goal that the effect is really staggering" (15:107).

In Eliot's life at the time, it seems that special significance is attached to the number thirteen. The election riot that forms the basis of *Felix Holt* occurred when Eliot was thirteen years old; there had been thirteen years between the deaths of her parents; by 1866, it had been thirteen years since the beginning of her affair with Lewes in 1853. The number thirteen thus seems to serve as the focus for the association and condensation of feelings related to these significant events in Eliot's life. Indeed, Eliot took note of the number in her inscription to Lewes when she presented the manuscript of *Felix Holt* to him: "From George Eliot (otherwise Polly) to her dear husband, this thirteenth year of their united life, in which the deepening sense of her own imperfectness has the consolation of their deepening love" (*FH* 71).

Eliot's reliving of the election riot through the writing of *Felix Holt* suggests that her mind had attached more than political significance to the historical event; the riot had almost certainly served as no less than an enactment of her inner state at age thirteen—the point in human life that typically symbolizes the departure from childhood. Eliot portrays age thirteen as such in *The Mill on the Floss*. In the chapter titled "The Golden Gates Are Passed," Maggie and Tom are shown to have grown rapidly out of childhood. Maggie is described as "tall now, with braided and coiled hair: she was almost as tall as Tom, though she was only thirteen" (265). At this point in the story the two must leave school to go home because of their father's financial failure and disability following his accidental fall from his horse. The chapter ends with the poignant statement that "they had gone forth together into their new life of sorrow, and they would never more see the sunshine undimmed by remembered cares. They had entered the thorny wilderness, and the golden gates of their childhood had for ever closed behind them" (270).

In Mary Anne Evans's life, thirteen was the age at which she "had mastered everything offered" at Mrs. Wallington's Boarding School in Nuneaton, where she had formed her long-lasting friendship with her teacher Maria Lewis, and had left to go to the Franklins' school in Coventry. Eliot's years at the Franklins' were academically very successful. Yet, as the pattern of her development suggests, her opportunity for further intellectual growth was more than likely accompanied by increased anxiety at the prospect of leaving Miss Lewis, and of living farther away from home. To the separation anxiety aroused at such a turning point in an adolescent's life is added the anxiety that accompanies sexual development. The oedipal situation, with its merging of intense feelings of love and hate toward parent figures, is revived. The middle-aged Eliot's attempt to separate the idealized Felix from the rage in the crowd in *Felix Holt* thus represents her attempt to separate herself from the strong feelings of adolescence, which have been revived and associated with present emotional reactions.

It had also been thirteen years since the publication of *Bleak House*, in 1853, the year of the beginning of her affair with Lewes. It seems likely that Eliot would associate the publication of Dickens's novel with the beginning of the affair, not only because both events occurred in the same year, but because Dickens's character Lady Dedlock was such a powerful Victorian symbol of the fallen woman. As Haight writes in his chapter that describes Eliot's decision to live openly with Lewes, "The most trifling violation of the sexual code by a Lady Dedlock or a Little Em'ly inevitably brought death or banishment" in the literature of the time (*Biography* 146); after Marian's elopement with Lewes, "The storm of horror that it produced matched the revulsion from the 'fallen woman' which Dickens was exploiting so profitably in Mrs. Dombey, Little Em'ly, and Lady Dedlock" (166).

Emery refers to Eliot's "imaginative success with Mrs. Transome, whose isolated state of despair emerges from the author's experience" (138). Perhaps the beginning of the affair with Lewes is associated not only with the story of the fictional character, but with the radicalism and loss of control that had characterized the election riot in 1832. Moreover, the affair with Lewes, a married man, may also have been associated with her state of mind at the time her father was dying, when she had experienced the "sensual and devilish" "vision of [her]self" (*Letters* 1:284) that foreshadowed her shifting attachments to men after his death. The oedipal fantasy in the election riot scene in *Felix Holt* suggests the revival in the author's mind of the "devilish visions" that derive from the intense, conflicting (love-hate) emotional reactions to loss. The author's fear of the mob that is evident in her novel could thus be said to be a projection of her fear of the powerful impulses coming from within herself.

Fifteen is another number that seems to hold significance for the author at this time. In *Felix Holt*, fifteen years is the interval between Harold Transome's departure and return to Transome Court. In *Silas Marner*, fifteen years is the interval between Silas's expulsion from Lantern Yard and his loss of his gold coins, a time when his childhood losses are also reexperienced. In Eliot's life, fifteen years is the interval between the deaths of her twin siblings and the death of her mother. In 1866, the publication date of Felix Holt, she would turn forty-seven, the age of her mother when she died—a time when, judging from Bowlby's studies of adults who have lost parents in adolescence, the survivor may likely suffer an anniversary reaction of some kind (3:158). In both novels, the pain of maternal loss returns to be reexperienced in the present—in *Felix Holt*, for Mrs. Transome, in the form of the return of her son Harold, from whom she had been separated for fifteen years; for Esther, in the form of Mrs. Transome, who symbolizes her deceased mother. In both novels, the aggression felt by the author toward the lost, needed mother is projected onto the "dead" mother of the story. Moreover, in the scene where Esther recognizes Mrs. Transome's "joyless embittered age" as increasingly affecting herself the longer she remained at Transome Court, the author remarks, "And many of us know how, even in our childhood, some blank discontented face on the background of our home has marred our summer mornings. Why was it, when the birds were singing, when the fields were a garden, and when we were clasping another little hand just larger than our own, there was somebody who found it hard to smile?" (585–86). In this passage, Eliot seems to be making a direct comment about the effect on herself in early childhood of her mother's depression, which I believe followed the deaths of the twins. Thus through the creation of Esther, the author once again enacts her wish to "separate [her]self from [her] past history" (epigram, chap. 21, *FH* 310)—or to leave behind the trauma of maternal loss, first by emotional separation, and fifteen years later by death. The portrayal of the change in Esther also repeats the author's conversion experience, which had occurred at age fifteen at the Franklins' school, and which had undoubtedly served to defend against her sense of loss of closeness to loved ones. Eliot's creation of *Felix Holt*, then, illustrates Pollock's observation that creativity can be an integral part of the mourning process—a process which is reflected in the repeating patterns that can be discerned in an artist's work (615).

The past that is repeated in the present in *Felix Holt* is both political and psychological, but it is the psychological theme that predominates. Mrs. Transome and Rufus Lyon are linked by their sense of dread that the secret of their past experience of loss of control will be revealed to others. When their secrets are finally confessed to their children, Mrs. Transome, although initially rebuffed, is (with Esther's help) eventually reunited with her son (598); Lyon, by contrast, is immediately released from his own inferno of painful memory by Esther's asking for forgiveness if she had not loved him enough: "He had been going to ask forgiveness of her who asked it for herself. In that moment of supreme complex emotion one ray of the minister's joy was the thought, 'Surely the work of grace is begun in her'" (355). At the end of the novel, Mrs. Transome and her son remain at Transome Court, while Lyon leaves the village of Treby Magna to join the newlyweds Felix and Esther in their new home at an undisclosed location. By creating in *Felix Holt* the sense "of life releasing itself from integument" (Coveney 59), the author dramatizes her vision of the potentiality of individual human growth as the means to overcome the "savage beast" of rage that underlies the secret dread of loss of control.

Eliot's vision of society as a necessarily "slow-growing system of things" is cut off at the scene of the election riot, much as her own growth had been inhibited by the underlying rage that followed from her sense of loss; her vision of society is thus an extension of her experience of her family. In the portrayal of the idealistic Felix Holt, Eliot proposes a new kind of radicalism as a substitute for the radicalism espoused by those engaged in the fight for the working man's suffrage. Felix's radicalism lies in his choice not to join in the rush for money and position in the new middle class; he chooses rather to become a "demagogue of a new sort," who will devote his own life to making life better for those around him. Perhaps Eliot intends to convey the message that society will be slowly changed by individuals like Felix, and like Esther, who are "reformed" slowly, from within. Yet her vision of the potential for growth in the individual is undercut by her harrowing vision of the riotous mob. Underlying the message of hope is a darker vision of society, something like the darkness in Dickens's *Bleak House*—although for Eliot the darkness lies as much at the heart of the working man's mob as it does in the decadence of the aristocratic Transome Court. *Felix Holt*, with its "incomplete fusion" of the personal and political sides of the narrative, reveals the author's underlying despair over the possibility of the "reformed" individual's participation in the group. For Eliot, the cost of individuation is perceived to be the sense of disconnection that follows from the loss of love.

SIX

The Vast Wreck of Ambitious Ideals in *Middlemarch*

After the publication of *Felix Holt,* George Eliot finally completed and published *The Spanish Gypsy,* in May of 1868. By the end of 1868, she had made her decision to write *Middlemarch,* but its writing was delayed, first by a trip to Italy in the late winter and early spring of 1869, then by Thornie's illness and return from Natal to the Priory in early May, and, finally, by his death on October 19. Both Eliot and Lewes suffered keenly from their loss. Eliot's work proceeded slowly during 1870; by the end of December, about one hundred pages were written. By the summer of 1871, however, during their stay at a rented house in the country at Shottermill, "Marian wrote with less torment from diffidence and self-mistrust than she had felt in many years" (Haight, *Biography* 433).

Jerome Beaty's manuscript study of Eliot's writing process concludes that the novel as we know it combined two separate works, an English novel, "Middlemarch," begun about July 1869, and a short story, "Miss Brooke," begun in December 1870. Beaty believes that Eliot made her decision to combine the two into "one great novel of provincial life in the last years before the first Reform Bill" on December 31, 1870. In early 1871 her work involved "a vast amount of rethinking and replanning, some rewriting, and some new writing in order to make the two separate stories fuse smoothly"; by March 19, she had completed 236 pages of the new work (11). Additional evidence of Eliot's writing process can be found in the notebooks that contain her reading notes before and during the writing of the novel. The *Quarry for Middlemarch* edited by Anna Theresa Kitchel contains Eliot's detailed notes on medical and political information, as well as the time-schemes and character relationships in the novel. Two notebooks which record Eliot's extensive

The Vast Wreck of Ambitious Ideals in *Middlemarch* 133

literary and historical research from the period 1868 to 1871 have been transcribed and edited by John Clark Pratt and Victor A. Neufeldt. Still another notebook that records Eliot's notes on philology, mythology, and art that pertain to *Middlemarch* has been edited by Joseph Weisenfarth.

Eliot's editor John Blackwood, who was very enthusiastic about the early parts of the manuscript, accepted Lewes's idea of publishing *Middlemarch* in eight parts, in order, as Lewes reasoned, "to furnish the town with talk for some time, and each part thus keep up and swell the general interest" (*Letters* 5:145–46). Book I was published in December 1871; the rest followed in 1872, with the last, Book VIII, published in December. The success of the novel surpassed even that of *Adam Bede*; the new work was "acclaimed a masterpiece" by critics (Haight, *Biography* 444). Blackwood had been unfailing in his encouragement throughout the publication process. Upon reading Book VI he wrote, "I cannot adequately express my admiration. . . . Every book seems to go on becoming what one could not have thought possible—better than its predecessor" (*Letters* 5:293). After the complete novel was available to the public, Henry James, among the reviewers, wrote that the work is "a splendid performance. It sets a limit . . . to the development of the old-fashioned English novel" (qtd. in Haight, *Biography* 444). Other contemporaries mentioned the book in their letters. Emily Dickinson wrote to a cousin, "What do I think of Middlemarch? What do I think of glory? . . . The mysteries of human nature surpass the 'mysteries of redemption'" (qtd. 445). Sigmund Freud, always a great reader, commented some years later that *Middlemarch* "appealed to him very much"; he found that it "illuminated important aspects of his relations with Martha [who became his wife]" (Jones 116). Eliot herself had written in her journal on January 1, 1873: "No former book of mine has been received with more enthusiasm—not even *Adam Bede,* and I have received many deeply affecting assurances of its influence for good on individual minds" (*Letters* 5:357).

The quantity, variety, and quality of the predominantly positive modern criticism of *Middlemarch* reflect its position as one of the great works of literature in the English language. At the same time, there have been criticisms of certain aspects of the novel, particularly, as W. J. Harvey explains ("Criticism" 143), of Eliot's unconvincing characterization of Will Ladislaw, the second husband of her heroine, Dorothea.

134 The Vast Wreck of Ambitious Ideals in *Middlemarch*

Closely related to the issue of Ladislaw's characterization is the frequent criticism that Dorothea's marriage to him is an unsatisfactory ending to the novel. To feminists (and others) like Ellin Ringler, this ending seems to undercut "the implications of [the] novel" up to that point (59). Despite such objections, however, twentieth-century critics, like most of Eliot's contemporaries, have generally regarded the novel as a masterpiece.

The story of *Middlemarch* begins in 1829, in that "relatively narrow and cramped society of provincial England just before the Reform Bill of 1832," as Harvey expresses it in his "Introduction" to the novel (10). Through its portrayal of the web of connections among the characters in the midlands village of Middlemarch, the novel stresses the influence of society and historical setting on individual lives. The stories of the principal characters Dorothea and Lydgate, which Harvey calls "twin studies in defeated aspiration" (8), are interwoven with the stories of the other characters. Dorothea is an idealistic young woman, inclined toward self-denial, who aspires to do some great good in the world despite the inadequate education that was typical at the time, even for women of "good" families. Lydgate, educated to be a medical man, aspires to be more than a "common country doctor" (171). Interested in the reform of the medical practices of his day, he also dreams of himself as a "discoverer" (175): "Such was Lydgate's plan of his future: to do good small work for Middlemarch, and great work for the world" (178). My purpose in this chapter is to explain the characters' failure to achieve their aspirations by illuminating the psychological dilemma they share with each other, and with the interconnecting characters in the world of *Middlemarch*. In so doing, I want to show how the trauma of loss of love determines the human "fear of success." I also want to show how the "melancholy" vision of the society of Middlemarch, as many contemporary reviewers saw it (Haight, *Biography* 446), is an extension of the sense of loss that Eliot shared with loved ones.

Lydgate's vocational aspirations are accompanied by a weakness for women, in the form of a tendency toward a "fitful swerving of passion," along with a "chivalrous kindness which helped to make him morally lovable" (180). These traits are illustrated by the flashback to his encounter with Mme. Laure, a French actress whom he had met during his student days in Paris, before he came to Middlemarch. Laure had played

The Vast Wreck of Ambitious Ideals in *Middlemarch* 135

the part in a melodrama of a woman who accidentally kills her lover by "mistaking him for the evil-designing duke of the piece." Lydgate came to the theater to watch the melodrama repeatedly, until finally it became his only relaxation from his scientific experiments. One evening, the drama became confused with reality when, "at the moment when the heroine was to act the stabbing of her lover . . . the wife veritably stabbed her husband, who [played the part of the lover]" (180).

Leaping onto the stage to rescue her from the "swooning" fall that followed the stabbing, Lydgate became involved in Laure's real life. Although some of her admirers believed her guilty of murder, he continued to believe fervently in her innocence. After a legal investigation turned up no motive for a murder, Laure was released by the authorities, and soon left Paris for Avignon, where Lydgate found her, "acting with great success . . . under the same name, looking more majestic than ever as a forsaken wife carrying her child in her arms." Following "the sudden impulse of a madman," he proposed to her. By way of response, Laure explained to him the incident on the stage: "My foot really slipped," she said. When Lydgate called it an accident, she explained, "*I meant to do it.*" Still trying to find excuses for her behavior, Lydgate was horrified to hear her reason: "He wearied me; he was too fond: he would live in Paris and not in my country; that was not agreeable to me." Finally, in response to Lydgate's further questions, Laure added, "I did not plan: it came to me in the play—*I meant to do it*" (182). His illusions dashed, Lydgate was thus forced to see his first-adored woman "amid the throng of stupid criminals." Laure concluded their conversation by saying, "You are a good young man. . . . But I do not like husbands. I will never have another" (183).

Despite his resolution to maintain a scientific attitude toward women after his experience with Laure, Lydgate repeats his Paris mistake in Middlemarch, where he has settled in the hope of having time to pursue his research while practicing medicine. Although he has planned to remain unmarried for several years, he soon falls prey to Rosamund Vincy's "melodic charm" (121). While Rosamond appears to be the opposite of Laure—blond instead of dark, slim instead of matronly—she plays the role of Laure in their married life. By thwarting his ambitions, for no apparent motive other than her desire to have her own way, she does "in essence if not in fact, [slowly] murder Lydgate," as Suzanne C. Ferguson puts it (513).

The story of Lydgate and Laure in Paris thus contains what turns out to be Lydgate's lifelong psychological situation. From a psychoanalytic perspective, Lydgate becomes obsessed with the actress because the murder scene in the melodrama symbolizes a traumatic scene in his life which he finds it necessary to repeat; each time he watches the scene, he sees his own unconscious fantasy on the stage. Laure's actual murder of her husband precipitates Lydgate's attempt to participate in the scene; he becomes involved with his heroine's real life—a mistake which soon results in the shattering of his illusions about her. After such an experience, Lydgate determines not to marry before he is well established as a medical practitioner—until he meets Rosamond in Middlemarch and begins to repeat the scene in the melodrama again. His marriage to Rosamond inevitably results in the shattering of his illusions about her, along with the loss, as well, of his vocational aspirations. His self-induced melodrama finally ends with his own untimely death at age fifty.

The narrative provides clues as to the underlying cause of Lydgate's psychological situation. Earlier in the chapter we learn that "he had been left an orphan when he was fresh from a public school. His father, a military man, had made but little provision for three children, and when the boy Tertius asked to have a medical education, it seemed easier to his guardians to grant his request by apprenticing him to a country practitioner than to make any objections on the score of family dignity" (172). We are also told that Lydgate had been a "quick" child who loved to read, and had decided on his vocation early, at about age ten, upon discovering an anatomy book in his home library (173). His father's death, occurring just at the time when he needed help in getting launched with his medical education, thus involved not only the loss of a parent, but a devastating change in his prospects for the future. Furthermore, although his mother is never mentioned, the implication is that she had died earlier; thus the loss of the father was added to that of the mother.

The narrative suggests, then, that the death of Lydgate's father at a critical turning point in his life resulted in his unacknowledged sense of doom about his future. His idealizations of women help to defend against his sense of loss, which the narrative intimates includes the shame of a lower social position than he had imagined before his father's death. The scene in the melodrama is a disguised enactment of the oedipal fantasy; thus the scene suggests the oedipal guilt that is the adolescent

The Vast Wreck of Ambitious Ideals in *Middlemarch*   137

son's reaction to the father's death. Yet in the disguised oedipal scene of the melodrama, it is the idealized matronly figure, not the son, who wishes to kill the father, or authority figure. The anger felt by the son (Lydgate) in response to the combined losses of his parents is projected onto the "evil-designing duke" and the murdering woman of the scene. That the lover is killed instead of the authority figure satisfies the observer's need for punishment for murderous impulses toward the father. Lydgate's obsession with the scene suggests that his devastating losses have kept him, in his imagination, at the scene of his father's death—a scene which he must experience repeatedly until he masters the trauma of loss by resolving his emotional reactions, including the anger and guilt that are projected onto the stage. However, when his idealized heroine acts out her impulse to kill her real-life husband, Lydgate loses control of his own impulses, and begins to act out the son's role as rescuer in his oedipal drama. His later discovery of the actress in Avignon, on stage again as the forsaken wife with a child in her arms, prompts him further to act out his desire to become the mother's husband; but he is rejected by the actress. His heroine's rejection repeats his original loss of his mother and only intensifies his accumulating sense of loss. Thus Lydgate finds it necessary to repeat the scene again with another woman, who is chosen for her murderous potential. His thwarted ambitions and his untimely death are his self-punishment for the fulfillment of his murderous wishes in the oedipal scene of his father's death.

One critic, Simon During, suggests that Eliot's story of Laure in Paris constitutes an allusion to the real-life story of Henriette Cornier, in 1825 a twenty-seven-year-old servant living in Paris, who severed the head of a nineteen-month-old child. Her bizarre crime provoked extensive debates among psychiatric and legal experts as to its nature and cause. Widely publicized, the crime also resulted in an epidemic of imitative crimes committed by others shortly afterward. During believes that the story of Laure in *Middlemarch* is meant to be a fictional version of one of the crimes imitative of Henriette's action, and that the story thus adds to the novel's verisimilitude. Laure's words of explanation to Lydgate echo Henriette's to her investigators. During writes that "questioned soon after and covered with blood, Henriette answered apathetically, first, [in French], 'The idea came to me!,' and then, 'I intended to kill her'" (86).

Psychoanalysts in the twentieth century can explain a sudden, irresistible impulse to kill as a manifestation of the repetition-compulsion, and as such, a reenactment of one or more traumatic events in the murderer's earlier life (e.g., the "Texas Killer," in Rose 55–58). However, the nineteenth-century psychiatrists who examined Cornier could discern no motive for her killing. Etienne Esquirol, later the author of the leading textbook (in Western Europe in the first half of the nineteenth century) on mental disorders, diagnosed Cournier as suffering from "monomania," which he defined as "a chronic cerebral affection . . . characterized by a partial lesion of the intelligence, affections or will" (320). In the section of his text on "homicidal monomania," he explains that people suffering from the disorder often slay loved ones; he writes: "We can understand this phenomenon, only by admitting the suspension, temporarily, of all understanding; all moral sensibility and volition" (365).

Although Rosamond, like Laure, and like the real-life Cornier, has no apparent motive for her "murder," the narrative suggests possible reasons for her brutality toward her husband. Descriptions of Rosamond, which repeatedly emphasize her "nymph-like figure" and her "infantine blondness" (123, 188, 470), suggest failed development, which in Eliot's portrayal seems to be the result of parental overindulgence. Both Rosamond's parents are shown to be powerless in the face of her charms. "I never give up anything that I choose to do," she says to Lydgate in defiance of her father's plan to interfere with their marriage. Her finishing-school education has only added to her sense of superiority over the people in her hometown, including her parents. Although as "the flower of Mrs. Lemon's school," she is "accomplished" by the standards for women in her day, "even to extras, such as the getting in and out of a carriage" (123), her prospects for a vocation are limited to the ornamental role played by married women in her society. The attitude of the villagers toward women's education is reflected in the words of Mrs. Plymdale, the mother of one of Rosamond's suitors, who secretly thinks that "Rosamond had been educated to a ridiculous pitch, for what was the use of accomplishments which would be all laid aside as soon as she was married?" (196–97).

Although marriage is Rosamond's goal, the narrative intimates that she dislikes men. In an early scene, when her mother observes that she is "hard on [her] brothers," Rosamond responds, "Brothers are so unpleasant" (125). Certainly she is unable to feel concern for her brother Fred during his illness; she can think only of the opportunity it will provide her to be near his doctor, Lydgate (297). Her assumption that every man she meets, including Lydgate, will fall in love with her reveals not only her capacity for self-reference, but also her need to "make conquests and enslave men" (474)—a need which perhaps reflects her rage over her own dim prospects as a female. Even after her marriage, the need persists; she is willing to risk her reputation in her attempt to gain Will Ladislaw's devotion. Rosamond's inflated sense of herself and her need for control suggest the pathological narcissism of Kernberg's theory, although the portrayal of her is not so detailed as that of Tito in *Romola*, or of Gwendolen in *Daniel Deronda*.

Rebuffing the suitors in her hometown, Rosamond wants to marry a stranger who will carry her off to a life of higher society. She tells her mother that she will "not marry any Middlemarch young man" (125). Soon Lydgate becomes her ideal, in part because he is "altogether foreign to Middlemarch" (145). She believes his "good birth" distinguishes him from his Middlemarch rivals, "and presented marriage as a prospect of rising in rank and getting a little nearer to that celestial condition on earth in which she would have nothing to do with vulgar people" (195). It becomes clear as they get to know one another that "Rosamond was occupied with Lydgate not exactly as he was in himself, but with his relation to her" (196)—and for the exciting life she imagines he will be able to provide her.

In their relationship with one another, Rosamond and Lydgate, like Hetty and Arthur, serve as extensions of one another's fantasies. Lydgate's need to rescue the "weak and suffering" prompts his proposal to Rosamond just at the time when he had resolved to spend less time with her, because he sees "a certain helpless quivering [in reaction to his long absence] which touched him quite newly" (335). He enjoys his initial feeling of superiority over her, "confess[ing] to himself that he was descending a little in relation to Rosamond's family" (384), yet feeling it "delightful to be listened to by a creature who would bring him . . . affection—beauty—repose—such help as our thoughts get from the summer sky and the flower-fringed meadows." Failing to take seriously Rosamond's own need to dominate, Lydgate assumes the "innate submissiveness of the goose as beautifully corresponding to the strength of the gander" (391).

Rosamond's capacity for murder without apparent motive is suggested by the incident of her self-induced miscarriage, which occurs after she goes horseback riding against her husband's medical advice, because "the gratification of riding on a fine horse, with Capt. Lydgate, Sir Godwin's son, on another fine horse by her side, and of being met in this position by anyone but her husband, was something as good as her dreams before marriage" (630). When Lydgate learns what has happened, he "secretly wondered over the terrible tenacity of this mild creature," and he feels "gathering within him an amazed sense of his powerlessness over Rosamond" (631). Soon after, consciously connecting Rosamond with Laure, he wonders, "Would *she* kill me because I wearied her?" (638). Her "murder" of him takes the form of a ruthless obstinacy that crushes his hopes. Her lack of empathy for his aspirations ("I often wish you were not a medical man," she says [497]), and her refusal to help economize while he is getting started in his career, leave him feeling "the biting presence of a petty degrading care, such as casts the blight of irony over all higher effort" (633). Rosamond wants to leave Middlemarch in the hope of his making a better living elsewhere; Lydgate tries to convince her of the reality that they have no means to go anywhere else. Their burden of debt adds to Lydgate's "degrading preoccupation which was the reverse of all his former purposes" (697). The two become increasingly unable to communicate. When Lydgate reluctantly decides that they have no alternative but to sell their expensive house and auction the furnishings, Rosamond cancels the plans without telling him (700–708). When Rosamond suggests asking his uncle, Sir Godwin, for a loan, Lydgate refuses; yet when he receives a letter of refusal from Sir Godwin soon after, he realizes that Rosamond has asked for the loan herself, just at the time when he had begun to consider visiting his uncle in person to ask for help. After their argument about the incident, Lydgate acknowledges to himself that "she had mastered him" (719). Despite Rosamond's change for the better after Dorothea, seeing that their marriage is deteriorating, intervenes on Lydgate's behalf, he comes to accept "his narrowed lot with sad resignation. He had chosen this fragile creature, and had taken the burthen of her life upon his arms. He must walk as he could, carrying that burthen pitifully" (858). In the "Finale" we learn that Rosamond had won the battle over Lydgate's career: before his premature death of diphtheria, he had established a successful medical practice, alternating between London and "a continental bathing-place," and had written a treatise on gout, "a disease which has a good deal of wealth on its side"; but he had always thought of himself as a failure: "He had not done what he once meant to do" (893).

In keeping with Kohut's theory, Eliot's portrayal of Rosamond suggests that her need to dominate Lydgate is the result of her own incomplete self-development. Prepared by her upbringing and education to expect self-completion through marriage, Rosamond's unrealistic expectations cause her to feel humiliated by her husband's financial difficulties and his less than glorious social position. The narcissistic rage that follows from her own sense of inadequacy, then, is at the root of her brutality toward Lydgate.

Whereas Rosamond is not shown to be conscious of any murderous wishes toward her husband, the portrayal of Bulstrode's conscious conflict between the "desire" to murder his old acquaintance, Raffles, and the "intention" not to do so (758) shows Eliot's awareness of the way in which the unconscious mind can help turn a murderous wish into a murderous act.

Bulstrode is a respectable banker and philanthropist who combines the rigorous practice of his evangelical version of Christianity with harsh judgments of others. He is known to be "a man who half starves himself, and goes the length of family prayers," but who also likes "to be master" (159); he is "evidently a ruler" in Middlemarch (184). When Raffles comes to town and threatens to destroy his reputation by telling the truth about his past, it becomes apparent that one reason for Bulstrode's ardent practice of religion is a guilty conscience over the origins of his wealth. We learn that as a young banker's clerk, he had been a member of a Calvinistic dissenting church, "having had striking experience in conviction of sin and sense of pardon." "Brother Bulstrode," as he was called, was "distinguished" among those in the small sect, with the result that he came to believe that "God intended him for special instrumentality." He was thinking of the ministry as a possible vocation, and "inclined toward missionary labour." As "an orphan educated at a commercial charity-school," however, he was susceptible, the narrative intimates, to the influence of "the richest man in the congregation" who befriended him and offered him the opportunity to join his pawnbroker's business. Soon after he began his new job, Bulstrode became aware that the firm dealt with stolen goods; but he rationalized that making profits out of "lost souls" might be "God's way of saving his chosen." Thus the practice of his religion became bound up with his dishonest dealings. Over the years since that time when he had "found himself carrying on two distinct lives, . . . his soul had become saturated with the belief that he did everything for God's sake, being indifferent to it for his own" (663–65).

When his boss died, Bulstrode succeeded in marrying his widow "without reservation of property," by concealing from her the whereabouts of her daughter (to whom she had hoped to leave her money), and by paying off Raffles for keeping his secret. Even after her death, Bulstrode continued to lead his double life. Instead of putting an end to the family business, he kept it going for thirteen more years, until it finally collapsed. Not deliberately hypocritical, he was "simply a man whose desires had been stronger than his theoretic beliefs," and who had "gradually explained the gratification of his desires into satisfactory agreement with those beliefs" (667).

Raffles's threat to reveal his past provokes Bulstrode to offer Will Ladislaw, who he has learned is the daughter's son (and thus the rightful heir to his fortune), a settlement. Ladislaw, however, knowing that his mother had run away to avoid having anything to do with her father's business, refuses (672). Bulstrode is further humiliated when Caleb Garth, having heard the story of his past from Raffles (who by now is very ill), refuses to work for him at Stone Court. Shortly after this incident, he feels "the intense desire . . . that the will of God might be the death of that hated man [Raffles]" (750).

When Lydgate diagnoses alcohol poisoning, Bulstrode offers to take care of Raffles. He tries to follow Lydgate's medical orders at the same time he struggles with his murderous wish: "Should Providence in this case award death, there was no sin in contemplating death as the desirable issue—if he kept his hands from hastening it—if he scrupulously did what was prescribed" (757). Making a distinction between intention and desire, he reasons that "intention was everything in the question of right and wrong," and he "set himself to keep his intention separate from his desire. He inwardly declared that he intended to obey orders" (758). When Lydgate returns to check Raffles, he prescribes small doses of opium, emphasizing the point at which the doses should cease. He also orders that no alcohol be given. Before Lydgate leaves, Bulstrode, not fully aware of his own "diseased motive," offers him the loan he needs, and Lydgate, unsuspecting, accepts (761).

Bulstrode begins to administer the opium according to Lydgate's directions. He soon feels so tired that he calls the housekeeper, Mrs. Abel, to relieve him, and explains to her how to administer the opium. An hour and a half later he realizes that he had forgotten to tell her "when the doses of opium must cease" (762). Bulstrode's forgetting to tell Mrs. Abel of Lydgate's complete instructions is an example of one of Freud's "parapraxes" (or, "Freudian slips"), which he describes in his *Introductory Lectures* as "psychical acts [that] arise from mutual interference between two intentions" (16:60). Freud explains that "a conflict between two purposes and a forcing-back of one of them . . . takes its revenge by producing a parapraxis" (16:71).

Bulstrode is still deliberating what to do, when Mrs. Abel knocks on his door and asks for brandy for Raffles. Pausing while she persists in urging him, he finally gives her the key to the wine cooler. The next morning, seeing Raffles on the verge of death, he hides the opium phial and puts the brandy back in the wine cooler himself. When he returns to watch Raffles die, "he felt more at rest than he had done for many months. His conscience was soothed by the enfolding wing of secrecy, which seemed just then like an angel sent down for his relief" (764).

When Bulstrode falls into disgrace as a result of the villagers' suspicions of his crimes, his wife's reaction contrasts sharply with Rosamond's response to her husband's (less disgraceful) troubles. "After an instant of scorching shame in which she felt only the eyes of the world . . . she was at his side in mournful but unreproaching fellowship with shame and isolation" (806). Her "loyal spirit" enables her to "say of his guilt, I will mourn and not reproach. But she needed time to gather up her strength; she needed to sob out her farewell to all the gladness and pride of her life. . . . she had begun a new life in which she embraced humiliation. She took off all her ornaments and put on a plain black gown, and instead of wearing her much-adorned cap and large bows of hair, she brushed her hair down and put on a plain bonnet-cap, which made her look suddenly like an early Methodist" (807).

Dorothea Brooke's plain dressing and habitual self-denial suggest that, like Mrs. Bulstrode after her husband's disgrace, she lives in a state of mourning. Indeed, she and her sister Celia, like so many of Eliot's characters, are orphans. They had been educated, "since they were about twelve years old and had lost their parents, on plans at once narrow and promiscuous, first in an English family and afterwards in a Swiss family at Lausanne, their bachelor uncle and guardian [Mr. Brooke] trying in this way to remedy the disadvantages of their orphaned condition" (30). Dorothea's situation mirrors Lydgate's: the education that had followed from her orphaned status has not adequately prepared her for the great work that she aspires to do. Also like Lydgate, Dorothea's ongoing need for her lost parents, who had apparently died early in her life, helps to explain her lifelong psychological situation.

Just as the word "infantine" (or "infantile") is used repeatedly to describe Rosamond's physical appearance, so the word "childlike" is used repeatedly to describe Dorothea. It is her "childlike ideas about marriage," in fact, that cause her to want a husband to be "a sort of father" (32). Wishing to participate in the work of a great man, she idealizes the middle-aged scholarly clergyman Mr. Casaubon, who has spent his life researching what others vaguely understood to be "a great work concerning religious history" (33). Dorothea's choice of Casaubon also suggests her avoidance of her own adult sexuality. Her lack of interest in accepting her share of her mother's jewels (33–36) is perhaps symbolic of her delayed sexual development. When she learns that Sir James Chettam, who in the eyes of others is a far more appealing match than Casaubon, is in love with her, "The revulsion was so strong and painful in Dorothea's mind that the tears welled up and flowed abundantly. All her dear plans were embittered, and she thought with disgust of Sir James's conceiving that she recognized him as her lover" (59).

Dorothea's distaste for anything associated with sensuality is also suggested by her incapacity to appreciate works of art. During her wedding trip to Rome, she is unable to enjoy "the gigantic broken revelations of that Imperial and Papal city" (225). When she meets Will Ladislaw, an aspiring artist, in an art museum there, she tells him: "There are comparatively few paintings that I can really enjoy. At first when I enter a room where the walls are covered with frescoes, or with rare pictures, I feel a kind of awe—like a child present at great ceremonies where there are grand robes and processions; I feel myself in the presence of some higher life than my own. But when I begin to examine the pictures one by one, the life goes out of them, or else is something violent and strange to me" (238).

Perhaps Dorothea's most surprising trait, in light of her idealism and

The Vast Wreck of Ambitious Ideals in *Middlemarch*   145

her tendency toward renunciation, is her quick anger. When she finally agrees to accept only a ring and bracelet from her mother's jewels, she explodes at Celia's innocent question about whether she intends to wear them in public (36). She shows her "temper" again when Celia is critical of Casaubon after they first meet him (42). Soon after, when Celia, not knowing that Dorothea has become engaged to him, criticizes Casaubon again, "Dorothea's feelings had gathered to an avalanche" (72). Her anger soon becomes directed toward Casaubon himself. Even before their marriage, she grates at his statement that he "should feel more at liberty" to pursue his research if she would take along a companion on their wedding trip (113). After their marriage, she quickly becomes disillusioned about the value of his research, which never seems to result in any written conclusions. During their weeks in Rome she becomes "more and more aware, with a certain terror, that her mind was continually sliding into inward fits of anger or repulsion, or else into forlorn weariness" as she begins to perceive their marriage as an "enclosed basin" (228). Their first argument follows from Casaubon's sensitivity to Dorothea's urging him to "make up your mind what part of [your notes] you will use, and begin to write the book which will make your vast knowledge useful to the world." After their angry exchange, they are not able to speak further, and Dorothea, struggling with her feelings, yearns to get beyond her "anger and despondency" (235).

Upon their return to their home in England, the conflicts between Dorothea and her husband become focused on Ladislaw, who is Casaubon's cousin, the grandson of his mother's sister. When Ladislaw sends a letter, Casaubon tries to fend off a visit by telling Dorothea, "I trust I may be excused for desiring an interval of complete freedom from such distractions as have been hitherto inevitable, and especially from guests whose desultory vivacity makes their presence a fatigue" (316). The heated discussion that follows precipitates Casaubon's first "attack" (317), and afterward, as he is recovering, Dorothea naturally feels penitent (319). Lydgate tells her after he sees Casaubon that "anxiety of any kind would be precisely the most unfavourable condition for Casaubon" (323). After Casaubon himself finally asks Lydgate about his health, Dorothea, although not a party to the conversation, senses how he must feel, and approaches him in the garden. When she attempts to "[pass] her hand through his arm" (462), Casaubon rebuffs her advance. Her reaction is to feel "a rebellious anger stronger than any she had felt since her marriage" (463). "In such a crisis," we are told, "some women begin to hate" (464). Dorothea, however, struggles with her feelings, and, characteristically, manages to restrain herself. Later that night, when her husband comes upstairs from the library, she feels "something like the thankfulness that might well up in us if we had narrowly escaped hurting a lamed creature" (465).

Having learned the realities of the status of his health from Lydgate, and realizing that he will more than likely die before his "Key to All Mythologies" is complete, Casaubon attempts to persuade Dorothea to promise to finish it for him. Understanding that such a project would be a waste of time, she manages to postpone a reply until the next day, and then spends the night in a state of intense conflict (519–21). She finally decides that "she could not smite the stricken soul that entreated hers" (523)—yet he dies before she has time to assent to his request.

Carol Christ's observation that "Eliot repeatedly uses the device of providential death to avoid and prohibit aggression" in her characters (136) applies to the timing of Casaubon's death, which allows Dorothea to escape her impossible dilemma. Other critics have also addressed the issue of Dorothea's inhibited aggression. Kristin O. Lauer sees Dorothea as absorbing her rage toward Casaubon, who cannot possibly live up to her unrealistic expectations, in "ever more self-effacing suffering and martyrish, uncomplaining submission" (338). Sandra M. Gilbert and Susan Gubar also observe that Dorothea's outward compliance masks her indignation and scorn, and that she is terrified of the murderous potential of her anger (511). David Parker sees in the statement, "she could not smite the stricken soul that entreated hers," Dorothea's "fantasized violence towards Casaubon and fearful stifling of it" (73). Simon During, connecting the story of Laure's murder of her husband to Dorothea's submerged murderous thoughts toward Casaubon, asserts, "With [the psychiatric category of] monomania . . . murder is no longer a matter of conscious motives" (93); he suggests that Dorothea, no less than Rosamond, "murders" her husband.

Dorothea's "English and Swiss Puritani[cal]" upbringing has not prepared her for the "deep impressions" that the Roman "ruins and basilicas, palaces and colossi, set in the midst of a sordid present" make upon her during her wedding trip: "All this vast wreck of ambitious ideals, sensuous and spiritual, mixed confusedly with the signs of breathing forgetfulness and degradation, at first jarred her as with an electric shock, and then urged themselves on her with that ache belonging to a glut of confused ideas which check the flow of emotion. Forms both pale and glowing took possession of her young sense, and fixed themselves in her memory even when she was not thinking of them, preparing strange associations which remained through her after-years" (225). Dorothea's impressions, as Emery observes (155), suggest the oedipal child's reactions to the primal scene—the image of parental intercourse that Otto Fenichel describes as a "primal fantasy"—that is, a fantasy that will be produced in the mind whether or not the scene is actually witnessed (92). In his discussion of the Oedipus complex, Fenichel explains the effect of the loss of parents on a young child's development. He describes "a frequent and intense unconscious connection between the ideas of sexuality and death, the two being connected by the conception of 'secrets of the adults'; this may create an intense sexual fear, due to the idea that sexual fulfillment may bring death" (94).

In a conversation with Ladislaw on one of his visits in Rome, Dorothea speaks again of her incapacity to enjoy art: "The painting and sculpture may be wonderful, but the feeling is often low and brutal, and sometimes even ridiculous." She says that even when she sees something "noble," it only makes her feel "it the greater pity that there is so little of the best kind among all that mass of things over which men have toiled so." Then she says: "I see it must be very difficult to do anything good. I have often felt since I have been in Rome that most of our lives would look much uglier and more bungling than the pictures, if they could be put on the wall" (252). Ladislaw responds energetically: "You talk as if you had never known any youth. It is monstrous—as if you had had a vision of Hades in your childhood, like the boy in the legend. You have been brought up in some of those horrible notions that choose the sweetest women to devour—like Minotaurs" (253). Dorothea's "vision of Hades" that has destroyed her hope is her orphaned child's "unconscious connection between the ideas of sexuality and death" (because the parents who would normally be part of her oedipal drama are dead). Her reaction to the sights in Rome is a reexperiencing of her feelings of loss (of her parents) after her own wedding. The sexual inhibition that has caused her to choose an equally sexually inhibited husband (who secretly believed that "the poets had much exaggerated the force of masculine passion" [87]) is her self-punishment for her oedipal guilt; her marriage to Casaubon serves to repeat and reinforce her sense of loss.

Dorothea's association of sexuality with death also creates in her a sense of social isolation. At the funeral for old Mr. Featherstone (Rosamond and Fred's uncle), Dorothea associates the village scene with her experience in Rome: "Aloof as it seemed to be from the tenor of her life, [the funeral] always afterwards came back to her at the touch of certain sensitive points in memory, just as the vision of St. Peter's at Rome was inwoven with moods of despondency." As one of the "country gentry" Dorothea feels, like the oedipal child at the primal scene, isolated from the participants, in this case, the villagers at the funeral, and she is "not at ease in the perspective and chilliness of that height." The "dream-like association of something alien and ill-understood [the scenes at Rome, and the funeral scene in Middlemarch] with the deepest secrets of her experience seemed to mirror that sense of loneliness which was due to the very ardour of Dorothea's nature" (360).

Just as Lydgate's obsession with the actress in the murder scene reveals his psychological state, so Dorothea's preoccupation with the "degradation" in Roman art reveals hers; just as Lydgate watches his melodrama repeatedly, so Dorothea repeatedly returns to the scene of her own oedipal drama. The narrative begins to build toward another symbolic primal scene when Dorothea first sees Ladislaw with Rosamond at her house during Lydgate's absence—although, preoccupied with her thoughts of her husband, she soon dismisses her own "confusedly unhappy reaction" (472). Much later, after Casaubon's death, Dorothea finds them together again, this time in a suggestive attitude: "Close by [Ladislaw] and turned towards him with a flushed tearfulness which gave a new brilliancy to her face sat Rosamond, her bonnet hanging back, while Will leaning towards her clasped both her upraised hands in his and spoke with low-toned fervour" (832). Although Dorothea reacts with "jealous indignation and disgust," she is finally able, upon later reliving the scene in her mind, and "forcing herself to dwell on every detail and its possible meaning," to resolve her painful feelings. Then she looks out her window at the landscape, which includes "a man with a bundle on his back and a woman carrying her baby" and, in contrast to her sense of alienation at Featherstone's funeral, feels "a part of that involuntary, palpitating life" (845–46).

The Vast Wreck of Ambitious Ideals in *Middlemarch* 149

In Emery's view, Dorothea's confrontation of primal-scene emotions after she sees Ladislaw and Rosamond together "becomes a means of release from the defensive pattern established to deal with them" (178)—a release which then enables her to be "finally overcome by her passion for a man" (182). My own view, however, is that the presentation of Dorothea's resolution of her feelings is undercut by her return to the primal-scene situation again in the final love scene with Ladislaw.

During the scene with Ladislaw a storm gathers. The description of the storm suggests another symbolic primal scene, this time projected onto the natural world: "The evergreens . . . were being tossed, and were showing the pale underside of their leaves against the blackening sky" (867). At one point during the conversation between Dorothea and Ladislaw, "there came a vivid flash of lightning which lit each of them up for the other—and the light seemed to be the terror of a hopeless love. . . . and so they stood, with their hands clasped, like two children, looking out on the storm, while the thunder gave a tremendous crack and roll above them, and the rain began to pour down" (868). Rather than a portrayal of a passionate love scene between two adults, then, the scene conveys a picture of two innocent children joined together to watch the passionate storm at a safe distance.

Many critics have expressed dissatisfaction with the portrayal of the Dorothea-Ladislaw relationship. Barbara Hardy sees the portrayal as "incomplete," because of the author's denial of sexuality in their relationship ("Implication" 31). Others, as I suggested earlier, see Dorothea's marriage to Ladislaw as an inappropriate ending to the novel. Laurence Lerner questions whether Dorothea's "'active conscience and great mental need' would really be satisfied in marriage, even happy marriage" ("Dorothea" 244–45); John Kucich asserts that Dorothea's marriage to Ladislaw "abolishes her desires for an epic life" (57). The marriage allows her to continue her lifelong pattern of self-denial, as she gives up both her inheritance from Casaubon and her own vocational aspirations to become "absorbed into the life of another [who himself became an 'ardent public man,' eventually elected to Parliament], and . . . only known in a certain circle as a wife and mother" (894).

Brian Swann compares the structure of *Middlemarch* to the structure of a dream. He observes that "in the novel's multiform connective tissue

... each character possesses something of each of the others. They are 'various small mirrors' reflecting each other, and 'one life'" ("Realism" 302). I would add that Dorothea, Lydgate, Bulstrode, and Ladislaw, all orphans, are linked throughout the novel by their interconnecting enactments of the oedipal drama. Bulstrode acts out the oedipal wish by marrying his boss's widow, a much older woman, and gaining her inheritance by hiding the whereabouts of her daughter. Ladislaw enacts the oedipal son's hatred for the father and idealization of the mother by transferring his childish wishes onto Casaubon and Dorothea. Although Casaubon serves as a father figure for Ladislaw, both Casaubon and Ladislaw attempt to deny the father-son dynamic by repeatedly emphasizing to acquaintances that they are only second cousins, not uncle and nephew, as others typically assume. Will's decision to be independent of Casaubon, who had taken care of him and his mother after his father's death, only intensifies their hatred for each other (395). Ladislaw idealizes Dorothea with the same intensity that characterizes his hatred of Casaubon. Although he dislikes her at their first meeting at Lowick before her marriage because of her association with Casaubon, and because he thinks she is critical of his painting, his attitude changes when he sees her in Rome on her wedding trip. Suddenly her voice is "divine" to him. Once again, not wanting to acknowledge the father-son dynamic with Casaubon, he bristles when his friend Naumann calls her his "aunt," just as he had earlier bristled upon hearing Casaubon called his "uncle." Contemptuous of Casaubon for luring such a young woman into a marriage, Ladislaw sees her as "an angel beguiled" (241); hating Casaubon for this "virgin sacrifice," he himself wants to be her "slave" (396). In contrast to Rosamond, whom he sees simply as "altogether worth calling upon," Dorothea is the "perfect woman," of whom he is the "devout worshipper" (473–74).

Despite his hatred for Casaubon and his ardor for Dorothea, Ladislaw does not entertain "the ordinary vulgar vision . . . that Dorothea might become a widow" (509)—not only because he is "unwilling to entertain thoughts which could be accused of baseness," but also because he "could not bear the thought of any flaw appearing in his crystal: . . . there was something exquisite in thinking of her just as she was." In other words, part of Dorothea's appeal is that she is unattainable. Thinking of Dorothea as "forever enthroned in his soul," he determines to stay in Middlemarch to protect her from "whatever fire-breathing dragons might hiss around her" (510–11). Soon after, however, when he goes to church to get a glimpse of Dorothea with Casaubon, and then regrets causing her embarrassment, he realizes with pain just how inaccessible she is (513).

Although Ladislaw has no conscious wishes for Casaubon's death, his actions suggest that, like the oedipal child, he does everything he can to put a strain on the couple's marriage. When he calls on Dorothea in Rome, he wastes no time in letting her know that he thinks Casaubon's research is long out of date. Soon after, in their conversation about Dorothea's incapacity to enjoy art, he expresses his anger that she "will go and be shut up in that stone prison at Lowick" (253). He also explains in more detail, in answer to her question, his opinion of Casaubon's research. "It is no use now to be crawling a little way after men of the last century," he says almost brutally (255). Later, back in Lowick, again expressing his opinion that Dorothea should not be shut up in a gloomy house helping Casaubon with his research, he cannot refrain from verbalizing his opinion that Casaubon does not like anyone "to overlook his work" because he has so little self-confidence. He also asserts that Casaubon "dislikes me because I disagree with him" (400).

Ladislaw's story of his parents, too, is a disguised oedipal enactment; as he tells it, Dorothea listens "with serious intentness, like a child watching a drama for the first time" (402). The story also constitutes an internal allusion to the story of Laure, the actress who runs away after she murders her husband and is later found playing the role of a mother with a child in her arms. Ladislaw tells Dorothea that he remembers little about his father except "one day . . . when he was lying ill, and I was very hungry." His father had "made himself known to Mr. Casaubon, and that was my last hungry day. My father died soon after, and my mother and I were well taken care of." He goes on to say: "It is curious that my mother, too [like his grandmother], [had run] away from her family . . . to get on the stage. . . . She was a dark-eyed creature with crisp ringlets, and never seemed to be getting old" (401–2). Ladislaw's story, like Laure's drama, contains the oedipal fantasy that after the father dies, the child keeps the mother, forever enshrined as a young actress on his stage, to himself. As Dorothea listens to the story, she sees Ladislaw as Lydgate sees Laure (and later Rosamond): as an actor in her own oedipal drama—that is, as an extension of her own fantasies. Ladislaw is the child in Laure's drama, and Dorothea, like Lydgate, identifies with him. Thus after Casaubon's death she chooses to marry someone in her own situation: a psychological twin, who shares both her oedipal guilt and her longing for her lost mother.

If Dorothea "murders" Casaubon, then so does Ladislaw. A psychoanalytic reading of their story suggests that they are (symbolically) siblings who murder their father and who, lacking a mother, marry each other.

Esquirol defines monomania as a break in the unity of the psyche; During adds the explanation that "in monomania, will [is] separated from emotion, reason from will, emotion from reason" (88). As I indicated in the chapter on *Silas Marner,* the human mind may protect itself from the effects of trauma by isolating affect from event: a traumatic event may be remembered at the same time that feelings about it are repressed. Ladislaw's story of his father's death is an example: in his strictly factual account, there is no hint of grief or guilt, despite his association of his own better life with the loss of his father. The sequence of events in his story comes close to suggesting that his own good fortune *followed* from his father's death, yet he seems to feel no guilt. That he feels himself to be "a sort of gypsy . . . belonging to no class" (502), however, suggests the sense of alienation, albeit romanticized, that follows from loss. That his anger is frequent and explosive suggests the underlying rage that follows from narcissistic injury. His worship of Dorothea juxtaposed with his contempt for Casaubon, and later with his harsh judgment of Rosamond, suggests a split in the psyche that, according to During, also characterizes the "monomaniac." In Dorothea, there is a similar split between her anger and her idealism; in Bulstrode, who is aware that he has led "two distinct lives," between theory and action; in Lydgate, the scientist, between reason and emotion: he cannot apply his capacity for rational thought to his relationships with women.

Rose explains that "among the chief effects of trauma, the phenomena of psychic splitting stand out; and at the heart of mastery lies the matter of reintegration" (ix). He goes on to say that for the creative writer, "fictional characters, like doubles, also represent aspects of the self, split off and displaced to the outside world" (21). For the author of *Middlemarch,* who, like Ladislaw, idealizes Dorothea and judges Rosamond, and who assigns murders to Laure, Rosamond, and Bulstrode while absolving Dorothea and Ladislaw of even the thought of murder, creating a world in which all the characters' lives are closely interconnected is an attempt at reintegrating unacceptable impulses with idealized self and object images. It is also an attempt to fathom the source of the frightening impulses within herself—an attempt to discover her own "Key to All Mythologies." Fenichel writes of the oedipal fantasy of the child who has suffered parental loss: "If the parent of the same sex has died, this is felt as a fulfillment of the Oedipus wish, and that creates intense feelings of guilt. If the parent of the opposite sex has died, the frustrated Oedipus love most often creates a fantastic idealization of the deceased" (94). I would add that in the case of a female who loses a mother, the oedipal guilt is also accompanied by an (unconscious) "fantastic idealization" (representing longing) of her. The author's own oedipal fantasy, revived by her losses at later stages of her life, is not only displaced onto her male character, Lydgate, but is divided among the other characters. The author's fear of acting on the impulses that follow from her sense of loss is reflected in the way she portrays her characters acting on theirs. Laure, with no apparent motive, acts on her sudden impulse to murder her husband; her action is one of the crimes imitative of Cornier's impulsive murder of the child. Lydgate's acting out of his oedipal drama in his relationships with women is precipitated by Laure's murder of her husband; when his wish to kill his father seems to be fulfilled, he punishes himself by seeking out the murdering woman. Rosamond unconsciously "murders" Lydgate, with no apparent motive. Bulstrode, who has a motive for murder but intends not to, acts out his murderous wish by means of a Freudian slip. Only Dorothea, the idealized heroine (with her psychological twin Ladislaw), who represents both the idealized self and mother of the author's oedipal fantasy, is prohibited from acting on hers. The author's insistence on Dorothea's innocence reflects her fear of the possibility (as seen in the portrayals of the other characters) of acting on her own dangerous impulses.

The tone of *Middlemarch*, which ends Dorothea's story with her feeling that "there was always something better which she might have done, if she had only been better and known better," is "melancholy," as many critics, both Victorian and modern, have expressed it (Haight, *Biography* 446; Emery 142). I would argue that there is a connection between the sense of shared loss among the characters in the novel, and the sense of shared loss between Eliot and Lewes before and during the writing of

Middlemarch, which helps to explain the "melancholy" tone of the novel.

In January 1869, close to the time when Eliot was ready to start working on *Middlemarch*, she and Lewes heard from their twenty-five-year-old son Thornie, who had gone to Natal to make his living as a farmer, that he was suffering from severe and persistent pains in his back. Because of unexpected losses incurred on a recent hunting trip, he needed money to come home for medical treatment (Ashton, *GHL* 247–48). Lewes sent him the money right away, but despaired of the length of time it would take Thornie to receive his letter and make the trip back to England. At the end of January, Lewes's eighty-two-year-old mother, Mrs. Willim, became ill; Lewes visited her almost every day, until the end of February, when she seemed well enough for him and Eliot to leave England for a trip to the Continent. Their trip to Italy in March and April was cut short, however, largely because of Lewes's anxiety over his mother, but also because of bad weather, their own illnesses, and Lewes's increasing impatience with the annoyances of travel in Italy (Haight, *Biography* 415). They returned to England on May 5, and three days later, Thornie arrived, six weeks earlier than expected. Shocked at the severity of his illness, they called upon James Paget, Serjeant-surgeon-extraordinary to Queen Victoria, for help, but neither he nor J. R. Reynolds, an authority on disease of the nervous system, was able to diagnose the tuberculosis of the spine that was causing his trouble. For the six months until his death on October 19, as his condition slowly worsened, the best that could be done was to administer morphia for his pain (416-18). Their letters during the period reflect their ongoing concern over Thornie's suffering (*Letters* 5:34–60). During that time, Eliot, too distracted to do much work on *Middlemarch*, turned to writing poetry, "Brother and Sister," and "The Legend of Jubal," while sitting at Thornie's bedside; she was with him when he died (Haight, *Biography* 420–21). As she wrote in a letter dated December 10, "Death had never come near to me through the twenty years since I lost my Father, and this parting has entered very deeply into me" (*Letters* 5:71). She also wrote on November 25 that "I have a deep sense of change within, and of a permanently closer companionship with death" (5:70).

During the winter that followed, Eliot could do little writing; it took even longer for Lewes to recover his capacity to work on his *Problems of*

The Vast Wreck of Ambitious Ideals in *Middlemarch*   155

Life and Mind. In March they went again to the Continent, returning home on May 6. During the summer, spent in various places near the sea, Eliot wrote "Armgart," a poem that, according to Haight, reflects her "depression and 'almost total despair of future work'" (*Biography* 429). To add to her sense of despair, the Franco-Prussian War broke out in July 1870. She wrote on September 12: "We think of hardly anything but the War, and spend a great portion of our day in reading about it" (*Letters* 5:114), and on September 26: "I am getting more and more gloomy about the war" (8:488). The year ended with the death of Lewes's mother on December 10 (Haight, *Biography* 431). Although neither the Leweses nor their biographers dwell on this last event, it is hard to imagine, given Lewes's fondness for his mother and his still fresh grief for Thornie, that it would not have contributed substantially to their load of grief. Although Eliot wrote a friend that "this death has had none of the bitterness that belonged to the parting with Thornie" (*Letters* 5:131), the effect of their accumulated losses is evident in a statement written shortly thereafter, that "physically I feel old, and Death seems to me very near. The idea of dying has no melancholy for me, except in the parting and leaving behind which Love makes so hard to contemplate" (135).

That Eliot shared Lewes's grief over his losses of son and mother is also suggested by the self-described "Siamese-twin condition" of their relationship (3:27), which I believe had its basis from the beginning in their shared sense of loss. There are noticeable parallels in their backgrounds: Lewes's father had vanished to Bermuda shortly after his birth (Ashton, *GHL* 9); his two older brothers had died relatively young; he was very close to his mother (viii). Eliot's mother had virtually disappeared from her life after the deaths of twin siblings when she was a toddler; in her childhood, she had been very close to her father and brother. Lewes was estranged from his wife, and saw his children infrequently (although he continued to support them all); Eliot was estranged from her remaining siblings. The death of Thornie followed closely upon the twentieth anniversary of her father's death, and the tenth anniversary of her sister Chrissey's death. The intensity of Eliot's pain at the time of Thornie's death was more than likely, given the timing, associated with revived feelings about her own earlier losses; indeed, the oedipal enactments that pervade *Middlemarch* argue strongly that the loss of Thornie occurred in the context of revived feelings associated with the losses of other family members, particularly her father, whom she had also nursed for a long time while he was dying.

When Lewes and Eliot were in Rome during the spring of 1869, the year of Thornie's death, they met John Walter Cross (whom Eliot married after Lewes's death), "a tall, handsome fellow, twenty-nine years old," with his mother in Rome (Haight, *Biography* 415). The story in *Middlemarch* of Dorothea's meeting of Ladislaw in Rome suggests the possibility that as part of her anniversary reaction to her father's death, in keeping with the pattern she followed after 1849, Eliot once again found herself in an (imagined) oedipal triangle, this time attracted to the young John Cross. Richard Ellman, believing that Ladislaw has traits of both George Eliot and George Lewes, also believes that he has characteristics of John Walter Cross, "[who] must have delighted her" at the time of their meeting. "The contrast of Ladislaw's youth and Casaubon's age, of the passionate unscholarliness of the first and the uneasy ferreting of the second, would then be an idealized registration of the effect on George Eliot of her meeting with Cross. . . . Momentarily, even the beloved Lewes must have appeared to disadvantage beside this taller, handsomer, sharper-sighted, younger banker" (762). It could be argued that Dorothea's story, among other things, dramatizes the author's (unconscious) wish to be rid of the old husband and marry the young one— a fantasy that would repeat the oedipal enactment of taking the husband (her psychological twin) from the mother (Agnes) in her initial relationship with Lewes. Interestingly, as the real-life story evolved after Lewes's death in 1878, Ellman reports that "since Cross's mother and one of his sisters had died soon after Lewes, he and George Eliot could share each other's grief" (762). Thus her marriage to Cross in 1880, like her relationship with Lewes, seems to have had its basis in their shared sense of loss.

Dorothea and Lydgate, Eliot's "twin studies in defeated aspiration," punish themselves for their oedipal fantasies by choosing marriage partners who will put an end to their high ambitions. Their poor choices are a reflection of their psychological immaturity. Moreover, their psychological immaturity, judging from the work of psychoanalysts like Joyce McDougall and George H. Pollock, who stress the connection between mourning and development, is the result of their failure to complete the necessary process of mourning for their deceased parents. The interconnecting characters in the novel are in similar predicaments. Bulstrode, the orphan who aspires to be a missionary, gives up his vocation when he is offered the opportunity to join his rich friend's business; Ladislaw, the "gypsy" who aspires to be an artist, becomes instead "an ardent public man" after his marriage to Dorothea. Although the portrayal of the characters in *Middlemarch* reveals something of the author's own psychological dilemma, the quality and lasting success of her masterpiece also suggest that, despite her own melancholy over past and recent losses, both her fiction writing and her partnership with Lewes provided her with the means to fulfill her aspirations. Lydgate may have "always regarded himself as a failure," and Dorothea may have felt that "there was always something better which she might have done, if she had only been better and known better," but Eliot was able to say of her own accomplishment: "I have finished my book and am thoroughly at peace about it—not because I am convinced of its perfection, but because I have lived to give out what it was in me to give and have not been hindered by illness or death from making my work a whole, such as it is" (*Letters* 5:324).

Eliot seems to intend to portray her characters' growth into their acceptance of the realities of their lot, as they find their places in society. Dorothea, we learn in the "Finale," "never repented that she had given up position and fortune to marry Will Ladislaw" (894). The value of her life is seen in the "incalculably diffusive" effect of "her being on those around her." The author adds the final statement that "the growing good of the world is partly dependent on unhistoric acts; and that things are not so ill with you and me as they might have been, is half owing to the number who lived faithfully a hidden life, and rest in unvisited tombs" (896).

Yet the vision of society in Eliot's "one great novel of provincial life" is darker than the final assertion of "the growing good of the world" would suggest. The provincial society in the world of *Middlemarch* is actually portrayed as a tightly knit group of individuals, bound together by their shared sense of loss, and doomed to mediocrity. The group is seen as conspiring to inhibit the growth of any individuals, like Lydgate, who might have the potential to become extraordinary. When he enters the Middlemarch community, his attempts at reform are regarded with suspicion. One villager declares that "the most ungentlemanly trick a man can be guilty of is to come among the members of his profession with innovations which are a libel on their time-honoured procedure" (487), and another describes the new young doctor as "want[ing] to make a noise by pretending to go deeper than other people" (494). To judge from Eliot's portrayal of provincial society, the only way to achieve individual aspirations is to leave the group behind, as Eliot had left behind her own family and society. Moreover, the author's melancholy vision of society extends beyond the realm of the midlands village of Middlemarch. Seen through the eyes of Dorothea on her wedding trip to Rome, and portrayed in the limited lives and lost dreams of the characters in the symbolic world of *Middlemarch*, human life is too often "ugly" and "bungling," and human history, when it is done, leaves behind only a "vast wreck of ambitious ideals" set "in the midst of a sordid present."

SEVEN

The Pattern of the Myth of Narcissus in *Daniel Deronda*

Shortly after the completion of *Middlemarch,* George Eliot, visiting in Homburg, Germany, observed a young woman among a group of gamblers, "completely in the grasp of this mean, money-raking demon." As she wrote in a letter to her editor John Blackwood, "It made me cry to see her young fresh face among the hags and brutally stupid men around her" (*Letters* 5:314). The image of the young woman was destined to become the germ of her next novel, *Daniel Deronda,* which opens with her character Gwendolen, a young Englishwoman, in a similar scene. As in her earlier novels, Eliot tells the story of her individual character in the larger context of her place in society and history. In this last novel, *Daniel Deronda,* she relates her young Englishwoman's sense of alienation to the larger social theme of the alienation experienced by Jews in England and other Western European societies, by developing a set of Jewish characters whose lives intersect with Gwendolen's. According to Gordon Haight, the "lively concern with the idea of Jewish nationalism" that is evident in the novel had grown out of a friendship with Emanuel Deutsch, a cataloguer in the British Museum, whose own "enthusiasm for a Jewish national home" had developed out of visits to the Middle East in 1868 and 1869. His death in 1873 occurred just as Eliot was planning her new novel, and in Haight's view, influenced her portrayal of Mordecai, the dying scholar who inspires Deronda's decision to settle in Palestine (*Biography* 470–71).

Eliot added to her already substantial knowledge of Judaism her study of Hebrew history, language, and literature in preparation for writing the novel (472). For details for the English setting of "her only novel of contemporary life" (458), she and Lewes traveled to Wiltshire, including Salisbury, Stonehenge, Devizes, and Marlborough, where she gained "a

159

rich store of material to draw from for the background of *Daniel Deronda*" (475). For legal details, she consulted the lawyer Frederic Harrison, as she had done while she was writing *Felix Holt* (476). She made her first "Sketches towards *Daniel Deronda*" in early 1874; the writing was completed by June 1876. *Daniel Deronda* was published in eight parts during February-September of 1876. Throughout the writing of the novel, Eliot had characteristically experienced recurring depressions and ill health. At the same time, Lewes, in a more positive frame of mind, was working energetically on his *Problems of Life and Mind*, volume 2 of which was published early in 1875.

Blackwood's response to *Daniel Deronda* was enthusiastic from the outset, and continued to be so as he received each part of the manuscript (*Letters* 6:143, 144, 182, 221, 227, 239, 261, 262, 271, 295, 305). Among many other positive comments, he observed a new technique in Eliot's fiction writing that reflects her gift for psychological analysis; of her characterization of Gwendolen he wrote, "[Gwendolen's] running mental reflections after each few words she has said to Grandcourt are like what passes through the mind after each move at a game, and as far as I know a new device in reporting a conversation" (182). Upon receiving the last section of the book, he wrote Lewes: "Grand, glorious, and touching are too mild words for this last book. In fact criticism and eulogism are out of place. I feel more than ever what I have often said to critics: 'Bow and accept with gratitude whatever George Eliot writes'" (262). The successful sales of the book suggest that most readers agreed with him. As Haight notes, "The publication of this last of her novels marked the zenith of George Eliot's fame. She was regarded as the greatest living English novelist" (*Biography* 491).

Blackwood had also written at one point that he was "puzzling and thinking over [the Mordecai] phase of the Tale" (*Letters* 6:222). Indeed, some of Eliot's contemporaries were not only puzzled by but critical of what Barbara Hardy calls the "conspicuously ideological and symbolic" presentation of "the Jewish problem" ("Introduction" 10). Eliot was gratified, however, by letters from many prominent Jews, who appreciated the extent of her knowledge of Judaism and her positive portrayal of Jewish people. Among them were Dr. Hermann Adler, Rabbi of the Bayswater Synagogue; Haim Guedalla, one of the leaders of the Jewish community in London; Abram Samuel Isaacs, an American Jew at the Theological Seminary in Breslau; and Abraham Benisch, editor of the

The Pattern of the Myth of Narcissus in *Daniel Deronda*   161

Jewish Chronicle (Haight, *Biography* 486). It is worth noting also that Sigmund Freud held in high regard Eliot's portrayal of Jews in *Daniel Deronda*; he was amazed "by its knowledge of Jewish intimate ways that 'we speak of only among ourselves'" (Jones 116).

Although Eliot clearly intended "everything in the book to be related to everything else there" (*Letters* 6:290), the unity of the novel has been an issue among modern critics, many of whom, including F. R. Leavis and Ruby Redinger, have seen the novel as having two plots: the Gwendolen story and the Jewish story. Among the critics who have defended the novel's unity, however, are Nancy Pell, who has identified "the themes of patriarchal power and the daughters' resistance to it . . . in both parts of the novel" (432), and H. M. Daleski, who points to the motif of the forsaken child which ties together the stories of several of the characters. Daleski also makes the distinction, however, between the unity of the novel and "the striking discrepancy in the quality of the two parts into which the novel falls." He sees the Gwendolen part "as among the best things George Eliot ever did," and the Jewish part as "among the worst" (67). Defending the Jewish section of the novel as "the part that gives the entire work its unity and significance," however, Joan M. Chard notes that both Gwendolen and Deronda are "uncertain of their identities." She argues that "the personal quest for identity and vocation is linked in this novel with the historic and national consciousness of the Jewish people, whose journey out of exile through the wilderness to the promised land has become a paradigm of the human pilgrimage" (38). My purpose in this chapter is to show how psychoanalytic insights illuminate the novel, particularly the characterization of Gwendolen, and contribute to the discussions of the novel's unity. I also want to show how the portrayal of Gwendolen's resolution of her psychological dilemma may reflect Eliot's own resolution of conflict, as evidenced in the self-described loss of her "personal melancholy" (*Letters* 6:310) following the completion of her last novel.

Underlying the story of Gwendolen Harleth in *Daniel Deronda* is the pattern of the myth of Narcissus. At the beginning of the novel Gwendolen is a female Narcissus, self-centered and cold in her relationships with other men and women. Unlike the mythological Narcissus, however, who finally dies pining away for his own image, Gwendolen is cured of her narcissistic disorder and begins to grow into a mature adult with a capacity to care for herself and others. A consideration of both the myth and the psychoanalytic theories about narcissism can help readers appreciate the depth of insight into human motivation that informs Eliot's prepsychoanalytic creation of her most fully developed character, Gwendolen. The writings of Heinz Kohut and Otto F. Kernberg, in particular, whose theories represent the two contemporary schools of thought on the subject, support the idea that Eliot has portrayed in Gwendolen what a modern psychologist would call a narcissistic personality.

According to Ovid's version of the myth, Narcissus is an attractive sixteen-year-old, much admired, but unloving in return. One of many rejected youths prays that Narcissus might fall in love and "not win over/The creature whom he loves!" Nemesis, the Goddess of Vengeance, answers the prayer: Narcissus looks into a pool of water, falls in love with his own reflection, pines away, and dies, because he cannot separate himself from "that image/Vain and illusive" (68–73).

Gwendolen, like Narcissus, is much sought after. Her "glance" has a "dynamic quality" that attracts people to her (35). Yet however much she delights in being admired, she does not reciprocate. She does not like girls or women, because she finds them uninteresting. She attracts men to her, only to reject them; she does not want them to touch her. When Rex Arrowpoint attempts to tell her that he loves her and tries to "take her hand," she says, "Pray don't make love to me! I hate it!" (114). After she rejects Rex, she breaks down and sobs to her mother, "[W]hat can become of my life? There is nothing worth living for! . . . I can't love people. I hate them. . . . I can't bear anyone to be very near me but you" (115). She realizes, at least momentarily, that her contempt for others is a sign of a deficiency in herself.

The relatively recent (1980) introduction of the diagnostic category, "narcissistic personality disorder," in the *Diagnostic Manual* of the American Psychiatric Association "finally gave formal psychiatric recognition to the importance of the concept of narcissism in mental disorders" (Russell 138). The manual lists five interrelated diagnostic criteria (DMS-III 317), and Gwendolen displays all five. The first is her exaggerated sense of her own importance, which in Eliot's portrayal is one result of the way she is treated in her family. She is her mother's first and most favored child, the "pet and pride of the household." She thinks of her

The Pattern of the Myth of Narcissus in *Daniel Deronda* 163

four younger sisters, the children of her mother's second marriage, as "superfluous." She is in the habit of having her own way, and she is determined not to let anyone else interfere with her happiness (chapter 4).

Second are Gwendolen's fantasies of unlimited success, power, and beauty. In the opening scene at the gambling table, Gwendolen has "visions of being followed by a cortege who would worship her as a goddess of luck and watch her play as a directing augury" (39). She is accustomed to taking for granted "that she knew what was admirable and that she herself was admired" (40). Wherever she goes, she delights in the "homage" she receives from men, as "an indispensable and agreeable guarantee of womanly power" (68).

Third is her need for constant attention and admiration—a need reflected by her manner of participation in the charades at the neighborhood party in her family's new home at Offendene. When the group is trying to think of what show to put on, Gwendolen's only thought is to choose a scene that "suited her purpose of getting a statuesque pose in this favorite costume" (89). She insists on being the center of attention: there is to be "just enough acting of the scene to introduce the . . . music as a signal for her to step down and advance"; and the scene is to end with Leontes kneeling and kissing "the hem of her garment" (90).

Fourth are Gwendolen's feelings of rage, inferiority, humiliation, or emptiness in response to criticism or defeat. Many examples of this kind of reaction occur in the early sections of the novel. She resents Deronda in the opening scene because she thinks he is "measuring her and looking down on her as an inferior" (38). She feels "anger," "resistance," and "bitter vexation" when she learns she must come home because of the loss of the family fortune (45). She reacts with "the vexation of wounded pride" when Deronda buys back and returns to her the necklace she has sold (49). She feels humiliated when Herr Klesmer, an accomplished musician, tells her she doesn't have enough talent to be a successful actress. Without her former grandiose image of herself, she is left feeling empty and bored. "All memories, all objects" and even her own reflection in the glass "seemed no better than the packed-up shows of a departing fair" (306).

Finally, there is her sense of entitlement and lack of empathy. Instead of feeling sympathy for her mother when the family suffers the financial loss, Gwendolen feels sorry for herself, as "rightfully the chief object of her mamma's anxiety" (45). When Rex falls in love with her, she cannot understand what he feels because she has never experienced "painful love" herself (101). Moreover, when he has a fall from his horse, Gwendolen, unable to feel genuine concern for his welfare, thinks only of her own enjoyment of the ride.

According to contemporary psychoanalytic theory, a narcissistic disorder results from early childhood narcissistic injuries, or disappointments in love, which have been severe enough to interfere with normal development. Kohut and Kernberg differ as to whether the interference takes the form of developmental arrest or pathological development. Kohut defines the narcissistic disturbance as a fixation "on archaic grandiose self configurations and/or on archaic, overestimated, narcissistically cathected objects" (*Analysis* 3). Therapy involves a gradual strengthening of the "self," a process of "transmuting internalization" through which the self acquires the capacity to take over the functions that the archaic self-object formerly provided. Kernberg, on the other hand, argues that the interference is a pathological development, not a developmental arrest. He describes a process of "refusion" and "condensation" of "ideal self, ideal object, and actual self images" which enables the narcissistic personality "to deny normal dependency on external objects and on the internalized representations of the external objects" (231). The self-concept of such a person is a "fantasy construction which protects him from . . . dreaded relationships with all other people" (257). Kernberg also emphasizes the rage that is the reaction to early disappointments, and that becomes reactivated every time the person is "disappointed." Unlike Kohut, he believes that this rage must be confronted directly during therapy. Whether one sides with Kohut or Kernberg, the narcissistic disorder has to do with a person's difficulties in completing that separation between self and parent images which is necessary for a full adult life.

Eliot's rich portrayal of Gwendolen in the context of her family and society includes several injurious events and circumstances which could be said to contribute to the sense of abandonment and low self-esteem that underlie the haughty exterior of her narcissistic personality. Evidence in the text suggests, for example, that the death of Gwendolen's father has assumed an importance in her mind (as portrayed by Eliot) that is integral to her disorder, which so mysteriously combines coldness, fear, and rage. Her father had died when she was still in "long clothes" (52), and she has no memory of him. Knowledge of the effects of a missing parent on a child's development is not new to psychoanalysis. Fenichel describes three consequences: (1) an increased attachment to the remaining parent, usually ambivalent in nature; (2) a "frequent and intense unconscious connection between the ideas of sexuality and death," which "may create an intense sexual fear," or "even a masochistic trend in which dying (reunion with a dead parent) may become a sexual goal"; (3) the regression to the oral phase which accompanies mourning and which may imply (if it occurs at an early age) "permanent effects in the structure of the Oedipus complex and character." He gives an example of a woman patient "whose father had died when she was a baby [and who] had a tendency to hate everybody": men because none were like her idealized father, and women "because her mother had taken the father for herself, letting him die before the daughter had had any opportunity to enjoy him" (94).

Fenichel's remarks are appropriate to Gwendolen's situation. There are few references in the novel to her father, but they are significant. We learn that when Gwendolen was twelve years old, her mother had shown her a picture of her father, and recalled "with a fervour which seemed to count on a peculiar filial sympathy," the fact that "dear papa" had died when Gwendolen was a baby. Gwendolen, only able to think of the stepfather she had known throughout her childhood, changed the subject and asked her mother why she married again. "It would have been nicer if you had not," she said. Astonished, her mother said, "You have no feeling, child!" After this incident, Gwendolen, "hurt and ashamed," never again dared to ask a question about her father (52–53). Years later, after the stepfather's death and the family's subsequent move to Offendene, Gwendolen goes hunting by horseback one day without permission. When she and her mother discuss the incident afterward with Mr. Gascoigne, her mother asks her not to "do it again," and then turning to Mr. Gascoigne adds, "Her father died by an accident, you know." Gwendolen, "kissing her merrily, and passing over the question of the fears which Mrs. Davilow had meant to account for," says, "Children don't take after their parents in broken legs" (107–8). Once again, by avoiding the subject of her father's death, Gwendolen denies the importance of her loss. At Leubronn, when Gwendolen learns of the loss of the family fortune, she decides to sell a necklace made of turquoises "that had belonged to a chain once her father's. But she had never known her father; and the necklace was in all respects the ornament she could most conveniently part with" (48). Gwendolen's lack of feeling about her one tangible reminder of her father betrays her lack of awareness of any feelings of grief or loss over her father's death. Her willingness to sell the necklace constitutes a denial of his importance to her. Just before she goes out to sell the necklace, she has made her preparations to return home from Leubronn, and happens to look at herself in the mirror. Narcissus-like, she "sat gazing at her image . . . till at last she . . . leaned forward, and kissed the cold glass which had looked so warm. How could she believe in sorrow?" (47). The loss of the fortune is associated with and reactivates her sense of loss of her father, because in her life it is fathers who provide fortunes. She defends herself against this sense of loss by gazing at her image in the mirror.

The importance of the loss of her father is evident in many ways. Fenichel emphasizes the child's increased, yet ambivalent, attachment to the remaining parent. Gwendolen has not wanted to share her mother either with a new father or her "superfluous" sisters. Mrs. Davilow's "apologetic state of mind for the evils brought on her by a step-father" (71) reinforces Gwendolen's sense of entitlement. Yet her feelings about her mother are ambivalent. She frequently refers to her mother's "unhappiness," for example, upon their arrival at Offendene, when she says, "Can nobody be happy after they are quite young? You have made me feel sometimes as if nothing were of any use" (57). Gwendolen is attached to her mother, but she is also disappointed in her.

Fenichel also emphasizes the connection in the child's mind between the ideas of sexuality and death. Gwendolen's fear of death is surprising in its intensity, given her customary self-assurance. She is terrified by the "picture of an upturned dead face from which an obscure figure seemed to be fleeing with outstretched arms," which is discovered behind a panel of the wainscot when the family is exploring the drawing room in their new home at Offendene (56). When she first sees the picture, Gwendolen "shudders silently," and then turns her fear into an angry attack on her younger sister, who had opened the panel. But her reaction is less guarded the next time the panel is opened, accidentally, by a "thunderous chord" on the piano during the performance of the tableau. Gwendolen falls to her knees, trembling, and has to be led away from the group (91). Eliot comments on Gwendolen's recurring fears, "when, for example she was walking without companionship and there came some rapid change in the light. Solitude in any wide scene impressed her with an undefined feeling of immeasurable existence aloof from her, in the midst of which she was helplessly incapable of asserting herself" (94–95). Eliot does not offer any explanation for Gwendolen's fear of the painting, but the details of the intensity of her reaction, taken together with the information about her missing father, would suggest that Gwendolen identifies with "the obscure figure fleeing with outstretched arms" and that her unremembered father is the "upturned dead face." The connection between Gwendolen's fear of death and her fear of sexuality will become clear later in the discussion of her marriage to Grandcourt.

The subsequent losses in Gwendolen's life add to her sense of injury. Her father's remaining family does not supply any source of comfort; they are "so high as to take no notice of her mamma" (52). Nor is Gwendolen able to form any kind of attachment to her "unlovable" stepfather. Before his death he has "for the last nine years joined his family only in a brief and fitful manner, enough to reconcile them to his long absences." He has been effectively as absent as her original father, and Gwendolen apparently feels no grief at his death (52).

Another injurious circumstance in Gwendolen's life is her family's frequent household moves, apparently a result of her stepfather's (Captain Davilow's) occupation (52). Eliot comments: "A human life . . . should be well rooted in some spot of native land, where it may get the love of tender kinship for the face of earth. . . . [T]hat prejudice in favor of milk with which we blindly begin, is a type of the way body and soul must get nourished at least for a time" (50). With every household move, a child feels cut off from people and environment in the same way she has earlier felt cut off from a parent. It is significant that Eliot connects rootedness to a place with the attachment of a baby to its mother's breast. Melanie Klein has written that mourning reactivates the "infantile depressive position" that occurs when the infant reaches the stage of being able to recognize her mother as a "whole object." At that time the infant experiences what amounts to a loss of her mother as an external and internal object (Segal 126). The loss of a father during infancy would reinforce and be reinforced by this loss of the mother; and these losses would in turn be reactivated later by frequent household moves—the loss of familiar, comforting surroundings.

Eliot's portrayal of Gwendolen in her social setting provides still another reason for her sense of injury: her society's treatment of women. One comes away from the novel with a clear understanding of the Victorian woman's dependence on men—fathers, husbands, brothers, and uncles—not only for happiness and status, but for basic survival. Without a man, without a fortune, a woman's existence was precarious. Yet marriage was not necessarily a happy state. From Gwendolen's point of view, it meant putting one's life in the control of another person. She is well aware of her society's treatment of women, and she hates being a female. She says, "Girls' lives are so stupid: they never do what they like" (101). Consequently she devalues the women in the story who have produced only daughters (Mrs. Mallinger and her own mother, Mrs. Davilow). She also devalues the role of married women, generally, who she thinks lead "dreary lives." While she enjoys being sought after by men, she does not actually want to be married (68).

Gwendolen, then, having lost her sense of connection to her father, family, land, and society, suffers from a sense of abandonment and low self-esteem that underlies her egotistical behavior. Her hatred of others is a projection of her hatred of herself. Gwendolen's only real attachment, to her mother, is excessively close, as Nancy Nystul also suggests in her Kleinian analysis of her character (47). On her wedding day Gwendolen tells her mother that she will always love her "better than anybody else in the world" (403). As she later tells Deronda, "I was very precious to my mother—and he [Grandcourt] took me away from her" (837). Her mother feels the same kind of attachment to her, the "flower of her life." Yet her attitude, like Gwendolen's, is ambivalent. She both loves and fears her daughter: "Your will has always been too strong for me," she says (129).

In Kohut's terms, Gwendolen's overattachment to her mother amounts to a developmental arrest; she is unable to move toward the stage of adult female sexuality in which she can experience mature love. The depths of Gwendolen's attachment, as well as the ambivalence of her feelings, can be inferred not only from the scenes with her mother, but also less directly from her excessive guilt about Lydia Glasher, the mother of Grandcourt's children. Although Lydia does not appear very often in the novel, she is ever-present as the source of Gwendolen's torment. She becomes for Gwendolen a Medusa, or symbolic mother figure, who turns Gwendolen to stone in her relationship with

Grandcourt by claiming him, the father figure, for herself. Lydia convinces Gwendolen that Grandcourt is obligated to marry her, his former mistress, and make their son his heir. But Gwendolen's guilt about Lydia, who had left her own husband and first child to live with Grandcourt, is out of proportion to the actual situation. Neither Lydia nor Grandcourt has any love left from their old passion: Lydia wants to marry Grandcourt only for her children's sake (387), and Grandcourt gives up any intention of marrying Lydia before he meets Gwendolen (386), although he willingly continues to support her and the children. Gwendolen's torment derives in part from Grandcourt's failure to reassure her about his past relationship; she fears competing with a former attachment (343). But her excessive guilt also reflects a deeper fear. Internal allusions in the novel connect Gwendolen's fearful reactions to Lydia and to Grandcourt with her fear of the upturned dead face in the painting. At their first meeting at the archery match, Lydia wants Gwendolen to decide not to marry Grandcourt (189–90). At Ryelands on their wedding day, Gwendolen receives the diamonds and letter from Lydia (407). The details of the scenes at the archery match and at Ryelands "repeat and transform some of the elements" of the earlier scene in which Gwendolen reacts so violently to the painting (Poole 303–5). Thus Eliot connects Gwendolen's fear of the sight of Lydia and later of Grandcourt with her fearful reaction to the upturned dead face. The later "Medusa-apparition" scene, when Lydia deliberately appears with two of her children before Gwendolen and Grandcourt when they are out riding (668), evokes in Gwendolen a reaction that calls to mind the three earlier scenes and adds to the evidence of a connection between her fears about her dead father, which Thomas P. Wolfe emphasizes in his Freudian analysis of her character (28–29), and a less apparent fear of her mother. Gwendolen is shocked when Grandcourt ignores Lydia and the children; she realizes she would be in Lydia's socially isolated position if she took the step of separating from her husband: she feels trapped in the marriage. Grandcourt's visible abandonment of Lydia and her children reenacts Gwendolen's inner sense of abandonment: her father, by dying, has abandoned his wife and child. Moreover, Lydia's punishment of her for marrying Grandcourt enacts her childhood fear of her mother's punishment for desiring the father. After the Medusa scene, Gwendolen's rage at Grandcourt becomes nearly unbearable, as she begins to wish for his death, which seems to Gwendolen the only way out of her predicament. The wish for the father's death is associated with the fear of the mother's punishment.

Another aspect of Gwendolen's fixation is her dread of becoming a mother herself. Her guilt about Lydia (in this case over the possibility of causing Lydia's son to lose his inheritance) is again closely associated with the wish that Grandcourt might die (736). Eliot vividly describes the rage that Gwendolen feels when she is on the yacht with Grandcourt, who has her so firmly under his control.

And the intensest form of hatred is that rooted in fear, which compels to silence and drives vehemence into a constructive vindictiveness, an imaginary annihilation of the detested object, something like the hidden rites of vengeance with which the persecuted have made a dark vent for their rage, and soothed their suffering into dumbness. Such hidden rites went on in the secrecy of Gwendolen's mind, but not with soothing effect—rather with the effect of a struggling terror. Side by side with the dread of her husband had grown the self-dread which urged her to flee from the pursuing images wrought by her pent-up impulse. The vision of her past wrong-doing [taking Grandcourt away from Lydia], and what it had brought on her, came with a pale ghastly illumination over every imagined deed that was a rash effort at freedom, such as she had made in her marriage [737].

Gwendolen is simultaneously enraged with Grandcourt and terrified of her murderous impulses toward him. Furthermore, her rage at her husband and her guilt about her sexual impulses are intermingled. Eliot verbally links Gwendolen's "pursuing images wrought by her pent-up impulse" with the figures in the painting. Gwendolen is the figure fleeing from "the upturned dead face"—that is, from her own impulses (both incestuous and murderous) toward her dead father who has existed only in her imagination.

Pre-oedipal and oedipal conflicts are simultaneously at work. Contemporary psychoanalytic theory emphasizes the role of pre-oedipal issues in the resolution of the Oedipus complex. Melanie Klein was perhaps the first to see sexual development as "bound up with . . . object relations and with all the emotions which from the beginning mould [the child's] attitude to mother and father" (Klein 419). The Oedipus complex, she believed, begins to develop during the phase when the infant begins to perceive the mother as a whole object. "People are recognized . . . as individual . . . and as having relationships with one another; in particular, the infant becomes aware of the important link that exists between his father and his mother. This sets the stage for the oedipus complex" (Segal

103). Although other theorists may differ from Klein on the timing of the Oedipus complex, most, including Kohut, now emphasize the role of pre-oedipal conflicts in its resolution. As Kohut puts it, "Behind the oedipal disturbances lie flawed self-object responses" ("Introspection" 405). Gwendolen, because of the conditions of her life beginning in infancy and reinforced by later experience, is not able to move from the pre-oedipal to the oedipal attachment, resolve the Oedipus complex, and become an adult female with a capacity for mature love.

During their courtship, Gwendolen is mysteriously attracted to Grandcourt. She begins to feel "a wand over her" (158) in his presence; he appeals to her more than the other men she has met, and she is assuming that she will become engaged to him. After she learns of the relationship with Lydia, however, she feels that "all men are bad" (192) and determines not to marry him. When she returns to Offendene after her trip to Leubronn, Grandcourt resumes the courtship despite her family's financial loss. She realizes when he finally comes to propose that she does not want to let him go: she feels "alarm at the image of Grandcourt finally riding away. What would be left her then? Nothing but the former dreariness. She liked him to be there" (346). Although most critics assume that Gwendolen marries Grandcourt for financial reasons, the text makes it clear that her reasons for marrying him go deeper than her own and her mother's financial need, which Gwendolen herself recognizes as only an "excuse" (665) for the decision. When her mother says, "I trust you are not going to marry only for my sake," Gwendolen is "irritated at this attempt to take away a motive. Perhaps the deeper cause of her irritation was the consciousness that she was not going to marry for her mamma's sake—that she was drawn toward the marriage in ways against which stronger reasons than her mother's renunciation were yet not strong enough to hinder her" (357). Gwendolen and Grandcourt are like Narcissus and Echo. The roles are interchangeable: the Gwendolen who was once Narcissus is punished by Nemesis and becomes an Echo. She cannot let Grandcourt go. In Ovid's myth, Echo, punished by Juno for trying to cover up Jove's affairs with the nymphs, is able to say only "the last thing she hears" (*Metamorphoses* 68). She cannot start a conversation (i.e., she cannot take initiative), nor can she "fail to answer other people talking" (i.e., she is overly compliant). Echo is infatuated with Narcissus; she is also trapped inside herself, unable to express her feelings for him. She is forced by Juno into a passive role for encouraging Jove's affairs with the other nymphs. This is perhaps a disguised way of saying that Echo's own wishes about Jove, the father, are being punished by Juno, the mother. The punishment is a kind of passivity, representing castration or mutilation (or effectively, a degree of impotence or frigidity), like the punishment for looking at the Medusa (turning to stone). Gwendolen's mysterious attraction to Grandcourt is like Echo's infatuation for Narcissus: Gwendolen is attracted to Grandcourt *because* he has, and will continue to have, power over her. Gwendolen, passive in her relationship with him, is punishing herself for her own incestuous impulses. In marrying Grandcourt, Gwendolen is also reinforcing the pattern of male behavior that exists in her mind. Like her own father and stepfather, Grandcourt has left the woman who bore his children.

Grandcourt is attracted to Gwendolen for similar mysterious reasons. He wants to marry her, even though he is aware that she does not love him. Their personalities mirror one another; each is attracted to the other's pride and coldness. After their marriage he becomes increasingly domineering and jealous (of her friendship with Deronda), as she becomes increasingly paralyzed with fear, guilt, and anger. Each is trapped by the other. Grandcourt is Gwendolen's double, her mirror image, the "upturned dead face" in the portrait which causes her to "flee with outstretched arms."

In the story of Narcissus, the youth goes to a sheltered pool, surrounded by grass and untroubled by men or beasts. Here Narcissus looks into the pool and falls in love with the image that keeps him "spell-bound" (Ovid 70). The pool symbolically represents the sheltering mother. Narcissus is bound by an image that fuses himself and his mother; it is a shadow or memory of that time when they seemed to be one person. He finally dies an early death: he wanes slowly until nothing is left of his body.

Gwendolen is bound to Grandcourt as Narcissus is bound to his image. Otto Rank has written about the use of doubles in Western literature, in particular about the use of mirrors, shadows, portraits, and twins. This use of the double motif "appears an effluence of narcissistic ties, of self-infatuation, which, just as in the child, plays a large role among primitive peoples, and which we also see in the neurotic individual" (Erich Stern, qtd. in Rank xviii). Rank also emphasizes the connection between narcissism and the fear of death. He writes that "the idea of death . . . is denied by a duplication of the self incorporated in the shadow or in the reflected image" (83); and that often in literature a character will resort to suicide, which he carries out on his double, in order to escape this fear of death.

Gwendolen's look in the mirror is a defense against her sorrow—a denial of the importance of her loss of her father, and a denial of her own fear of death. She is looking at the combined image or fantasy of herself and her parents, to whom she is still psychologically attached. In other words, her self-image is a fantasy construction, a fusion and condensation of herself, her mother, and her missing father. By marrying Grandcourt, her double, she does not have to let go of her fantasy. Yet she also wants to slay the image that controls her. When Grandcourt drowns, Gwendolen later confesses to Deronda, "I saw my wish outside me" (761). She also refers to "a dead face" and says, "I shall never get away from it" (753). Once again, Eliot makes a connection with the "upturned dead face" (her father) in the portrait. Gwendolen's wish for Grandcourt's death is a disguised wish for her own death, the death of her fantasy construction—a death that represents her only hope of "release" from her dilemma. Narcissus says that death will take his trouble away; he pines away looking into a pool of water. Gwendolen has wanted her "trouble" to be taken away; Grandcourt dies by drowning in the "pool of water."

Gwendolen, released from the control of her double, lives to be cured of her disorder. Her growth is facilitated by Daniel Deronda, with whom she has a "transference" relationship, which, as Laurence Lerner ("Education" 361) and Eugene Hollahan ("Therapist" 65) also suggest, is like the relationship between patient and therapist. But Grandcourt is part of her "therapy" too. As Gwendolen's double, he is the first object of her transference. Gwendolen focuses on him all the rage that has resulted from her childhood narcissistic injuries. Through her relationship with him Gwendolen becomes acutely conscious of that rage, which Kernberg emphasizes must be confronted directly in therapy. After Grandcourt dies, Deronda plays the role of therapist who listens to her confession of her rage and her murderous impulses. Through Deronda, Gwendolen completes the transference: her infantile attachments have become reactivated; he becomes for her a fused and condensed symbol of both father and mother, a man "moved by an affectionateness such as we are apt to call feminine" (367). He is the first person apart from her mother that Gwendolen feels able to love. In the process of coming to care for Deronda, she is also moving toward a more realistic view of herself. Gwendolen experiences both the "idealizing" and "mirroring" transference, which Kohut says are two facets of the same developmental phase, and which may occur simultaneously or separately, and with differing degrees of emphasis, depending upon the individual in therapy (*Analysis* 107). In the idealizing transference, there is a "therapeutic activation of the omnipotent object" with whom the child attempts to remain attached (*Analysis* 37). In the mirroring transference, the "grandiose self" is reactivated. This is the phase in which the child attempts "to save the originally all-embracing narcissism by concentrating perfection and power upon the self" (*Analysis* 106). In Gwendolen's case, not only does she "fall in love" (idealizing transfer) with Deronda, but she also takes on a more realistic, yet also more positive self-image (mirroring transfer). In coming to know and love Deronda, Gwendolen is coming to know and love herself. Deronda is Kohut's "empathic therapist" who accepts her idealizing transfer, listens to her confession about her murderous impulses, eases her guilt about the cause of Grandcourt's death (764), and guides her toward a more realistic attitude toward herself, while at the same time assuring her of her potential to help others.

Part of the idealization is that Deronda serves as Gwendolen's superego, which is becoming integrated in her mind. This is a process of internalization which in a narcissistic personality has not yet been completed. As her superego, Deronda gives her advice when she needs it. When he advises her to be concerned about others she responds, "You mean that I am selfish and ignorant." Deronda does not deny her insight, but at the same time he encourages her growth: "You will not go on being selfish and ignorant" (502). Gwendolen comes to see all her actions through the impression they will make on Deronda. During her marriage, the thought of Deronda keeps her from "acting out the evil within" (746). After Grandcourt's death, she asks Deronda for advice about whether to accept any of the money left by his will; she wants "to secure herself against any act he would disapprove" (833).

Like a patient in therapy, Gwendolen imagines she is more important in Deronda's life than she really is. Their meetings have "a diffusive effect in her consciousness, magnifying their communication with each other, and therefore enlarging the place she imagined it to have in his mind" (647). Deronda responds to her too, however; he goes through a "countertransference." He is attracted to her, but realizes he must control his reactions while at the same time not abandoning her. He feels a "nervous consciousness that there was something to guard against not only on her account but on his own"; yet "her words of insistence that he 'must remain near her—must not forsake her' continually recurred to him" (683–84). He is strong enough not to have to avoid her; he accepts her idealization because he is genuinely interested in her welfare.

In working through the transference, Gwendolen must face the fact of Deronda's intended marriage to Mirah and his plans to go to Palestine. When she first learns about the marriage she is in despair. But just as a young female must accept the fact that her father belongs to her mother, so Gwendolen must accept the fact that Deronda belongs to Mirah. In coming to accept the reality of her impending separation from Deronda, Gwendolen is psychologically separating from her parents—a step that means her survival. Only by separating herself from their presence in her mind can she stop making herself the object of her own rage and murderous impulses. "I mean to live," she says to her mother after he leaves (879). Gwendolen has gone through a process like Kohut's "transmuted internalization" and become a more complete person.

Other characters in the novel are in situations that parallel Gwendolen's. Deronda must also resolve the question of his relationship to his parents. But unlike Gwendolen, he does not know who his real parents are. He must find them, confront the truth about them, and find a way to separate himself from his shadowed memory of them.

Until he finds and confronts his mother, Deronda is aimless, not yet settled on a vocation or marriage. His "many-sided sympathy" threatens "to hinder any course of action" (412). One aspect of this many-sided sympathy is his tendency to attach himself to people who need to be rescued. He spends so much time helping his friend Meyrick with his academic problems at Cambridge that he flunks out himself. He also rescues Mirah, whom he finds standing on the bank of a river, from suicide. Eliot connects his desire to rescue her with his search for his mother: "The agitating impression this forsaken girl was making on him stirred a fibre that lay close to his deepest interest in the fates of women—'perhaps my mother was like this one'" (231). Yet there is something beyond this need to rescue in his attraction to Gwendolen—"something due to the fascination of her womanhood." His imagination, at this point in the story, is "much occupied with two women, to neither of whom would he have held it possible that he should ever make love. Hans Meyrick had laughed at him for having something of the knight-errant in his disposition" (370). On the one hand, Deronda is a sensitive person who likes to help people. Yet on the other, he is something of a lady-killer. Like Gwendolen, he possesses that narcissistic quality of attracting and rejecting (in the sense of not seriously intending a relationship that can be permanent) the opposite sex. In his last scene with Gwendolen, when he finally "rejects" her by telling her he plans to marry Mirah, he recognizes his "cruelty" to her: "Deronda's anguish was intolerable.... 'I am cruel too, I am cruel,' he repeated" (877).

Deronda is also like Gwendolen in his sense of rootlessness. He does not know anything about his background, but as the novel progresses, he slowly discovers and accepts his Jewish heritage. The need to feel connected to a heritage and to a land is an extension of his original need for his mother. Deronda responds to the Jewish liturgy in the way that a child responds to its union with its mother: "the forms of the Judengasse, rous[ed] the sense of union with what is remote" (414). As Fenichel explains, "Certain narcissistic feelings of well-being [for example, religious or patriotic feelings] are characterized by the fact that they are felt as a reunion with an omnipotent force in the external world.... The longing [for such a connection] can be called the 'narcissistic need'" (40).

When Deronda finally finds his mother, he must confront her rejection of him. She says, "I did not wish you to be born. I parted with you willingly" (697). She explains that she rejected both the role of motherhood and her Jewish heritage because of her father's oppression of her. She is like Gwendolen in this: because she feels oppressed by a male-dominated culture, she has no interest in the customary female role. "I am not a loving woman," she says. She has also, like Gwendolen, been a femme fatale. "Men have been subject to me," she says (730). She is only able to be in male-female relationships in which one person has power over the other. The passage in which Deronda meets his mother occurs just before the scene in which Gwendolen, on the boat with Grandcourt, recognizes the full strength of his control over her, along with her own dread of becoming a mother. The two situations are parallel: a father's oppression is a factor in the "failure" of a daughter's "maternal instinct."

After Deronda directly confronts his mother's rejection, he becomes free of her hold on his mind. He can then find that "blending of personal love in current with a larger duty" (685) that he has been looking for. "I have always longed for an ideal task" (819), he tells Mordecai. He accepts his Jewishness; he helps Gwendolen, but lets her know the boundaries of their relationship; he proposes to Mirah; he takes on Mordecai's ideals and plans to go to the Middle East to work to establish a new state of Israel. He has succeeded in curing himself and finding the right combination of circumstances that will serve in his life as a substitute for the mother he never had.

Mirah's situation parallels both Gwendolen's and Deronda's. In her childhood her father has literally taken her away (from England to the Continent) from her mother, just as Gwendolen's marriage to Grandcourt has symbolically taken her away from her mother. At the time the novel takes place, Mirah is back in England looking for her mother. Like Deronda, she must face the reality of the loss of her mother—in her case, her mother's death; she must also "forgive" her father (by taking him into her household) before she is psychologically free to marry. She associates her Jewish religion and heritage with her mother and is able to find through it a satisfactory substitute, which, along with her marriage to Deronda, will serve throughout her life. Through this heritage she is able to retain her feeling of union with her mother: "If I got wicked I should lose my world of happy thoughts where my mother lived with me" (254). She associates her mother with her ideals: "When the best thing comes into our thoughts, it is like what my mother has been to me" (523).

Mordecai's situation parallels Gwendolen's, Deronda's, and Mirah's. In his case, an early death is the outcome of a life of oppression and rejection. He has been waiting for someone like Deronda, through whom his own life can be completed and extended after he dies. He refers to Deronda as "his new self" (551); and Deronda is described as "receptive" to him. His ties to his heritage and to his religion, which he passes on to Deronda, are substitutes for his attachment to his lost mother. He and Mirah, brother and sister, are psychological doubles, as are Gwendolen and Grandcourt. Mordecai, Mirah's double, dies, and Mirah is released to achieve psychological maturity on her own.

A principle source of the unity of *Daniel Deronda*, then, is in the psychological situation of the characters. Each must find a way to leave behind old, disappointing parental images and find replacements that will be sustaining throughout adult life.

The novel also illustrates what happens to the "maternal instinct" when a woman feels oppressed and/or abandoned by men. This brings us back to the myth of Narcissus. According to Ovid's version of the story, Narcissus's mother, the naiad Liriope, was raped by Cephisus, the river-god. Narcissus's birth is the result of the rape—a situation that implies both male dominance and male abandonment—feelings about which a mother, left without a mate, would all the more intensely transfer onto a child. Narcissus's "disorder" derives at least in part from the parenting of a mother who feels oppressed and abandoned, and yet is likely to be all the more closely attached to him because she has no husband or other children. Narcissus is also the child of a missing father. A child in this situation, suffering from grief, anger, and fears about his loss, defends himself by inventing a father in his mind to replace the one he has not had. Narcissus is not able to separate himself from a fantasy construction that includes the self, mother, and imagined father of his infancy. To be unable to separate self from parental images is to be unable to grow. Gwendolen, whose psychological situation parallels Narcissus's, is cured of her disorder. In the process of transferring her parental images onto Grandcourt and Deronda, she is able to separate herself from them: Grandcourt drowns and Deronda marries someone else. In working through the transference, Gwendolen comes to see herself clearly as she really is, and not as the image or fantasy construction she had formerly projected of herself. Her growing self-knowledge is her path to maturity.

Some critics, like Evelyn Butler, have interpreted the outcome of the novel as a punishment for Gwendolen, who is left alone after she loses Deronda. Eliot's intention to show that Gwendolen ultimately gains from her loss is clear in her response to Blackwood's positive assessment of the proofs of the first 256 pages of the novel: "It will perhaps be a little comfort to you to know that poor Gwen is spiritually saved, but 'so as by fire'. Don't you see the process already beginning? I have no doubt you do, for you are a wide-awake reader" (*Letters* 6:188). Besides reflecting Eliot's psychological acuity regarding the necessary losses entailed in the process of human growth, the novel, with its unconventional ending, reflects a "more acute assessment of marriage and of marriage plots" than do the "conventional modes of closure employed by the [Victorian] novel's standard love-plots," as Joseph Allen Boone expresses it (65–73). Other critics also view the novel as more "modern" than her earlier works. In his study of *The Novel and Society*, Grahame Smith sees in *Daniel Deronda* the beginnings of a movement away from "the great European achievement of the social novel." He observes that Eliot's last novel moves outside English society to a "wider international perspective" (210), at the same time that it marks the shift toward the portrayal of the "interior landscape" that characterizes the modern novel (212). Noting the connection between Gwendolen's inner world and the English society presented by the author, Smith also sees in Eliot's portrayal a "total rejection of her society" (209). Jean Sudrann, also emphasizing Eliot's sense of alienation, suggests that "George Eliot felt her own alienation in terms more 'modern' than Victorian, that she sought to define that experience by making it the central subject of her last novel, the only one to have a contemporary setting, and that she then had to bend to new uses the conventional forms of the novel to express the new subject matter" (433). As Sudrann interprets the ending, Gwendolen is left "solitary, certainly, and aware" for the first time of the "vastness" of the world beyond herself (454); and, "Her kindly parting from Deronda, releasing him from responsibility, shows a new—if feeble—action of will in 'asserting herself' in the immensity." In her view, Gwendolen "has passed through a crisis of alienation so that she may possess her self" (455).

After the publication of *Daniel Deronda*, Eliot wrote her lifelong friend Sara Hennell on her fifty-seventh birthday (November 22, 1876): "It is remarkable to me that I have entirely lost my *personal* melancholy. I often, of course, have melancholy thoughts about the destinies of my fellow-creatures, but I am never in that *mood* of sadness which used to be my frequent visitant even in the midst of external happiness. And this, notwithstanding a very vivid sense that life is declining and death close at hand" (*Letters* 6:310). Eliot's statement suggests the possibility that by the time *Daniel Deronda* was completed, she had experienced in herself at least a partial resolution of the sense of loss that she portrays in her character Gwendolen.

Joseph Weisenfarth explains that Eliot's "formal structure in which the dynamics of personal development proceed" seems indebted to Goethe's idea, expressed in the German epigraph of chapter 39, of placing oneself "before a wise man." He observes that "Gwendolen places herself before Deronda and he serves her, reluctantly, in the role of wise man; indeed, he becomes her Daniel. Deronda, in turn, places himself before Mordecai who serves him, willingly, as a wise man; he becomes his Ezra. The understanding that these wise men have of their charges leads to the regeneration of both Gwendolen and Deronda. They experience a 'transmutation of self'" (*Notebook* xxxviii). Weisenfarth notes that the phrase "transmutation of self" is used in the novel by Deronda to explain the legend of the Buddha who, upon seeing a tigress unable to feed her young, offered his body to be devoured by them. Deronda interprets the story to a group of friends, including Mirah, as "an extreme image of what is happening every day—the transmutation of the self" (523). In this scene Eliot's characters attempt to put into words the idea that is dramatized both in the legend of the Buddha and in the story of Gwendolen and Deronda. I would suggest that George Eliot's last novel, *Daniel Deronda,* enacts that painful process of the author's own self-transmutation, which she ultimately achieved through the creation of her works of art. To put it in psychoanalytic terms, the artist, during the creative process, enters into a transference, or fantasy, through which she can reenact and attempt to rework her own past. Through the process of Kohut's "transmuted internalization" she can, like Gwendolen in her relationship with Deronda, strengthen herself by reworking the missing elements in her experience of her parents. Through this process, her rage is diminished, and her "personal melancholy" eased, as her identity as an artist is achieved. Perhaps like Gwendolen, the author had, through the writing of her fiction, finally "passed through [her] crisis of alienation so that she [might] possess herself."

Conclusion

At the end of 1877, the year of Blackwood's publication of the "Cabinet Edition" of George Eliot's works, Eliot wrote in her journal:

Today I say a final farewell to this little book which is the only record I have made of my personal life for sixteen years and more. I have often been helped by looking back in it to compare former with actual states of despondency from bad health or other apparent causes. In this way a past despondency has turned to present hopefulness. But of course as the years advance there is a new rational ground for the expectation that my life may become less fruitful. The difficulty is, to decide how far resolution should set in the direction of activity rather than in the acceptance of a more negative state. Many conceptions of works to be carried out present themselves, but confidence in my own fitness to complete them worthily is all the more wanting because it is reasonable to argue that I must have already done my best. In fact, my mind is embarrassed by the number and wide variety of subjects that attract me, and the enlarging vista that each brings with it [*Letters* 6:440].

By June 1878, Eliot was writing *Impressions of Theophrastus Such*, a collection of eighteen essays on a variety of subjects, "connected only through the fictitious narrator," as Haight explains it (*Biography* 521). Upon reading the first chapter of the manuscript received in November, Blackwood was "delighted with it. . . . It is so readable, and clear as profound" (*Biography* 7:79–80). By this time, however, Lewes was seriously ill. His death followed soon, on November 30. Grief-stricken, Eliot decided to delay the publication of the essays; as she wrote Blackwood in January, "To me now the writing seems all trivial stuff." She agreed to correct the proofs, however, and have them "laid by for a future time" (93).

During the period immediately following Lewes's death, Eliot would not see anyone except their son Charles. After a week of reading for consolation, she set herself the task of completing Lewes's *Problems of*

Life and Mind, by "revising and putting in order for the press such portions of his manuscript as are at all in a state for publication" (7:115); it was published before the end of the year. By April she had also begun her plan to establish a studentship in Lewes's name "to supply an income to a young man who is qualified and eager to carry on physiological research and would not otherwise have the means of doing so.... I have been determined in my choice of the Studentship by the idea of what would be a sort of prolongation of *His* life. That there should always, in consequence of his having lived, be a young man working in the way he would have liked to work, is a memorial of him that comes nearest to my feeling" (128). Meanwhile, at Blackwood's urging, *Theophrastus* was to be published in May. By July, he wrote that "the splendid success of Theophrastus has been a most satisfactory thing to watch" (181). It had taken about six months before Eliot was able to resume interest in her own life. Yet she marked the first anniversary of Lewes's death by recording in her journal for the date November 29: "Reckoning by the days of the week, it was this day last year my loneliness began. I spent the day in the room where I passed through the first three months [after his death]. I read his letters, and packed them together, to be buried with me. Perhaps that will happen before next November" (7:227).

During the year following Lewes's death, Eliot's friendship with the twenty-years-younger John Cross, who had been a close family friend and financial advisor, had blossomed. Cross himself wrote later that beginning in April 1879: "I saw George Eliot constantly. My mother had died in the beginning of the previous December—a week after Mr. Lewes; and as my life had been very much bound up with hers, I was trying to find some fresh interest in taking up a new pursuit. Knowing very little Italian, I began Dante's 'Inferno' with Carlyle's translation." When Eliot learned of his interest, she offered to read with him, and they proceeded through the "Inferno" and the "Purgatorio" together. "The divine poet took us into a new world," Cross wrote. "It was a renovation of life" (7:139). By April 1880, the two had decided to marry. Although Eliot, fearing the disapproval of relatives and friends, had waited until close to the wedding date (May 6) to inform them, the response was entirely warm and enthusiastic. Even her brother Isaac wrote, "I have much pleasure in availing myself of the present opportunity to break the long silence which has existed between us, by offering our united and sincere congratulations" (280). Eliot responded, "It was a great joy to me to have your kind words of sympathy, for our long silence has never broken the affection for you which began when we were little ones" (287).

Although Eliot was well during their wedding trip to the continent, the occasion was marred by Cross's illness on June 16 in Venice, where he was reported to have jumped from the balcony of their hotel into the Grand Canal. Cross himself ascribed the cause to "this continual bad air, and the complete and sudden deprivation of all bodily exercise," although Haight concludes that his illness (from which he soon recovered) was "an acute mental depression" (*Biography* 544). Following their return to England in early August, Eliot wrote Charles by the end of the month that "Johnnie gets a little better every day, and so each day is more enjoyable. But I am decidedly less well than I was when abroad. There is something languorous in this climate or rather in its effects" (*Letters* 7:318). She became ill in September. Her health deteriorated quickly, and she died on December 22, "from failure of the powers of the heart supervening on a bad cold," as Cross wrote that night (350).

On the wedding trip Eliot had written her good friend Barbara Bodichon of her marriage as "a wonderful blessing falling to me beyond my share after I had thought that my life was ended. . . . Deep down below there is a hidden river of sadness but this must always be with those who have lived long—and I am able to enjoy my newly re-opened life" (7:291). Although judging from the tone of this and other letters, she was delighted with the love and companionship afforded by her new marriage, her life in England after the wedding trip was taken up with social visits and moving—activities which she had never enjoyed. There is no sign of any further plans for writing. The timing of her death, shortly after her sixty-first birthday, and shortly after the second anniversary of Lewes's death, suggests the extent of her identification with Lewes, who was also sixty-one when he died. Her sense of completion after the writing of *Daniel Deronda*, and her prophetic remark about her burial, "Perhaps that will happen before next November," also suggest her readiness for death. Her fiction writing career had coincided with her life of "dual solitude" with Lewes.

In the preceding chapters I have focused on some of the ways in which aggression is portrayed in George Eliot's novels. In *Adam Bede*, the interconnecting characters in the village of Hayslope express aggression indirectly in their victimization of Hetty; the individuals' sense of inadequacy is transformed into the group manifestation of narcissistic rage. In *The Mill on the Floss*, Maggie's narcissistic rage, which derives from her sense that she is devalued by her family and society, is transformed into her misuse of sexual power in her relationships with males when she becomes a young adult. In *Silas Marner*, the protagonist's compulsive weaving and hoarding contain the rage that is the reaction to his sense of loss. In *Romola*, extreme forms of aggression appear in Tito's treachery, Baldassarre's revenge, and Savonarola's visions of doom. In *Felix Holt*, the protagonist's political conservatism reflects his fear of the possibility of acting on his own aggressive impulses. In *Middlemarch*, Laure, Rosamond, and Bulstrode, each in a different way, act out their murderous impulses. In *Daniel Deronda*, Gwendolen's rage is evident in the incapacitating fear that is the source of her sexual inhibitions. I have argued that the author's denial of aggression in the idealized characters in the novels is an aspect of the defensive process of psychic splitting that is the human response to trauma. I have also argued that George Eliot's creative work was her constructive response to the trauma of loss.

On the basis of Mahler's studies of separation-individuation and Bowlby's studies of attachment, separation, and loss, I have suggested that Eliot's mother, suffering from her own loss of her twin infants in March 1821, was unable thereafter to focus adequate attention on the needs of her toddler, the young Mary Anne Evans. As I explained in the chapter on *Silas Marner*, there is no evidence either of Mary Anne's early interactions with her mother, or of her later memories of her; the correspondence from the two years following her death is missing, and Eliot rarely mentioned her mother in the years following. The patterns in the fiction, however, taken together with the facts of her biography, suggest an early sense of disconnection from her mother that was associated in her mind with the deaths of the twins, and later, with the deaths of each of her parents. Her early sense of disconnection also seems to have established in her behavior a self-reinforcing tendency to alienate herself from the rest of her family, and from her society.

Although Mary Anne's early childhood close attachment to her brother Isaac and her affectionate relationship with her father apparently served to compensate for the loss of closeness to her mother, her reaction to the experience of being sent away from the family to boarding school at age five was, as suggested by Bowlby's findings on the cumulative effects of childhood separations (2:52), no doubt exacerbated by her earlier experience. At the end of her life she still remembered the time at the boarding school as marking the beginning of her "low general state of health," her "fears at night," and the "liability to have 'all her soul become a quivering fear,' which remained with her afterwards [and] had been one of the supremely important influences dominating at times her future life" (Cross 8-9). Her remarks suggest that her early childhood separations contributed to a chronic state of anxiety from which she never fully recovered. That her early emotional separation from her mother was linked with the deaths of the twins also suggests that Eliot's own mourning over the loss of siblings, as well as her inevitable guilt, and her anxieties about the possibility of her own death, were combined with her separation anxiety. On the basis of Bowlby's studies of the effects of family loss on children, then, one could say that every time there was a new death in the family, the old state of mourning would be revived and intensified (3:160). Eliot's unresolved mourning for lost family members appeared in the form of the "intense sadness," for example, that marked the period of her life when she was struggling to begin writing *Romola*; her attempt to resolve her sense of loss is evident in *Silas Marner*, the story which intruded on her at that time.

Although Eliot's early emotional separation from her mother undoubtedly influenced the course of her later development, this circumstance of her life should be seen in the context of her experience of her whole family, as well as her experience of her society, as Kohut's theory would suggest, and as Eliot herself presents human development in her novels. The post-Freudian emphasis in psychoanalytic theory on the preoedipal period of development, and therefore on the important role of the primary attachment figure in the child's developing sense of identity, has resulted at times in what is now recognized to be unwarranted "mother-blaming." To blame Eliot's later problems, including her anxiety and depressions, on her mother's apparent depression in her early life would be a distortion of the realities of the complexity of human development; to do so would ignore, for example, the role of inborn traits that may have shaped her response to her environment. That Eliot subsequently identified with her father more than her mother was actually beneficial to her in a society which generally withheld educational and vocational opportunities from women; her sister Chrissey, who was said to be her mother's favorite of the two girls, and who had apparently identified with her mother, died young, after fulfilling the expected female role of marriage and child-bearing. Eliot's observation of her mother's and her sister's experience no doubt contributed to her skepticism about marriage and motherhood; her experiences with the Brays and the Chapmans contributed further to the development of her unconventional ideas. Yet, although she apparently had no desire to have children herself (Haight, *Biography* 205, 533; Eliot, *Letters* 5:52), she took pride in middle age in her role as step-mother to Lewes's children, and she seemed to be warmly attached to them, just as she remained deeply attached to Lewes, who became her lifelong partner, even though he was not able to become her husband.

Rose has observed that fictional characters "represent aspects of the self, split off and displaced to the outside world" (21). I would add that fictional characters may also represent images of others, which may be confused with images of the self. While a novel is a projection of its author's psychological state, the projection can be seen in more ways than one. In *Adam Bede*, for example, the idealized Dinah expresses interest in Hetty, but disappears until it is too late to help her. Besides reflecting in the two characters the author's conflicting images of herself, the novel, which was begun only a few months after Eliot's estrangement from her family, may also reflect the image of her relationship with her sister Chrissey, the beautiful daughter who had married a year after their mother died, leaving Mary Ann with the job of taking care of her father's household. Mary Ann had described Chrissey early in her marriage, as her troubles began to accumulate, as "meek and passive," perhaps in contrast to herself. Later, after her own life as a fiction writer had begun, Eliot continued to express concern for Chrissey, but (by informing the family of her relationship with Lewes) precipitated her own banishment (or disappearance) from Chrissey's life close to the date of her wedding anniversary, and just as the condition of her health was becoming serious.

Images of Chrissey also appear in *The Mill on the Floss*, in the beautiful, favored cousin Lucy, whose fiancé Maggie steals, and in Mrs. Moss, Mr. Tulliver's sister, "a patient, loosely-hung, child-producing woman," who in her brother's view had "quite thrown herself away in marriage and had crowned her mistakes by having an eighth baby" (*Mill* 139, 136). In *Middlemarch*, more positive memories of Chrissey take form in

Celia, Dorothea's level-headed (but by implication, more ordinary) sister. Images of Eliot's brother Isaac take shape not only in Tom in *The Mill on the Floss*, but also in the domineering best friend William Dane in *Silas Marner*, who betrays Silas by stealing his fiancée and causing his banishment from their religious community. In *Romola*, feelings toward Isaac are suggested in the character of the longed-for, dying brother Dino, who has been free to pursue his vocation as a friar, while the long-suffering *Romola* has taken full responsibility for their aging father. Dino dies early in the story, as *Romola*, the stronger of the two, eventually finds a way to live her life without a brother or a father.

Memories of Eliot's father, recalled from her early childhood, appear in the idealized carpenter, Adam Bede; images of the aging, dying father appear in the demanding Mr. Tulliver in *The Mill on the Floss* and in Bardo and, in much more distorted form, in Baldassarre in *Romola*. Images of Eliot's mother seem to be rare. As Haight observes, "Of [Eliot's] feeling for her mother one can gather little. Inferences drawn from the mothers in her novels are dangerous [because of the lack of evidence about Eliot's relationship with her]" (*Biography* 6). Although we cannot draw conclusions about the details of her early interactions with her mother, the author's experience of her mother's incapacitating sense of loss following the twins' deaths when she was a toddler is suggested by little Eppie's experience of the mother who is too incapacitated by her addiction to care for her young child; the author's experience is also suggested by the narrator's direct comment in *Felix Holt* about the "blank discontented face" remembered from early childhood that "found it hard to smile." More frequently, the author's longing for the lost mother is evident in the excessive idealizations of some of the heroines, like Dinah, Romola, and Dorothea, which suggest, in the light of Fenichel's explanation of the effects of missing parents on children, Bowlby's evidence of the effects of parental death on adolescents, and Kernberg's object relations theory of pathological narcissism, the author's fusion of her idealized self-image with the idealized image of the mother. The less extreme idealizations of the working men *Adam Bede* and *Felix Holt* also suggest the author's identification with the lost father.

Both George H. Pollock and David Aberbach stress the fact that Freud began writing *The Interpretation of Dreams*, in which he recounts his discovery of the Oedipus complex, in response to the death of his father in 1896. As Freud himself wrote, the book was "a portion of my own self-analysis, my reaction to my father's death—that is to say, to the most important event, the most poignant loss, of a man's life" (qtd. in Aberbach 44). Freud wrote much later, in 1931, that the work contains "even according to my present-day judgment, the most valuable of all the discoveries it has been my good fortune to make. Insight such as this falls to one's lot but once in a lifetime" (Brill 181). Pollock observes that it was about a year after his father's death that "Freud announced two elements of the Oedipus complex, the love for one parent and jealous hostility to the other" (115). Pollock suggests that "we see here in dramatic fashion a superb illustration of my hypothesis that the successful completion of the mourning process results in a creative outcome" (116). He also suggests that the creative works of individuals in a variety of fields, including the arts, may represent not only resolutions, but also "aspects of the mourning process itself" (127).

George Eliot's creative works reflect aspects of her own mourning process. A study of her life in relation to her fiction reveals a network of anniversary manifestations that reflect the organizing effect on her behavior of the repetition-compulsion in reaction to associated traumas. I have concluded that her decision to write fiction in 1856, twenty years after her mother's death, signified the beginning of her release from mourning—the point at which she was able to resume the psychological growth that had been interrupted by her unmourned traumatic losses. I also believe that the publication of *Daniel Deronda* in 1876, twenty years later, signified, if not the completion of the mourning process, then at least the fulfillment of her identity as an artist.

In her novels, Eliot repeatedly tells the story of a young, idealized heroine, typically about seventeen years old, who struggles to grow into adulthood, and whose success in doing so is contrasted with the failure of an extremely immature and/or villainous character. I would argue that this repeating pattern reflects the author's own attempts to grow beyond her fixation on the scene of her mother's death, which had occurred when she was sixteen. That Eliot began her life of dual solitude with Lewes at about age thirty-four also suggests the repetition in the author's life of seventeen-year cycles as part of her attempt to master the trauma of maternal loss. In another seventeen years, following Thornie's death, Eliot would conceive out of two separate works "one great novel of

Conclusion 189

provincial life," *Middlemarch*, which became her masterpiece, and which, through the stories of its interconnecting characters, including Lydgate, who could not escape the scene of his father's death, reflected her mind's attempt to integrate emotions and events.

I would argue that *Romola*, which Eliot conceived in 1860 and began to write in 1861, reenacts not only the period in Eliot's life following her move to London after her father's death, when she became infatuated by turns with Chapman, Spencer, and Lewes (1851–53), but also the period following Isaac's marriage and the move from the family home at Griff to Coventry in 1841. During that time, the expression of rebellion against her family that had been directed primarily at Isaac (in the form of her somber Calvinism) shifted to her father, when Mary Ann made the apparently sudden decision to reject Christianity altogether. Mary Ann's shifting infatuations, from her evangelical friend Maria Lewis to her free-thinking friend Charles Bray, beginning in 1841, and for the scholarly Dr. Brabant in November 1843, reflected her sense of dislocation, as well as her attempts to find replacements for her brother and her father. The move from Griff on March 17, 1841, was also very close to the twentieth anniversary of the births of Eliot's twin siblings on March 16, 1821. The household move and the loss of Isaac to marriage would thus be associated with the loss of the newborn twins and the painful separation from the mother that had followed. The associated traumas were relived again in the form of Marian's banishment from Chapman's household in London on March 24, 1851. Eliot completed *Silas Marner*, through which she reenacted the loss of parents and siblings, in March 1861. She returned to her research for *Romola*, which reenacts her sense of disconnection and loss, in April 1861. In writing these novels, Eliot was demonstrating that she had learned to attempt mastery of her traumas by creating works of fiction, rather than by repeatedly acting them out in her personal life, as she had done ten and twenty years earlier.

Marian's affair with Lewes in 1853 began about ten years after the incident with Dr. Brabant in 1843, when Brabant's wife and sister had sent Mary Ann away from their household. The banishment from Victorian society that resulted from her choice of Lewes was the culmination of a long-term pattern of banishments: from the Chapman's household, from the Brabant's household, from her father's household during their "Holy War"—all of which I believe echoed her sense of banishment from her mother's company following the twins' deaths. The significance for the author of the dates and numbers used in *Felix Holt*, which tells the story of an election riot that she had witnessed at age thirteen, and which, as a symbol of "radicalism," she apparently associated with her elopement with Lewes (thirteen years prior to the novel's publication date), suggests her guilt over her choice of a married man, the traumatic effects of her subsequent banishment from family and society, and, judging from her emphasis on Felix's capacity to control his rage through the use of words, her determination to stop "acting out the evil within" (*Deronda* 746).

Writing of his early observation of anniversary reactions, Freud describes a woman who had sick-nursed her husband (and other loved ones before him) until his death, and who afterward "celebrated annual festivals of remembrance at the period of her various catastrophes, and on these occasions her vivid visual reproduction and expressions of feeling kept to the date precisely" (2:163). Explaining her delayed reactions, Freud writes that besides the effects on the body of self-neglect and constant worry during the nursing period, there are the effects of "suppressing every sign of [her] own emotion." If the sick person dies, "and the period of mourning sets in . . . these impressions that have not yet been dealt with come into the picture as well" (162). Eliot had helped with nursing her mother as she was dying, and she had been wholly responsible for the care of her dying father. She was also at Thornie's bedside during the last months of his life. My analysis of *Middlemarch*, the work conceived shortly after Thornie's death (and twenty years after her father's death), suggests that the predominance of oedipal dramas in the novel follows from the intensity of the author's reaction to her revived sense of loss. Her preoccupation with murderous wishes in her characters reflects her fear, as portrayed in Bulstrode, of the possibility of acting on the powerful impulses that comprise the reaction to the loss of loved ones. Freud explains in his essay on anxiety that the human mind associates the infant's anxiety over separation and loss with the young child's (castration) anxiety of the oedipal period (20:138). By way of extending Freud's argument, I would add that the anxiety that accompanies the later loss of a loved one is also accompanied by a revival of oedipal fantasies, and moreover, that losses that occur before the oedipal period are associated with oedipal fantasies retroactively. Freud's own experience after his father's death, when he discovered the Oedipus complex as he analyzed his own dream material, is an example of how the mind associates loss with the oedipal drama. The conflicting love-hate (or longing and anger) impulses that are aroused in response to the adult's renewed sense of the child's loss of love take the form in the imagination of the oedipal fantasy: in response to the trauma of loss, the overwhelming love-hate impulses are split between the two parents and disguised as a drama in dreams and creative works.

Eliot's shifting infatuations in 1841 and 1851 reenacted the inner conflicts of her childhood; her novels dramatize them. In *The Mill on the Floss*, Maggie's shifting involvements with men reflect her attempts to grow beyond her intense childhood attachment to her brother, who had served as a substitute for both her parents. In *Romola*, the motherless title character leaves her marriage to Tito (her brother's replacement) at the same time that she grows out of her subjection to Savonarola (her father's replacement) to become the head of a family herself. In *Daniel Deronda*, Gwendolen reworks, in the transference with Deronda, the missing elements in her experience of her parents. The reward for her acceptance of the reality of her loss of Deronda is her sense of a separate self, gained through a process of "transmuted internalization." Eliot's novels thus illustrate Kohut's idea that the resolution of the Oedipus complex should be seen in the context of the development of a firm sense of self.

The young Mary Anne Evans's shaky sense of identity is suggested both by her name changes and their timing. If it is true that she changed the spelling of her name to Mary Ann on the day of her sister's wedding, then the timing would suggest a sense of dislocation brought on by her sister's departure from the household. The next change in the spelling of her name, to Marian, also suggests a connection to her sense of dislocation following her move to London in the spring of 1851, which was also the tenth anniversary of the move to Coventry before Isaac's marriage. Finally, the choice of the pseudonym, George Eliot, was made in 1856, the anniversary of her mother's death, and suggests her new sense of identification with Lewes. As she explained later to Cross, she chose the name because "George was Mr. Lewes's Christian name, and Eliot was a good mouth-filling, easily pronounced word" (Haight, *Biography* 220).

The timing of major events in the Evans family also suggests the possibility that each individual's anniversary reactions reflected a shared sense of loss among family members. Isaac married in the spring of 1841, the twentieth anniversary of the twins' deaths. Mr. Evans's decision to move with Mary Ann to Coventry on March 17, close to the day of the births on March 16, taken together with the timing of Isaac's decision to marry, suggests the possibility of the family's shared reaction to the earlier loss. Mr. Evans died on May 31, 1849, close to the date of the twelfth anniversary of Chrissey's wedding on May 30, 1837. Chrissey died on March 15, 1859, close to the day of the twins' births, the year of the tenth anniversary of her father's death, and as she was approaching the age of her mother when she died; thus the date of her death apparently combined reactions to three earlier family losses. Eliot's family pattern of interacting reactions to loss was perpetuated in her life with Lewes, whose background of family loss mirrored hers. Moreover, the pattern was reinforced when their son Thornie died soon after the twentieth anniversary of Mr. Evans's death. Eliot herself died close to the anniversary of Lewes's death, and at the same age. Her sense of loss was also shared by her husband John Cross, who had lost his mother close to the time when Eliot had lost Lewes. I would argue that Eliot's perception of the network of reactions to loss among family members is projected onto the web of interconnections among the characters in the world of *Middlemarch*, whose shared sense of loss is reflected in their network of oedipal dramas. Eliot's marriage to Cross, which can be seen as a reenactment of her own oedipal drama in response to Lewes's death, suggests an incomplete resolution of her lifelong psychological dilemma. However, a study of her life in relation to her fiction also shows how creative work provides a vehicle for mastery of trauma, even if the results are incomplete.

In Bowlby's view, anger is bound up with the anxiety reaction to loss and/or separation from attachment figures. In Kohut's terms, rage is the response to narcissistic injury, or to any experience that the mind interprets as loss of love. Kohut also believed that the rage will disappear as the structures of the self are completed by the process of "transmuted internalization." Eliot's sense of completion after the writing of *Deronda*, along with the disappearance of her symptoms of depression, suggest that she achieved through her creative work the strengthening of the sense of self that Kohut describes. The body of Eliot's fiction as a whole enacts her vision of the human potential for growth that she attempted to portray in her novel *Felix Holt*. The rapid artistic, intellectual, and personal growth that is evident in the progress of her novels leaves the reader with the sense of "life releasing itself from integument"—a feeling that reflects the psychological reality of the process of the author's gradual release from her state of mourning. Although we cannot know with certainty how completely Eliot ultimately resolved her sense of loss, it is apparent that in the attempt she achieved her position as an eminent English novelist, as well as her own clear sense of personal fulfillment. Her life, by any measure, was a personal and professional success.

Works Cited

Aberbach, David. *Surviving Trauma: Loss, Literature and Psychoanalysis.* New Haven: Yale University Press, 1989.
Akhtar, Salman, N. N. Wig, V. K. Varma, Dwarka Pershad, S. K.Verma. "Phenomenological Analysis of Symptoms in Obsessive-Compulsive Neurosis." *British Journal of Psychiatry* 127 (1975): 342–48.
Alexander, F. "Remarks about the Relation of Inferiority Feelings to Guilt Feelings." *International Journal of Psycho-Analysis* 19 (1938): 41–49.
Ashton, Rosemary. *George Eliot.* Oxford: Oxford University Press, 1983.
———. *G. H. Lewes: A Life.* Oxford: Clarendon Press, 1991.
Bamber, Linda. "Self-Defeating Politics in George Eliot's *Felix Holt.*" *Victorian Studies* 18 (1975): 419–35.
Barrett, Dorothea. *Vocation and Desire: George Eliot's Heroines.* New York: Routledge, 1989.
Beaty, Jerome. *"Middlemarch" from Notebook to Novel: A Study of George Eliot's Creative Method.* Urbana: University of Illinois Press, 1960.
Beer, Gillian. *George Eliot.* Bloomington: Indiana University Press, 1986.
Bonaparte, Felicia. *The Triptych and the Cross: The Central Myths of George Eliot's Poetic Imagination.* New York: New York University Press, 1979.
———. *Will and Destiny: Morality and Tragedy in George Eliot's Novels.* New York: New York University Press, 1975.
Bonaparte, Marie. "Time and the Unconscious." *International Journal of Psychoanalysis* 21 (1940): 427–68.
Boone, Joseph Allen. "Wedlock as Deadlock and Beyond: Closure and the Victorian Marriage Idea." *Mosaic* 17 (1984): 65–81.
Bowlby, John. *Attachment and Loss.* 3 vols. New York: Basic Books, 1982, 1973, 1980.
Brill, A. A., ed. *The Basic Writings of Sigmund Freud.* New York: Modern Library, 1965.
Butler, Evelyn. "*Daniel Deronda:* Why is Gwendolen Punished?" *Recovering Literature* 6 (1977): 51–65.
Carroll, David. "*Felix Holt:* Society as Protagonist." *Nineteenth-Century Fiction* 17 (1962): 237–52.

Works Cited

Carroll, David, ed. *George Eliot: The Critical Heritage*. New York: Barnes & Noble, 1971.

Caserio, Robert L. "The Featuring of Act as 'The Rescue': Story in Dickens and George Eliot." In *Plot, Story, and the Novel*. Princeton: Princeton University Press, 1979.

Chard, Joan M. "'A Lasting Habitation': The Quest for Identity and Vocation in *Daniel Deronda*." *The George Eliot Fellowship Review* 15 (1984): 38–44.

Chessick, Richard D., M.D. *Psychology of the Self and the Treatment of Narcissism*. Northvale, N.J.: Jason Aronson, 1985.

Christ, Carol. "Aggression and Providential Death in George Eliot's Fiction." *Novel* 9 (1976): 130–40.

Coen, Stanley J., "Sexualization as a Predominant Mode of Defense." *Journal of the American Psychoanalytic Association* 29 (1981): 893–920.

Cohen, Susan R. "History and Metamorphosis: Continuity and Discontinuity in *Silas Marner*." *Texas Studies in Literature and Language* 25 (1983): 410–26.

Coveney, Peter. "Introduction." In *Felix Holt, The Radical*. New York: Penguin Books, 1972.

Creeger, George. "An Interpretation of *Adam Bede*." *Journal of English Literary History* 23 (1956): 218–38.

Cross, J. W. *George Eliot's Life As Related in Her Letters and Journals*. Arranged and edited by her husband, J. W. Cross. New Edition. New York: AMS Press, 1965.

Daleski, H. M. "Owning and Disowning: The Unity of *Daniel Deronda*." In *Daniel Deronda: A Centenary Symposium*. Ed. Alice Shalvi. Jerusalem: Jerusalem Academic Press, 1976.

Diagnostic and Statistical Manual of Mental Disorders. 3d ed. (DSM-III). American Psychiatric Association, 1980.

Dodds, M.H. "George Eliot and Charles Dickens." *Notes and Queries* 190 (1946): 143–45.

Donovan, Robert Alan. *The Shaping Vision: Imagination in the English Novel from Defoe to Dickens*. Ithaca, N.Y.: Cornell University Press, 1966.

Draper, R. P., ed. *George Eliot: "The Mill on the Floss" and "Silas Marner."* Casebook Series. London: Macmillan, 1977.

During, Simon. "The Strange Case of Monomania: Patriarchy in Literature, Murder in *Middlemarch*, Drowning in *Daniel Deronda*." *Representations* 23 (1988): 86–104.

Edwards, Michael. "A Reading of *Adam Bede*." *Critical Quarterly* 14 (1972): 205–18.

Eliot, George. *Adam Bede*. Ed. Stephen Gill. New York: Penguin, 1980.

———. *Daniel Deronda*. Ed. Barbara Hardy. New York: Penguin, 1967.

———. *Felix Holt, The Radical*. Ed. Peter Coveney. New York: Penguin, 1972.

———. *The George Eliot Letters*. 9 vols. Ed. Gordon S. Haight. New Haven: Yale University Press, 1955–78.

———. *Middlemarch*. Ed. W. J. Harvey. New York: Penguin, 1965.

———. *The Mill on the Floss*. Ed. A. S. Byatt. New York: Penguin, 1979.
———. *Romola*. Ed. Andrew Sanders. New York: Penguin, 1980.
———. *Silas Marner*. Ed. Q. D. Leavis. New York: Penguin, 1967.
Ellman, Richard. "Dorothea's Husbands." *Middlemarch*. Norton Critical Edition. Ed. Bert G. Hornback. New York: Norton, 1977.
Emery, Laura Comer. *George Eliot's Creative Conflict: The Other Side of Silence*. Berkeley: University of California Press, 1976.
Ermarth, Elizabeth. "George Eliot's Conception of Sympathy." *Nineteenth-Century Fiction* 40 (1985): 23–42.
———. "Maggie Tulliver's Long Suicide." *Studies in English Literature* 14 (1974): 587–601.
Esquirol, Etienne. *Mental Maladies. A Treatise on Insanity*. Transl. E. K. Hunt, M.D. Philadelphia: Lea and Blanchard, 1845. Facsimile intro. Raymond de Saussure. New York: Hafner, 1965.
Fairbairn, W. R. D. *Object Relations Theory of the Personality*. New York: Basic Books, 1954.
Fenichel, Otto. *The Psychoanalytic Theory of Neurosis*. New York: Norton, 1945.
Ferguson, Suzanne C. "Mme. Laure and Operative Irony in *Middlemarch*: A Structural Analogy." *Studies in English Literature* 3 (1963): 509–16.
Freud, Sigmund. *The Standard Edition of the Complete Psychological Works of Sigmund Freud*. 24 vols. London: Hogarth, 1953–74.
Fulmer, Constance Marie. "Contrasting Pairs of Heroines in George Eliot's Fiction." *Studies in the Novel* 6 (1974): 288–94.
Garrett, Peter. *Scene and Symbol from George Eliot to James Joyce*. New Haven: Yale University Press, 1969.
Gay, Peter. *Freud: A Life for Our Time*. New York: Doubleday, 1989.
Gilbert, Sandra M., and Susan Gubar. *The Madwoman in the Attic: The Woman Writer and the Nineteenth-Century Literary Imagination*. New Haven: Yale University Press, 1979.
Graver, Suzanne. *George Eliot and Community: A Study in Social Theory and Fictional Form*. Berkeley: University of California Press, 1984.
Greenberg, Jay R., and Steven A. Mitchell. *Object Relations in Psychoanalytic Theory*. Cambridge, Mass.: Harvard University Press, 1983.
Greenstein, Susan M. "The Question of Vocation: From *Romola* to *Middlemarch*. *Nineteenth-Century Fiction* 35 (1981): 487–505.
Gregor, Ian. "The Two Worlds of *Adam Bede*." In *The Moral and the Story*. In collaboration with Brian Nicholas. London: Faber, 1962.
Haight, Gordon S. *George Eliot: A Biography*. New York: Penguin, 1985.
———. *George Eliot and John Chapman: With Chapman's Diaries*. New Haven: Yale University Press, 1940.
———, ed. *A Century of George Eliot Criticism*. Boston: Houghton Mifflin, 1965.
Hamilton, Edith. *Mythology*. New York: New American Library, 1942.
Hardy, Barbara. "Implication and Incompleteness in *Middlemarch*." In *Particu-

larities: Readings in George Eliot. Athens, Ohio: Ohio University Press, 1982.
———. "Introduction." *Daniel Deronda.* New York: Penguin, 1967.
———. "Life and Art in *The Mill on the Floss.*" In *"The Mill on the Floss" and "Silas Marner."* Casebook Series. Ed. R. P. Draper. New York: Macmillan, 1977.
———. *The Novels of George Eliot: A Study in Form.* London: Athlone, 1959.
Harris, Mason. "Arthur's Misuse of the Imagination: Sentimental Benevolence and Wordsworthian Realism in *Adam Bede.*" *English Studies in Canada* 4 (1978): 41–59.
———. "Infanticide and Respectability: Hetty Sorrel As Abandoned Child in *Adam Bede.*" *English Studies in Canada* 9 (1983): 177–96.
Harvey, W. J. *The Art of George Eliot.* London: Chatto & Windus, 1963.
———. "Criticism of the Novel." In *Middlemarch: Critical Approaches to the Novel.* New York: Oxford University Press, 1967.
———. "Introduction." In *Middlemarch.* New York: Penguin, 1965.
Herbert, Christopher. "Preachers and the Schemes of Nature in *Adam Bede.*" *Nineteenth-Century Fiction* 29 (1975): 412–27.
Hollahan, Eugene. "Therapist or The Rapist?: George Eliot's *Daniel Deronda* as a Pre-Freudian Example of Psychoanalysis in Literature." *Journal of Evolutionary Psychology* 5 (1984): 55–68.
Insel, Thomas R., ed. *New Findings in Obsessive-Compulsive Disorder.* Washington, D.C.: American Psychiatric Press, 1984.
Johnstone, Peggy Fitzhugh. "Loss, Anxiety, and Cure: Mourning and Creativity in *Silas Marner.*" *Mosaic* 25 (1992): 35–47.
———. "Narcissistic Rage in *The Mill on the Floss. Literature and Psychology* 36 (1990): 90–109.
———. "The Pattern of the Myth of Narcissus in *Daniel Deronda.*" *University of Hartford Studies in Literature* 19 (1987): 45–60.
———. "Self-Disorder and Aggression in *Adam Bede*: A Kohutian Analysis." *Mosaic* 22 (1989): 59–70.
Jones, Ernest. *The Life and Work of Sigmund Freud.* Ed. and abr. Lionel Trilling and Steven Marcus. New York: Basic Books, 1961.
Kernberg, Otto F. *Borderline Conditions and Pathological Narcissism.* New York: Jacob Aronson, 1975.
Kettle, Arnold. "*Felix Holt, The Radical.*" In *Critical Essays on George Eliot.* Ed. Barbara Hardy. London: Routledge and Kegan Paul, 1970.
Kitchel, Anna Theresa, ed. *Quarry for Middlemarch.* Berkeley: University of California Press. (Supplement to *Nineteenth-Century Fiction,* 1950.)
Klein, Melanie. *Love, Guilt and Reparation and Other Works, 1921–45.* New York: Dell, 1975.
Knoepflmacher, U. C. "George Eliot." In *Victorian Fiction: A Second Guide to Research.* Ed. G. H. Ford. New York: Modern Language Association, 1978.
———. *George Eliot's Early Novels: The Limits of Realism.* Berkeley: University of California Press, 1968.

Kohut, Heinz. *The Analysis of the Self.* New York: International Universities Press, 1971.

———. *How Does Analysis Cure?* Ed. Arnold Goldberg with Paul Stepansky. Chicago: University of Chicago Press, 1984.

———. "Introspection, Empathy and the Semi-circle of Mental Health." *International Journal of Psychoanalysis* 63 (1982): 395–407.

———. *The Restoration of the Self.* Madison, Conn.: International Universities Press, 1977.

———. "Thoughts on Narcissism and Narcissistic Rage." In *The Psychoanalytic Study of the Child*, vol. 27, Quadrangle Books. New York: *New York Times*, 1973.

Krieger, Murray. "*Adam Bede* and the Cushioned Fall: The Extenuation of Extremity." In *The Classic Vision: The Retreat from Extremity in Modern Literature.* Baltimore: Johns Hopkins University Press, 1971.

Kucich, John. "Repression and Dialectical Inwardness in *Middlemarch*." *Mosaic* 18 (1985): 45–62.

Laski, Marghanita. *George Eliot and Her World.* London: Thames and Hudson, 1973.

Lauer, Kristin O. "His Husband/Her Wife: The Dynamics of the Pride System in Marriage." *Journal of Evolutionary Psychology* 6 (1985): 329–39.

Leavis, F. R. *The Great Tradition.* New York: Stewart, 1950.

Lerner, Laurence. "Dorothea and the Theresa-Complex." *George Eliot: Middlemarch, A Casebook.* Ed. Patrick Swinden. London: Macmillan, 1972.

———. "The Education of Gwendolen Harleth." *Critical Quarterly* (1965): 355–64.

Levine, George. "*Romola* as Fable." In *Critical Essays on George Eliot.* Ed. Barbara Hardy. London: Routledge and Kegan Paul, 1970.

Lewes, George. *Problems of Life and Mind* (1879). *Significant Contributions to the History of Psychology, 1750–1920.* Vol. 6. Washington, D.C.: University Publications, 1977.

McDonnell, Jane. "'Perfect Goodness' or 'The Wider Life': *The Mill on the Floss* as Bildungsroman." *Genre* 15 (1982): 379–402.

McDougall, Joyce. "Parent Loss." In *The Reconstruction of Trauma: Its Significance in Clinical Work.* Ed. Arnold Rothstein. Madison, Conn.: International Universities Press, 1986.

Mahler, Margaret S. *The Memoirs of Margaret S. Mahler.* Compiled and edited by Paul E. Stepansky. New York: Free Press (Macmillan), 1988.

Mahler, Margaret S., Fred Pine, and Anni Bergman. *The Psychological Birth of the Human Infant.* New York: Basic Books, 1975.

Martin, Bruce K. "Rescue and Marriage in *Adam Bede*." *Studies in English Literature* 12 (1972): 745–63.

Meckier, Jerome. "The Victorian 'Multiverse' *Bleak House Felix Holt*." In *Hidden Rivalries in Victorian Fiction: Dickens, Realism, and Revaluation.* Lexington: The University Press of Kentucky, 1987.

Mintz, I. L. "The Anniversary Reaction: A Response to the Unconscious Sense of Time." *Journal of the American Psychoanalytic Association* 19/4 (1971): 720–35.

Mundhenk, Rosemary. "Patterns of Irresolution in *The Mill on the Floss*." *Journal of Narrative Technique* 13 (1983): 20–30.

Munich, Richard L. "Transitory Symptom Formation in the Analysis of an Obsessional Character." *The Psychoanalytic Study of the Child* 41 (1986): 515–35.

Myers, William. *The Teaching of George Eliot*. Totowa, N.J.: Barnes & Noble, 1984.

Nystul, Nancy. "*Daniel Deronda:* A Family Romance." *Enclitic* 7 (1983): 45–53.

Ovid. *Metamorphoses*. Transl. Rolfe Humphries. Bloomington: Indiana University Press, 1955.

Paris, Bernard. "The Inner Conflicts of Maggie Tulliver." In *A Psychological Approach to Fiction: Studies in Thackeray, Stendhal, George Eliot, Dostoevsky, and Conrad*. Bloomington: Indiana University Press, 1974.

Parker, David. "'Bound in Charity': George Eliot, Dorothea and Casaubon." *Critical Review* 26 (1984): 69–83.

Pell, Nancy. "The Father's Daughters in *Daniel Deronda*." *Nineteenth-Century Fiction* 36 (1981): 424–51.

Perlis, Alan. "Introduction." In *George Eliot: A Reference Guide, 1972–87*. Ed. Karen L. Pangallo. Boston: G. K. Hall, 1990.

Pollock, George H. *The Mourning-Liberation Process*. 2 vols. Madison, Conn.: International Universities Press, 1989.

Poole, Adrian. "'Hidden Affinities' in *Daniel Deronda*." *Essays in Criticism* 33 (1983): 294–311.

Pratt, John Clark, and Victor A. Neufeldt, eds. *George Eliot's Middlemarch Notebooks: A Transcription*. Berkeley: University of California Press, 1979.

Rank, Otto. *The Double*. Transl. and ed. Harry Tucker, Jr. Chapel Hill: University of North Carolina Press, 1971.

Redinger, Ruby. *George Eliot: The Emergent Self*. New York: Alfred A. Knopf, 1975.

Ringler, Ellin. "*Middlemarch:* A Feminist Perspective." *Studies in the Novel* 15 (1983): 55–61.

Roazen, Paul. *Freud and His Followers*. New York: New American Library, 1976.

Robinson, Carole. "*Romola:* A Reading of the Novel." *Victorian Studies* 6 (1962): 29–42.

Rose, Gilbert J. *Trauma and Mastery in Life and Art*. New Haven: Yale University Press, 1987.

Rothstein, Arnold, ed. *The Reconstruction of Trauma: Its Significance in Clinical Work*. Madison, Conn.: International Universities Press, 1986.

Russell, Gillian A. "Narcissism and the narcissistic personality disorder: A comparison of the theories of Kernberg and Kohut." *British Journal of Medical Psychology* 58 (1985): 137–49.

Sanders, Andrew. *The Victorian Historical Novel.* New York: St. Martin's Press, 1979.

Santangelo, Gennaro A. "Villari's *Life and Times of Savonarola:* A Source for George Eliot's *Romola.*" *Anglia* 90 (1972): 118–31.

Segal, Hanna. *Introduction to the Work of Melanie Klein.* New York: Basic Books, 1974.

Shuttleworth, Sally. "Fairy Tale or Science? Physiological Psychology in *Silas Marner.*" In *Languages of Nature: Critical Essays on Science and Literature.* Ed. L. J. Jordanova. New Brunswick, N.J.: Rutgers University Press, 1986.

Smith, David. "'In their death they were not divided': The Form of Illicit Passion in *The Mill on the Floss.*" *Literature and Psychology* 15 (1965): 144–62.

Smith, Grahame. "*Daniel Deronda.*" In *The Novel and Society: Defoe to George Eliot.* London: Batsford Academic and Educational Ltd., 1984.

Steig, Michael. "Anality in *The Mill on the Floss.*" *Novel* 5 (1971): 42–53.

Stern, Daniel N. *The Interpersonal World of the Infant.* New York: Basic Books, 1985.

Sudrann, Jean. "*Daniel Deronda* and the Landscape of Exile." *English Literary History* 37 (1970): 433–55.

Sullivan, William J. "Piero de Cosimo and the Higher Primitivism in *Romola.*" *Nineteenth-Century Fiction* 26 (1972): 390–405.

Swann, Brian. "*Middlemarch:* Realism and Symbolic Form." *English Literary History* 39 (1972): 279–308.

———. "*Silas Marner* and the New Mythus." *Criticism* 18 (1976): 105–22.

Taylor, Ina. *George Eliot: Woman of Contradictions.* London: Weidenfeld and Nicolson, 1989.

Thale, Jerome. *The Novels of George Eliot.* New York: Columbia University Press, 1959.

———. "The Sociology of Dodsons and Tullivers." In *George Eliot: "The Mill on the Floss" and "Silas Marner."* Casebook Series. Ed. R. P. Draper. New York: Macmillan, 1977.

Thomson, Fred C. "The Genesis of *Felix Holt.*" *Publications of the Modern Language Association of America* 74 (1959): 576–84.

Vance, Norman. "Law, Religion, and the Unity of *Felix Holt.*" In *George Eliot: Centenary Essays and An Unpublished Fragment.* Ed. Anne Smith. Totowa, N.J.: Barnes & Noble, 1980.

Weinstein, Donald. *Savonarola and Florence: Prophecy and Patriotism in the Renaissance.* Princeton: Princeton University Press, 1970.

Weisenfarth, Joseph. "Antique Gems from *Romola* to *Daniel Deronda.*" In *George Eliot: A Centenary Tribute.* Ed. Gordon S. Haight and Rosemary T. Van Arsdel. Totowa, N.J.: Barnes & Noble, 1982.

———. *George Eliot: A Writer's Notebook, 1854–1879.* Charlottesville: University Press of Virginia, 1981.

Werman, David S., and Theodore J. Jacobs. "Thomas Hardy's 'The Well-Beloved' and the Nature of Infatuation." *International Review of Psychoanalysis* 10 (1983): 447–57.
Willey, Basil. "George Eliot." In *A Century of George Eliot Criticism*. Ed. Gordon S. Haight. Boston: Houghton Mifflin, 1965.
———. *Nineteenth Century Studies*. New York: Columbia University Press, 1949.
Witemeyer, Hugh. *George Eliot and the Visual Arts*. New Haven and London: Yale University Press, 1979.
———. "George Eliot's *Romola* and Bulwer Lytton's *Rienzi*." *Studies in the Novel* 15 (1983): 62–73.
Wolfe, Thomas P. "The Inward Vocation: An Essay on George Eliot's *Daniel Deronda*." *Literary Monographs* 8 (1976): 1–46.
Woodward, Wendy. "The Solitariness of Selfhood: Maggie Tulliver and the Female Community at St. Ogg's." *English Studies in Africa* 28 (1985): 46–55.
Yeazell, Ruth B. "Why Political Novels Have Heroines." *Novel* 18 (1985): 126–44.
Young-Bruehl, Elizabeth. *Anna Freud: A Biography*. New York: Summit Books, 1988.

Index

Adam Bede, 3, 21, 22, 24–40, 41, 42, 43, 76–77, 86, 94, 105–6, 133, 183, 186, 187
"Address to Working Men," 123
Aggression, 2, 183–84; Bowlby on, 11; and characters in Bede, 29, 30–31, 32–34, 35–38, 184, Felix, 118–19, 184, Marner, 72, 73, 184, Middlemarch, 146, 184, Mill, 43–46, 48–59, 184, Romola, 90, 92, 93, 96, 98, 99, 100, 106, 107, 184; and Eliot, 2, 26, 39, 66–67, 110, 124, 129; Kernberg on, 8, 92, 107; Kohut on, 9, 27, 45. See also Eliot, George, aggression/rage; Rage
Anniversary reaction, 3–4, 18, 70, 77, 81, 109, 126, 129, 188, 190, 191–92
Anxiety, 11, 71, 72, 73, 77, 80, 87, 109, 128, 185, 190. See also Separation anxiety
"Armgart," 155
Attachment, 3, 6, 10, 184. See also Bowlby, John
Attachment figure, 10, 71
Attachment theorists, 6

Bain, Alexander, 1
Blackwood, John (editor and publisher), and Bede, 24, 25; and Deronda, 159, 160, 178; and Felix, 112; and Magazine, 123; and Marner, 69, 87; and Middlemarch, 133; and Mill, 41, 42; and Scenes, 19–21; and Theophrastus, 181–82
Bowlby, John, 3, 4, 10–11, 70, 79, 184, 185; on reactions to loss, 77, 80, 83, 108–9, 129, 192. See also Attachment; Loss; Separation
Brabant, Robert, 62, 189
Bray, Charles and Cara, friendship with Eliot, 15–17, 62–63, 66, 76, 82, 124–25, 186, 189
"Brother and Sister Sonnets," 22, 154
"Brother Jacob," 22

Chapman, John: editor of Westminster Review, 16–18, 63, 65, 109; relationship with Eliot, 16, 64, 107, 125, 186, 189
Chessick, Richard D., 92, 98, 100, 101
Christian Observer, 14
Cornhill Magazine, 86
Countertransference, 175. See also Transference
Coventry, 12; Eliot's 1841 move from Griff, 15, 61, 189, 191–92; Eliot's friendships at, 124–25; Franklins' school, 13, 125–26
Coventry Herald, 15, 62
Cross, John Walter, 12, 78, 156, 191; marriage to Eliot, 156, 182–83, 192. See also Depression; Loss

Daniel Deronda, 2, 18, 23, 159–80, 188, 191
Darwin, Charles, 1
Depression, 11; and John Cross, 183; and Eliot, 62, 69, 87, 108, 155, 185, 192; and Eliot's mother, 78–81, 129, 184–85, 187
Depressive position, 5

203

Dickens, Charles: *Bleak House*, 112, 128, 130; comments on *Bede*, 25; on *Scenes*, 20
Dickinson, Emily, 133
Durade, Francois D'Albert, 63

Eliot, George, aggression/rage, 2, 11, 26, 39, 66–67, 109, 110, 124, 129, 180, 184. *See also* Aggression
Eliot, George, biography, 11–23, 61–66, 68–69, 75–83, 107–10, 111–12, 123–30, 132, 153–57, 181–93
Eliot, George, depression, 62, 69, 87, 108, 155, 185, 192. *See also* Depression
Eliot, George, literary criticism of, 1–2; *Bede*, 25, 38, 39; *Deronda*, 160–61, 178–79; *Felix*, 113, 118–19; *Marner*, 69–70; *Middlemarch*, 133–34, 146, 149, 153; *Mill*, 41–44, 46, 59–61; *Romola*, 87–88, 90–91; *Scenes*, 20–21
Eliot, George, loss, 81–82, 110, 125, 128, 129, 130, 132, 134, 153–57, 189, 190, 192–93; Chrissey's death, 77, 81, 83, 109, 185–86; estrangement from family, 40, 75, 82–83, 109, 155, 184; father's death, 15, 40, 62–63, 76, 77, 81, 83, 107, 125, 128, 155, 187; George Lewes's death, 181–83; mother's death, 13, 40, 78–79, 81, 155, 187; Thornie's death, 132, 154–56, 188, 190; twin siblings' deaths, 11–12, 40, 78–81, 129, 155, 184, 185, 187, 189. *See also* Loss
Eliot, George, pseudonym, 10, 191
Eliot, George, writing process: *Bede*, 24–25; *Deronda*, 159–60; *Felix*, 111–12, 126–30; *Marner*, 68–69, 84–85; *Middlemarch*, 132–33; *Mill*, 41–42; *Romola* 86–87, 89–90, 109–10; *Scenes*, 18–20, 22
Eliot, George, writings: *Adam Bede*, 3, 21, 22, 24–40, 41, 42, 43, 76–77, 86, 94, 105–6, 133, 183, 186, 187; "Address to Working Men," 123; "Armgart," 155; "Brother and Sister Sonnets," 22, 154; "Brother Jacob," 22; in *Christian Observer*, 14; in Coventry *Herald*, 15, 62; *Daniel Deronda*, 2, 18, 23, 159–80, 188, 191; *The Essence of Christianity* (transl. of Feuerbach), 17; *Ethics* (transl. of Spinoza), 17; *Felix Holt*, 22, 111–31, 132, 160, 187, 190; in *Fraser's*, 18; "History of *Adam Bede*," 24; "How I Came to Write Fiction," 18; *Impressions of Theophrastus Such*, 22, 181, 182; "Janet's Repentance," 20, 21, 24; in *Leader*, 17, 18; "The Legend of Jubal," 22, 154; "The Lifted Veil," 22; *The Life of Jesus* (transl. of Strauss), 15; *Middlemarch*, 22, 23, 89, 132–58, 159, 186, 189, 190, 192; *The Mill on the Floss*, 3, 21, 22, 41–67, 68, 69, 75, 77, 82, 86, 105–6, 108, 113, 127, 186, 187, 191; "Mr. Gilfil's Love Story," 19; "The Natural History of German Life," 18; *Romola*, 22, 68–69, 86–110, 111, 113, 185, 187, 189, 191; "The Sad Fortunes of the Reverend Amos Barton," 19; in *Saturday Review*, 18; *Scenes of Clerical Life*, 19–21, 24; *Silas Marner*, 3, 21, 68–85, 86, 109, 111, 123, 126, 129, 152, 184, 185, 187, 189; *The Spanish Gypsy*, 22, 111, 132; *Tractatus Theologico-Politicus* (transl. of Spinoza), 16; in *Westminster Review*, 16, 17, 18, 63–66, 109, 125
Essence of Christianity, The, 17
Ethics, 17
Evans, Chrissey (Eliot's sister), 12, 13, 14, 19, 63, 75–78, 81–83, 109, 185, 186, 192. *See also* Eliot, George, loss; Loss
Evans, Isaac (Eliot's brother), 12, 14, 61, 63, 75, 78, 80, 82, 124, 125, 126, 182, 184, 187, 189, 191, 192. *See also* Eliot, George, loss, estrangement from family
Evans, Marian (Eliot), 16, 17, 63–66, 76, 128, 189, 191
Evans, Mary Ann (Eliot), 13, 15, 61–63, 75–76, 123–26, 189, 191, 192
Evans, Mary Anne (Eliot), 11, 75, 78, 80, 184, 191
Evans, Mr. Robert (Eliot's father), 15, 76, 124, 191, 192. *See also* Coventry; Eliot, George, loss; Griff; "Holy War"
Evans, Mrs. Robert (Eliot's mother), 13, 19, 78–81. *See also* Depression; Eliot, George, loss; Loss

Fairbairn, W. R. D., 11
Felix Holt, 22, 111–31, 132, 160, 187, 190

Fenichel, Otto, 73, 147, 153, 165–66
Feuerbach, Ludwig, 17
Franklins' School, 13, 125, 127
Fraser's Magazine, 18
Freud, Anna, 4, 5, 7
Freud, Sigmund, 3, 4, 70; anniversary reactions, 190; *Beyond the Pleasure Principle*, 71, 81; on *Deronda*, 161; *Inhibitions, Symptoms, and Anxiety*, 71, 190; *Interpretation of Dreams*, 187; *Introductory Lectures*, 143; on *Middlemarch*, 133; *Notes Upon a Case of Obsessional Neurosis*, 72; on numbers, 126; on obsessive-compulsive behavior, 3, 73; on Oedipus complex, 187–88; on parapraxis, 143; on repetition-compulsion, 71, 81, 84; on separation anxiety, 10, 71, 190; on trauma, 10, 73, 126
Freudian slip. *See* parapraxis
Frustration-aggression hypothesis, 11

Griff, 12, 14, 61, 189

Hennell, Sara, 60, 62, 66; Eliot's correspondence with, 63, 76, 77, 82, 179
"History of *Adam Bede*," 24
"Holy War," Eliot and her father, 15, 62, 66, 124, 189
"How I Came to Write Fiction," 18

Impressions of Theophrastus Such, 22, 181, 182
Individuation, 131. *See also* Separation-individuation
Infatuation, 53–58, 64, 65, 66, 191

James, Henry, 87, 133
"Janet's Repentance," 20, 21, 24

Kernberg, Otto F., 3, 7–8; on aggression/rage, 8, 107, 164, 173; on narcissism/narcissistic personality, 7, 91–93, 96, 99, 109, 162, 164; on the self, 7, 91–93, 96, 164; on splitting, 39; theory applied to characters in *Deronda*, 162, 164, 173, *Felix*, 122, *Middlemarch*, 139, *Romola*, 96, 97, 99, 100, 102, 103, 107, 109; theory applied to Eliot, 187
Klein, Melanie, 4–5, 7, 167, 170

Kohut, Heinz, 3, 8–10, 26–27, 101, 107; on aggression/rage, 9, 27, 31, 45, 164, 192; on narcissistic personality disorder, 8, 164; on narcissistic rage, 40, 45, 60, 141; on principle of complementarity, 8; on the self, 26, 27, 174; on self-disorder, 27; on self-object, 27; on self-psychology, 8, 26–27, 39, 40; theory applied to characters in *Bede*, 26–27, 31, 38, 39–40, *Deronda*, 162, 164, 168, 174, 175, 180, 191, *Mill*, 45, 60, *Middlemarch*, 141; theory applied to Eliot, 185, 192; on transmuting internalization, 9, 38, 164, 175, 180, 191

Leader, 17, 18
"Legend of Jubal, The," 22, 154
Lewes, Agnes Jervis (GHL's wife), 17, 65, 156
Lewes, Bertie (GHL's son), 111
Lewes, Charles (GHL's son), 68, 83, 111, 181, 183
Lewes, George Henry, 1; biography, 153–57, 181–83; *The Fortnightly*, 125; *Life of Goethe*, 17, 18; *Problems of Life and Mind*, 154–55, 160, 181–82; relationship with Eliot, 16–21, 25, 41, 61, 65–66, 68–69, 82–83, 86, 87, 107, 108, 111, 125, 127, 128, 132, 153–57, 159, 186, 188, 189, 190, 191, 192; relationship with Agnes Jervis Lewes, 17, 65; *Seaside Studies*, 18, 19. *See also* Eliot, George, loss, estrangement from family; Loss
Lewes, Thornie (GHL's son), 111, 132, 154–56, 188, 190, 192
Lewis, Maria: Eliot's correspondence with, 14, 15; Eliot's friendship with, 62, 189; and Wallington's School, 12, 61, 124, 125, 127–28
Life of Jesus, The, 15
"Lifted Veil, The," 22
Liggins, Joseph, 20
London: Eliot's 1851 move from Coventry, 16, 63–66, 107, 189, 191; Eliot's 1860 move, 68; Eliot's 1863 move to North Bank, 111
Loss, 3; Bowlby on, 11, 77, 80, 83, 108–9, 129, 192; and characters in *Deronda*,

Loss, (Continued)
165–67, 173, *Marner*, 74, *Middlemarch*, 134, 136, 137, 147, 148, 152; Freud on, 71, 73, 190–91; and John Cross, 156; and Eliot, 81–82, 110, 125, 128, 129, 130, 132, 134, 153–57, 189, 190,192–93; and Eliot's mother, 12, 78–80, 184, 187; and Eliot's sister Chrissey, 75, 76, 83; and George Lewes, 154–56. *See also* Eliot, George, loss
Lytton, Edward Bulwer: on *Mill*, 42; on *Rienzi*, 89

Magazine, Blackwood's, 123
Mahler, Margaret S., 3, 5–7, 70, 79–81, 184
Middlemarch, 22, 23, 89, 132–58, 159, 186, 189, 190, 192
Mill on the Floss, The, 3, 21, 22, 41–67, 68, 69, 75, 77, 82, 86, 105–6, 108, 113, 127, 186, 187, 191
"Mr. Gilfil's Love Story," 19
Mourning, 3–4, 5, 11, 18, 70, 71, 108, 110, 129, 143, 156, 167, 188, 193
Mourning-Liberation Process, The, 3

Narcissism, 2, 86–110, 139, 162, 173. *See also* Chessick, Richard D.; Kernberg, Otto F.; Kohut, Heinz
Narcissistic injury, 164, 173, 192
Narcissistic personality disorder, 7, 8, 161–65, 178
Narcissistic rage, 40, 41–67, 98–100, 141, 184; definition, 45. *See also* Rage
"Natural History of German Life, The," 18
Nuneaton: Election Riot, 112, 116; Wallington's School, 12, 20, 127

Object relations theory, 5, 7, 10
Obsession, 137, 148
Obsessive-compulsive disorder, 3, 72–74
Oedipus complex, 9, 147, 165, 170–71, 188, 191; oedipal conflict/guilt, 54, 70; oedipal drama/elements/enactments/ scene, 118, 137, 148, 150, 151, 153, 155, 190, 192; oedipal fantasy/wish, 128, 136, 153, 156, 190–91; oedipal triangle, 56, 156

Parapraxis (Freudian slip), 143, 153
Pollock, George H., 3, 5, 19, 70, 77, 126, 129, 188
Primal scene, 147–49

Rage, 3, 10, 11, 27, 31, 38, 47–59, 100, 107, 109, 115, 130, 139, 146, 152, 163, 164, 169, 170, 173, 180, 184, 192. *See also* Aggression; Narcissistic rage
Repetition-compulsion, 3, 57, 71, 77, 81, 84, 126, 138, 188
Romola, 22, 68–69, 86–110, 111, 113, 185, 187, 189, 191

"Sad Fortunes of the Reverend Amos Barton, The," 19
Saturday Review, 18
Savonarola: character in *Romola*, 90, 93, 97, 100–102, 105, 106, 107; historical figure, 68, 86, 88–89
Scenes of Clerical Life, 19–21, 24
Scott, Sir Walter, 13, 48, 86–87, 89
Self: and characters in *Bede*, 28–29, 38, 40, *Felix*, 122, *Marner*, 74, *Mill*, 60, *Romola*, 95, 96, 102; and Eliot, 39, 153, 192; Kernberg's theory, 7, 91–93, 96, 164; Kohut on, 9, 26–27, 174, 192
Self-disorder, 24–40; definition, 27
Self-object, 27
Self-psychology, 8–10, 26–27, 39, 40
Separation, 3, 6, 10, 71, 73, 79, 129, 184, 185, 189, 190. *See also* Bowlby, John
Separation anxiety, 10, 71–72, 128, 185. *See also* Anxiety
Separation-individuation, 3, 6, 79–81, 184
Silas Marner, 3, 21, 68–85, 86, 109, 111, 123, 126, 129, 152, 184, 185, 187, 189
Smith, Elder & Co., 86
Spanish Gypsy, The, 22, 111, 132
Spencer, Herbert, 1; friendship with Eliot, 16, 64–65, 107, 189
Spinoza, 16, 17, 18
Splitting, 39, 152, 184; and projection, 38, 109
Strauss, Friedrich, 15, 62

Tractatus Theologico-Politicus, 16
Transference, 38, 173, 174, 178, 180, 191

Transmuting internalization, 9, 38, 164, 175, 180, 191
Trauma, 10, 71, 73, 126, 134, 137, 152, 184, 188, 189, 191

Wallington's Boarding School, 12, 20, 112, 127
Westminster Review, 16, 17, 18, 63–66, 109, 125

www.ingramcontent.com/pod-product-compliance
Lightning Source LLC
Chambersburg PA
CBHW022054290426
44109CB00014B/1098